Recent Work in *Rural Archaeology*

Recent Work in RURAL ARCHAEOLOGY

Edited by P. J. Fowler

Moonraker Press

© 1975 Moonraker Press and Peter Fowler

First published in 1975 by Moonraker Press,
26 St Margarets Street, Bradford-on-Avon, Wiltshire

SBN 239 00140.0

Printed in Great Britain by Butler & Tanner Ltd,
Frome and London

This book illustrates some of the sorts of archaeological work at present taking place in the British countryside. It is tempting to say that the nine chapters demonstrate how the *past* of our rural landscape is being studied archaeologically and, in a sense, this would be true; but apart from the facts that many other students primarily of other disciplines are also studying the same subject and that archaeology cannot stand alone in this field, the results from such work as that described here significantly contribute to an understanding of how the landscape has come to be what it is today. In that sense these essays, far from representing backward-looking exercises of only academic interest, illustrate lines of approach to a better understanding of an increasingly scarce resource.

The topics here, nevertheless, are a personal editorial choice, representative, it is hoped, but certainly not comprehensive. Archaeological excavation plays some part in all the work described, but conventional 'finds' do not loom large as such, since all the contributors have stood back from the immediate means of obtaining their evidence and set their projects into wider contexts of social and environmental evolution. In so doing, they demonstrate their methods, the issues they are trying to illuminate, the problems that arise during the work and the significance, as they see it now, of their results so far. Several aspects, almost themes, of archaeology in the countryside carry through from essay to essay: the importance of environmental evidence in placing human activity in a context and, conversely, of recognising the human factor in a 'natural' succession; the concern with the destruction through modern land-usage of the primary evidence in the field; the awareness of the inadequacy of existing records and of the quantitative explosion in field data which has occurred in recent years through increased field survey, air photography and observation of archaeologically destructive—and revealing—agencies like deep-ploughing and road-building. Attempts, however inadequate at this stage, to interpret this greatly increased amount of information, most of it unpublished, are foreshadowed in some of the essays, and clearly the absorption over the next decade of this enormous amount of 'new' evidence must not only make all existing archaeological distribution maps out of date but will surely radically affect our thinking about populations, settlement patterns, continuity and rural economy.

In choosing the book's contents, some attempt was made to obtain topographical as well as chronological variety. With only nine chapters, however, full coverage of the country was impossible, and so the omission of various areas is not meant to imply that comparable work is not proceeding. Indeed, the opposite could be true: one reason for not inviting a contribution from the North East of England, for example, is that the highly relevant work there has already been fully published in detail and in general. Similar considerations applied in choosing the topics. The selection here is, for example, obviously light on the medieval period but this is deliberate in view of the comprehensive and wide-ranging book recently published on medieval villages. Two other recent books, respectively from the Council for British Archaeology and Rescue, a Trust for British Archaeology, also influenced our choice.

The illustrations, particularly with their extended captions, and the bibliographies are regarded as integral parts of this book and not just decoration. We are particularly indebted to Professor J. K. S. St Joseph for his air photographs. The bibliographies, which have deliberately not been standardised in their presentation, represent the contributors' various responses to an invitation to provide leads to the source material on their particular sites and areas and to the background which has informed the work they describe. The material for this book was assembled during 1972 and in most cases the work described is continuing.

University of Bristol, February, 1973

Books referred to in the Preface
M. Beresford and J. G. Hurst (eds.) *Deserted Medieval Villages* (1971)
E. Fowler (ed.), *Field Survey in British Archaeology* (CBA, 1972)
G. Jobey in A. L. Rivet (ed.), *The Iron Age in Northern Britain* (1966), 89–109, and in C. Thomas (ed.), *Rural Settlement in Roman Britain* (CBA, 1966), 1–14
P. Rahtz (ed.), *Rescue Archaeology* (Penguin, 1974)

CONTENTS

List of Illustrations and Acknowledgements · · · · · · · · · · · · · · *page* 8

Contributors · · · · · · · · · · · · · · 10

Editorial notes · · · · · · · · · · · · · · 11

1 **The Somerset Levels** *by John Coles and Alan Hibbert* · · · · · · · · · · · · · · 12

2 **Settlement, Farming and Environment in South West England** *by Roger Mercer* · · · · · · · · · · · · · · 27

3 **Pattern and Interpretation: a view of the Wessex landscape** *by Collin Bowen* · · · · · · · · · · · · · · 44

4 **Religion and Settlement in Wessex, 3000–1700 BC** *by Geoffrey Wainwright* · · · · · · · · · · · · · · 57

5 **The Brochs of Scotland** *by Euan MacKie* · · · · · · · · · · · · · · 72

6 **The North-Western Interface** *by Barri Jones* · · · · · · · · · · · · · · 93

7 **Roman Settlements in the Nene Valley: the impact of recent archaeology** *by Christopher Taylor* · · · · · · · · · · · · · · 107

8 **Continuity in the Landscape? Some local archaeology in Wiltshire, Somerset and Gloucestershire** *by P. J. Fowler* · · · · · · · · · · · · · · 121

9 **The Origins of Rural Settlement in East Anglia** *by Peter Wade-Martins* · · · · · · · · · · · · · · 137

Index · · · · · · · · · · · · · · 158

List of Illustrations

Figures in the text

Chapter 1

1.1 Map: the Somerset Levels in the 3rd millennium bc

1.2 Diagram: pollen analysis of a Neolithic track in Somerset

1.3 Diagram: transect of vegetation changes in the Somerset Levels in the 3rd millennium bc

Chapter 2

2.1 Plan: land-clearance for cultivation, Carn Brea, Cornwall

2.2 Plan: settlement and field system, Stannon Down, St. Breward, Cornwall

Chapter 3

3.1 Plan: the Dorset Cursus

3.2 Plan: Hamshill, Barford St Martin, Wilts.

3.3 Plan: some 'Celtic' fields in central Dorset

3.4 Plan: some ancient boundaries between Bokerly Dyke and Whitsbury, Hants.

Chapter 4

4.1: Reconstruction of the Southern Circle, Durrington Walls, Wilts.

4.2: Comparative plans of four earthwork enclosures in Wessex

Chapter 5

5.1: Plan and section: broch at Dun Telve

5.2 Plan: broch at Dun Mor Vaul

5.3 Diagrammatic plan: Dun Telve

5.4 Diagrammatic plan: Dun Borodale

5.5 Diagrammatic plan: Ness

Plates

following page 32

1a: two brushwood footpaths, early 3rd millennium bc

1b: corduroy road, *c*2000 bc

1c: line of the Abbot's Way

1d: terminal of late 3rd millennium bc track

1e: multi-layer construction of Neolithic track

2a: cultivated land surface, Carn Brea, Cornwall

2b: ard-marks in a prehistoric field, Gwithian, Cornwall

3a: air photograph, Knoll Down, Damerham, Hants.

3b: air photograph, north east of Danebury, Hants.

3c: air photograph, Stonehenge, 1922

3d: air photograph, South Haven Peninsula, Studland, Dorset

3e: Bindon Hill and coast near Lulworth Cove, Dorset

3f: air photograph, Pimperne, Dorset

following page 80

4a: air photograph, Avebury, Wilts.

4b: air photograph, Stonehenge, Wilts.

4c: air photograph, Maiden Castle, Dorset

4d: air photograph, Hambledon Hill, Dorset

4e: air photograph, Mount Pleasant, Dorset

4f: air photograph, Woodhenge, Wilts.

5a: broch at Dun Telve

5b: broch at Dun Carloway

5c: Dun Mor Vaul under excavation

5d: Dun Ardtreck, under excavation

5e: Dun Ardtreck, entrance

5f: Dun Ardtreck, entrance

5g: Dun Ardtreck, door handle in position

5h: Dun Ardtreck, door handle in close-up

Figures in the text
Chapter 6
6.1 Map: The Upper Eden valley
6.2 Plan: settlements in the Highland Zone
6.3 Plan: the Waitby Dykes
6.4 Diagram: bone identifications from Mediolanum and Margidunum

Chapter 7
7.1 Map: Roman settlements in the Nene Valley, 1931–1972

Chapter 8
8.1 Map: Fyfield and West Overton in the Saxon period
8.2 Map: Vale of Wrington, Somerset
8.3 Plan: fields and settlement, Scars Farm, Wrington
8.4 Plan: Roman fields, Lye Hole, Wrington
8.5 Plan: field system, Brean Down, Somerset
8.6 Plan: fields and closes around the Roman villa, Barnsley Park, Glos.

Chapter 9
9.1 Village plan: Longham
9.2 Village plan: Longham in the 16th century
9.3 Village plan: Weasenham St Peter
9.4 Village plan: Weasenham St Peter in the 9th century
9.5 Village plan: Mileham
9.6 Village plan: Mileham in the Saxon period

Plates
following page 112
6a: air photograph, Northshield Rings, near Peebles
6b: air photograph, Caer Caradog, Cerrig-y-Drudion, Denbigh
6c: air photograph, near Pembridge, Hereford
6d: air photograph, Ewe Close, Westmorland
6e: air photograph, Waitby, near Kirby Stephen, Westmorland
6f: air photograph, Waitby, near Kirby Stephen, Westmorland
6g: air photograph, Housesteads, Northumberland
6h: air photograph, near Burwens, Crosby Ravensworth, Westmorland

7a: air photograph, Great Billing, Northants.
7b: air photograph, Ashton, near Oundle
7c: air photograph, Thorpe Achurch, south of Oundle
7d: air photograph, Woodford, north of Irthlingborough
7e: air photograph, Orton Waterville, near Peterborough

following page 128
8a: boundary ditch, Overton Down, Wilts.
8b: late prehistoric fields, Fyfield Down, Wilts.
8c: boundary stone, Fyfield/Clatford parishes, Wilts.
8d: *Raddun* medieval farm under excavation, Fyfield Down, Wilts.
8e: air photograph, Row of Ashes Farm, Butcombe, Somerset
8f: air photograph, Westmead, Row of Ashes Farm, Butcombe
8g: air photograph, Brean Down, Somerset
8h: air photograph, Cadbury Congresbury, Somerset
8i: air photograph, Barnsley Park, Glos.
8j: field boundary, Barnsley Park, Glos.

9a: air photograph, West Dereham church, Norfolk

Contributors

H. C. Bowen O.B.E., M.A., F.S.A., is on the staff of the Royal Commission on Historical Monuments (England)

J. M. Coles M.A., Ph.D., F.S.A., is Lecturer in Archaeology, University of Cambridge

P. J. Fowler M.A., F.S.A., is Reader in Archaeology, University of Bristol

F. A. Hibbert M.A., Ph.D., F.S.A., is Lecturer in Biology, Liverpool Polytechnic

G. D. B. Jones M.A., Ph.D., F.S.A., is Professor of Archaeology, University of Manchester

E. W. MacKie M.A., F.S.A., is on the staff of the Hunterian Museum, University of Glasgow

R. J. Mercer M.A., F.S.A., is on the staff of the Directorate of Ancient Monuments and Historic Buildings, Department of the Environment

C. C. Taylor B.A., F.S.A., is on the staff of the Royal Commission on Historical Monuments (England)

P. Wade-Martins B.A., Ph.D., is Director of the Norfolk Archaeological Unit

G. J. Wainwright B.A., Ph.D., F.S.A., is on the staff of the Directorate of Ancient Monuments and Historic Buildings, Department of the Environment

Acknowledgements for illustrations
Aerofilms 6g; Airviews (M/cr) Ltd 6a; J. M. Coles 1a, 1b, 1c, 1d, 1e; Cambridge University Collection per Professor J. K. S. St Joseph 3d, 3f, 4a, 4b, 4c, 4d, 4f, 7a, 7b, 7c, 7d, 7e, 9a; P. J. Fowler 8a, 8d, 8e, 8j; N. U. Grudgings 8b, 8c; J. E. Hancock 8f, 8h, 8j; G. D. B. Jones 6b, 6c, 6d, 6e, 6f, 6h; E. Mackie 5a, 5b, 5c, 5d, 5e, 5f, 5g; R. J. Mercer 2a; National Monuments Record 3a, 3b, 3c, 3e; Royal Commission on Historical Monuments (England) Fig. 3.1, 3.2, 3.3, 3.4; Society of Antiquaries of London Fig. 4.1, 4.2; Society of Antiquaries of Scotland Fig. 5.1; A. C. Thomas 2b; Mrs S. Wainwright 4e; West Air Photography, Weston-super-Mare, 8g.

1 In the present state of studies, the use of 'dates' deriving from radio-carbon estimates is complex and uncertain. In this book, BC indicates an absolute date in calendar years (usually approximate as shown by *c* before it), and bc indicates an uncalibrated date in radio-carbon years based on a half-life of 5568 years. Such 'dates' are, by definition, approximate in that they give the central year in a period of time (often between 50 and 150 radio-carbon years) within which there is a 66% probability that the radio-carbon 'date' lies. Such dates can be recalculated on the basis of a new 'half-life' of 5730 years and also calibrated with variations between radio-carbon and calendar years (*see* Table 1, p. 30). In general, from 1500 bc, radio-carbon 'dates' become progressively too young in relation to absolute dates the further we move back in time until by the early sixth millennium BC they are some 700–800 years out *i.e.* a radio-carbon date of 5200 bc = *c* 6000 BC. Complications are increased because the variations are not constant. Work on these problems continues. Meanwhile, *see* I. U. Olsson (ed.) *Radio-Carbon Variations and Absolute Chronology*, Proc. 12th Nobel Symposium, Uppsala, 1969 (1970), and recent, current and doubtless future numbers of, for example, *Proc. Prehist. Soc.* and *Antiquity; see also* C. Renfrew, *Before Civilization* (1973), Appendix on Radio-Carbon Dating, 255–68.

2 The system of abbreviations used is that advocated by the Council for British Archaeology (obtainable from CBA, 8 St Andrews Place, London NW1).

3 The metric system of measurement is used but not comprehensively, imperial values tending still to be favoured by the contributors for area measurements.

1 The Somerset Levels

John Coles & Alan Hibbert

The continuous growth of peat in the Somerset Levels over a period of approximately four thousand years has left an area which has entombed material from prehistoric human activities as well as fossilising the remains of plants in close association with such artifacts. By studying the plant fossils throughout this period, a picture of the environment with which prehistoric peoples had to contend may be deduced. Further, the changes in this natural scene caused by Man himself may be both characterised and localised within the Levels, through both archaeological and palaeobotanical investigations. In this chapter we examine both of these disciplines, because either one alone cannot reveal the fullest possible picture about human activities in the area in the third millennium BC.

The Levels themselves are not entirely peat. The part with which we are concerned, between the Polden Hills and the Wedmore Ridge, contains various 'islands' of permanently dry land, consisting either of outcrops of Lias rock (at Westhay and Meare) or of ridges of sand (at Burtle and other places). Such dry areas, and the northern and southern boundaries of hills, would have supported permanent settlements in the past just as they do today, while the marshy ground of the Levels themselves would have provided complementary sources of food and other raw material.

fig. 1·1

Archaeological work in the Levels has developed over the years on a scale related, partly by chance, to the exploitation of peat by commercial enterprises. The distribution of ancient finds in the Levels reflects the extent of industrial activity as much as that of archaeological research. Almost all of the stray finds of prehistoric origin have been made by men or women cutting or stacking peat, and most of the ancient wooden roadways have been revealed initially by the removal of peat for drainage or other purposes. That archaeologists have often been on hand to observe and record such finds, and to investigate some of them further, is a tribute as much to the unusual interest of the finds as to the persistence of the prehistorians.

fig. 1·1

The first archaeologist to realise the potential of the Levels was H. S. L. Dewar. He compiled records of finds made by peat cutters from the late 1940's, and carried out small-scale excavations of wooden structures in the peat. Sir Harry Godwin also recorded archaeological and palaeobotanical material from the Levels, through a consistent policy of research and excavation. The results

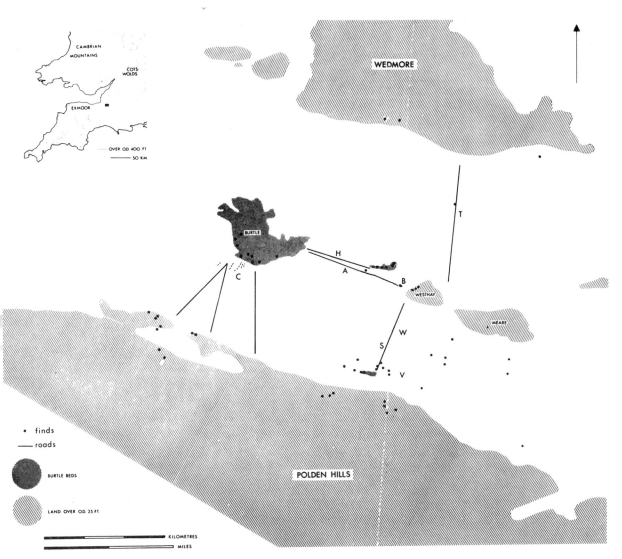

Fig. 1·1 Map of the northern part of the Somerset Levels. Stray finds of Mesolithic and Neolithic flints, potsherds, stone and flint axes, wooden bows and other artifacts are shown, as well as the routes on the main Neolithic tracks and roads. Key to this map and to fig. 1·3: A, Abbot's Way; B, Bell area; C, Chilton tracks; H, Honeygore track; S, Sweet track; T, Tollgate and Blakeway tracks; V, Viper's track; W, Westhay track. All of these are of the 3rd millennium bc except for T, V and W, which are of the 1st millennium bc; the routes of these late tracks are not shown.

of their joint endeavours were published in 1960 and 1963. Featured in these papers were the ancient trackways of the third millennium BC, and four such structures were recorded. It is a measure of the increased exploitation of peat in this area, and the vigilance of local archaeologists, that in 1972 almost forty trackways of the third millennium are known to exist. The discoveries of C. F. Clements are particularly notable and abundant. The positions of some of these are shown on the map; it must be emphasised that only small parts of most of these have been seen, and the prolongation of some of the route lines on the map is nothing more than an informed guess.

The excavation of these trackways is a job requiring some patience and much care. The wooden bearers, rails, pegs and bundles are all in remarkably good states of preservation, considering their age, but they are soft and easily damaged. Since 1964, trackways of the third millennium BC have been traced by borings, and excavated at intervals, by the Department of Archaeology, University of Cambridge.

Almost all of the trackways so far discovered have been made on a simple principle: that a bundle of twigs or brushwood thrown down will provide, for **pl. 1a** a time, reasonably firm footing over marshy, occasionally treacherous, ground. The wood selected for such treatment was mainly birch, the stems, branches and twigs ranging in diameter from 10 to 2 cm. Occasionally, transverse timbers were placed on the wet ground before the bundles were dropped into position; modern brushwood trackways generally have such transverse bearers which support the main thickness of wood. The bundles were held in place by pegs, of birch, which were driven into the marsh along the sides of the bundles, so that they did not project above the walking surface.

Trackways of this simple type appear to have been made in the early part of the third millennium bc according to radio-carbon dates, and indeed they were made again in the first millennium BC. In several areas of the Levels, multiple tracks were built, and in at least one case a pair of tracks join each other as they approach, or leave, the islands of dry ground. In another area, tracks overlie one another, separated by only two or three cm of peat; we may speculate on the reaction of the builders of the latest track as they placed their bundles upon the unusually firm surface of marsh where the preceding trackways were faintly visible to the eye, and clearly evident to the foot. **pl. 1a**

A more elaborate type of trackway was constructed in the late third millennium. This is essentially a corduroy road, made of alder planks and split timbers laid transversely along the line of the road. The single dated example of this, **pl. 1b** the Abbot's Way, was discovered more than a century ago, and it has recently been traced over almost its entire surviving length of about one kilometre. It was built in short stretches, aligned to avoid the particularly wet patches of the by now developing raised bog, and the effect when viewed from one of its terminals is of a gently curving road, like a modern motorway. The planks **pl. 1c** and timbers of the Abbot's Way were again held in place by birch pegs driven into the marsh along the sides of the roadway. These pegs are likely to have been attached to longitudinal stringers, also of birch, that lay on top of the planks, the whole effect being one of stability. The Abbot's Way is the only road of the later third millennium, a time when the raised bog would have provided reasonably secure footing for normal human traffic. Estimates can be made of the quantities of wood needed for this very heavy road: about 20 km of 20 × 12 cm planks and split stems of alder and over 50,000 birch pegs up to one metre long and carefully sharpened at one end were required. At least one of these pegs had been accidentally driven in, with difficulty, upside down. To these quantities of wood must be added the time involved in felling and transporting the wood, and in laying the wood and driving the pegs. The last activity was accomplished with heavy wooden mallets, one example of which has recently been discovered in third millennium peat.

These two types of track, made by birch bundles or by split alderwood, are represented by almost all of the known trackways in the Levels. They appear to have been entirely successful in providing a firm passage across the areas of marshy ground in the Levels, and some show signs of fairly heavy use necessitating occasional repairs. They could not, however, cope with the edges of the fen or marsh, where open water conditions were likely to develop; such water would accumulate by drainage from the slopes of the higher land, and later from the raised bog. Therefore, as the trackways approached their terminals, conditions would tend to overwhelm any normal construction. In one area, such conditions have recently been investigated.

At Westhay, several trackways approach from the west. They are called the **fig. 1·1** Abbot's Way, and the Honeygore and the Bell tracks. Improvised methods for the Bell track at its terminal involved the building up of a mattress of wood, fully 0·5 metre thick, upon the ordinary track of bundled wood. The mattress consisted of alternating layers of ashwood stems and branches, laid transversely, and masses of birch, hazel and yew twigs, laid longitudinally. The area over **pl. 1d** which this elaborate structure was required was c. 10 metres long; there apparently still remained a small area, immediately off the 'shoreline', where even the mattress was unstable. Excavations reveal a mass of jumbled branches, twigs and pegs, as well as quantities of natural drowned wood where flooding must have been regular and serious. The reaction to this situation on the part of the track builders was to sink a quantity of heavy timber, tree-stems and branches, into the marsh, and then to lay upon this a platform of long tree stems to form a bridge-like structure over the final six metres of marsh. The platform remained intact while around it, the remnant of the mattress and ordinary trackway show the damage caused by excessive water. **pl. 1e**

The terminal portions of these trackways not only provide useful indications of past attempts to adapt to meet localised conditions; they also lead to the areas where permanent or temporary settlements are likely to have existed. The marshy areas of the Levels themselves were not suitable for any permanent occupation, not because people could not cope with the damp conditions, but because the Levels were without much doubt subject to seasonal and severe flooding. What historical documents we possess indicate that the Levels were uninhabitable, and downright inhospitable at times. They were described in 1826 as 'a gloomy waste of waters, or still more hideous expanse of reeds . . . impassable by human foot, and involved in an atmosphere pregnant with pestilence and death'. The Abbey of Athelney, founded in AD 878 in the fastness of the fens, was described as 'so inaccessible on account of bogs and inundation of the lakes that it cannot be approached except by a boat'. A late fifteenth-century account speaks of the Levels in describing how 'in the wynter season the medewes be so filled and replenysshed with water, that the bootes may go over at any place'.

The reason for this consistent flooding is not hard to find. The areas around the Levels—the Quantocks and Exmoor to the west, the Mendips to the north—have a high rainfall, and about 800 square miles of uplands drain into 233 square miles of lowland. The rivers draining the Levels towards Bridgwater Bay have extremely low falls, sometimes only one foot in one mile, and their outlets are often blocked by high tides. Recent records show conclusively that from November to February, flood-stages are reached in parts of the Levels even today, and were it not for the extensive and successful flood prevention schemes in operation, the northern Levels would be inundated.

In 1794, three times in the nineteenth century, and in 1936, very large areas of the Levels were totally covered by water, from Wedmore to the Poldens, and inland to near Glastonbury. Even in 1971, one could have punted from Wedmore to Burtle and beyond.

The flooding conditions of the recent past must be indicative of the situation in prehistoric times. If so, there can be no possibility of any successful permanent settlement within the low-lying area of the Levels, and we must look to the uplands for such sites. Surface indications suggest that these settlements are likely to be near the hamlets of today, both to north and south. In the **fig. 1·1** central region, however, the evidence of pollen analyses points to the sand of Burtle itself as a likely area for occupation on a fairly intensive scale (*below* p. 24). Today, the fertility of the sand beds, at Burtle, and on the smaller ones as well, is considered by those farmers actually working the land to be twice as great as that of the upland limestone and Lias fields, and well above that of the drained acidic peat. What then was the value of the Levels themselves to prehistoric man? We can approach this from two aspects, the archaeological evidence from the peat and the historical evidence from twelfth- to fourteenth-century records.

The pools, watery moors and natural streams and rivers always have been prolific sources of fish, fowl, reeds and rushes. The 'hangings', those fields just at the base of the uplands, where down-washed mineral soils were mixed with the peat, have always provided extremely fertile meadows, occasionally flooded but abundantly full of grass for cattle and other animals and eminently suitable for other crops. The higher, permanently dry, arable land complements these sources.

There is little trace in the archaeological record of fishing activities, but historical records and current yields suggest that eels and other fish such as pike, tench, roach, would have been a useful source of food to ancient man. The abundance of wildfowl in the Levels has been strangely neglected in most historical records, but the present variety and quantity of fowl may indicate its value to prehistoric man. Sudden floods in part of the Levels today bring in extremely large numbers of fowl from swans downwards to snipe, and the many archaeological discoveries of flint arrowheads and wooden bows in the peat must point to a great interest in hunting food of this kind.

Some of the peat itself would have been available for cutting and drying in the third millennium, and could have served as fuel or as building materials. Several wooden spades of this time have been recovered from within the Levels, and were probably put to this use. The moors would also have yielded alderwood, and some willow and ash, along its seasonally flooded edges, and early records indicate the importance of this for fuel and for a variety of building uses. Certainly in the third millennium stands of ash and alder were being cleared, as were oak and holly on the uplands and birch in the moors themselves.

The main activity in the Levels in the past may well have been pasturing. Seasonal grazing of cattle on the meadows of lush grass, recently clear of the winter floods, would have contributed greatly to the economy of Neolithic man, just as it did for medieval man and does for the present farmers. The use of these moors for intercommoning animals might well have involved some measure of agreement over areas for such exploitation even in prehistoric times; the contrast between the rather sparse grasses of the uplands and the short season of lush vegetation on the 'hangings' would have been great, and competition for particularly accessible areas, and those first free of water, certainly existed in medieval times. In the seventeenth century, the moors in winter were 'soe covered with water you would rather deeme them sea than lande', but in summer they were 'fertile and pleasant Moores and Meades' and were claimed to support the largest cattle in all of England. The common land 'enabled the poor man to support his family and bring up his children. Here he could turn out his cow and pony, feed his flock of sheep and keep his pig'; such is the record of a commoner in the recent past, and there are ecclesiastical complaints about this easy living leading to idleness and vice.

These lands, however, clearly could not in themselves serve to support communities over the entire year, and any permanent settlement would have had to rely upon a varied exploitation of all the resources of the region. Difficult times for cattle and sheep in the wet season, and flooding of the best arable lands, would have been alleviated by the abundance of wildfowl and fish, and it is this time, rather than the drier season, that is probably represented by the hunting equipment of the third millennium found in the Levels. Representative of somewhat drier conditions are probably the majority of wooden trackways traversing the Levels, and some of the finds that point to peat cutting, wood clearing and temporary occupations in the central part of the moors. Spades, axes, pottery and the like indicate actual working or camping in the moors, pursuits unlikely to have been possible in the winter.

The archaeological discoveries in the peat clearly cannot in themselves be truly representative of the total surviving behaviour of third-millennium man, and it is in and on the 'hangings' that the real evidence for exploitation must exist. To these two sources must also be added the uplands, the Wedmore Ridge and the Poldens, where more permanent occupations took place. The archaeological evidence, however, is likely to be imperfectly preserved in this last situation, and for this reason, the recent investigations have been concentrated upon the peat with its potential for yielding information about the habits and practices of ancient man that is unique at the moment in British archaeology.

The archaeological work of excavation and recording is not the only source of information that we possess about the activities of prehistoric man in the Levels. As much as for any area in Britain, the Levels demonstrate the interdisciplinary approach to studies of early man, studies involving, in this case, palaeobotanical work of a particularly important character. The reason for this importance is that the Levels consist of vast areas of peat in which the record of Man's environment through time is preserved. By studying the nature of the peat deposits, and the fossils contained within them, a great deal of information about past conditions can be built up. Plant communities represented in the organic deposits have specific requirements in order to flourish; this we know from studies of their present-day distribution. When such characteristic plant communities can be recognised from fossil remains, then the environmental conditions reflected by their present-day distribution may have assumed to prevail in prehistoric time.

Plants have been growing in the Levels since the withdrawal of the sea some six thousand years ago; under waterlogged conditions, the plant remains were not destroyed by bacteria but accumulated and gradually built up the deposits of peat that survive today. The activities of bacteria were severely curtailed by the lack of oxygen in the watery conditions, and so the plant debris survived. Often it is possible to recognise quite easily some of the plants preserved in this way; alongside these, fruits, seeds, and microscopic pollen grains are also preserved in a state which enables them to be identified. When taken together, all of these contribute to our further understanding of the environment which led up to their deposition.

Immediately above a marine clay, the peat deposits are characterised by the remains of plants originating from a reed-swamp accumulating under freshwater conditions. The water would not have been universally shallow and there would have been stretches of open water which had both floating leaved, and submerged, aquatic plants, remains of which are found in the peat. With the passage of time the gradual build up of plant debris, together with a trapping of silt fraction, would cause a progressive shallowing of the water. Under such new, changing conditions, new species invaded the area and competed more successfully. Remains of wood appear in the peat together with fossil stems of Sawtoothed Sedge (*Cladium*). This is the beginning of a change to fen-woodland conditions which accelerated as the water became less deep. Under such conditions stretches of open water would be restricted and would eventually disappear. Islands of more stable ground, dominated by the initial tree colonisers, were becoming established, later to spread over much of the Levels. This is indicated by the layer of wood-peat which is found almost everywhere in the area, following the reed-swamp peat. By looking at the microscopic structure of the wood remains it is possible to identify the tree from which it came; most of the wood occurring naturally in this fen-woodland comes from birch and alder trees, both of which are characteristic of similar fen-woodlands at the present time.

Above the fen-wood layer in the peat there is an abrupt change of peat type. This represents a totally different vegetation colonising the area. Remains of bog moss (*Sphagnum*), ling (*Calluna*), cotton grass (*Eriophorum*) and other plants characteristic of large raised bogs are found, bogs such as are seen today on the central plain of Ireland and around the Solway estuary. These are gently domed structures, generally tree-less, rising above the influence of drainage water in the area, relying almost entirely upon precipitation for their water and mineral matter. This is the third major vegetational type in the Levels, and indicates that the calcareous drainage water from the Mendips was not affecting the Levels at this time, yet that rainfall was sufficiently high (greater than 40 inches per year) to allow bogs to develop.

By looking at these three main types of vegetation which the peat types represent it is possible to outline three main types of environment which prehistoric people had to contend with in the area. By using radio-carbon dating we are also able to tell how long each phase lasted. Between 3500 bc and 2800 bc the area was one of reed-swamps with its associated areas of open water. Fen-woodland began to establish itself around 2800 bc progressively encroaching over the area until by 2200 bc there was a more stable woodland over most of the Levels. From this time, raised bog began to overwhelm the woodland, creating the third stage of the development which persisted until approximately 900 bc when renewed flooding by calcareous ground water overcame the area.

To this information, simply gained from a study of the peat types, we may add the more refined techniques of pollen analysis and a study of the other macroscopic remains, fruits and seeds.

Pollen may be deposited over widespread areas of the countryside, in particular wind-dispersed pollen. When it is encountered as a fossil in peat it therefore represents not only the plants growing locally but those growing further afield. We are, therefore, able to learn details of a much wider area by looking at the pollen. Generally speaking those plants growing locally have an abundant representation in the pollen 'rain' and one may establish such plants on this basis together with an analysis of the plants making up the peat type. Fruits and seeds may also be dispersed over some distance from their point of origin but their distribution is not generally as widespread.

There are not many fruits and seeds recorded as fossils from the peat; they are, however, characteristic of those associations of plants we would expect to encounter from a study of the peat types found here. There are then, three main groups bearing evidence, each complementing the other and each reinforcing our view of the prehistoric environment.

Pollen analysis is the most valuable of these techniques, not only reinforcing the evidence already gained from a study of the macro-fossils, but revealing more of the vegetation of the hills around the Levels and of the areas of dry land on the Levels themselves. From an analysis of the pollen content of successive samples taken from the peat a pollen diagram can be constructed. In this the pollen encountered is expressed as a percentage of the total tree pollen and, when considered as a whole, trends of change in the vegetation may be recognised. The role which certain plants play in this sequence of change may be established and the cause of change determined.

Although not representative of the total sequence of deposits, the pollen diagram from the Chilton Track 1 shows clearly the three main vegetation types already discussed and illustrates how such communities may be resolved on the basis of pollen representation. On the diagram, the peat type is also represented, and the diagram itself is divided into six categories representing pollen from trees, shrubs, cryptogams (ferns and mosses), herbaceous dry-land plants, mire plants and aquatics. From a depth of 95 cm to approximately 65 cm the peat was formed from plants characteristic of reed-swamp and open water. The representation of pollen from aquatic plants is at its highest during this phase. Alongside these, many mire plants were flourishing in areas of more shallow water; in particular, spores of the Marsh fern (*Thelypteris palustris*) are abundant, a plant characteristic of this stage of the development. At about 65 cm, wood remains appear in the peat together with remains of Saw-toothed Sedge (*Cladium*). Pollen from Aquatic plants cease to be continuously represented whilst mire plants remain fairly constant. The pollen of birch (*Betula*) steadily rises from this point indicating its dominance as a fen-wood species. Alder (*Alnus*) also assumes higher pollen values during the fen-wood stage. Spores of the Royal fern (*Osmunda regalis*), which is often found today in wet woods on peaty soils, appear at this time and reach their maximum values during this stage. As the peat type changes in the top 15 cm of the deposit to one characteristic of raised bog, there are the first records of pollen from plants of ling (*Calluna*), Crowberry (*Empetrum*) and an expansion in the percentage representation of *Sphagnum* spores.

fig. 1·2

Three palaeobotanical parameters have now been examined, involving the peat type, and both the macro- and micro-fossil assemblages; compiling all of these it is possible, with some degree of certainty, to reconstruct the sequence of changing environments which existed throughout the history of the Levels. It then becomes possible to consider why the building of Neolithic roads and trackways was necessary and how it was associated with changes in the surface characteristics of the Levels themselves. With the exception of the Abbot's Way and the complicated Bell complex, the remaining trackways are all associated in the peat with the fen-wood stage. The Bell platforms are associated with wood remains in the peat but in this particular area the stage persists for some considerable time. The area where this trackway has been investigated is close by the island of Westhay, in a situation where drainage patterns both from the bog and the island would converge to maintain a wetter area over a long period and support a wet fen woodland. Indeed, it is likely that there would even be a major drainage channel with open stretches of water at this point, which may well account for the complicated construction and reconstruction which has taken place (*above* p. 15).

In general, however, as the fen woodland was becoming established and areas of open water were receding, islands of more stable ground were appearing. The trackways were constructed at a time when areas of open water were disappearing and yet, without the aid of some construction such as a track, travel by foot alone was impossible. Seasonal water table fluctuations would add further difficulty in maintaining communications. Once the raised bog had developed, passage on foot would be reasonably feasible. The raised bog would be far from dry, and there would be the added hazard of deep pools scattered over its surface, but such difficulties could be overcome. Having established that, we are left to find the reason for the Abbot's Way occurring within such peat. It is possible that a more substantial roadway, as its construction implies, was necessary for purposes other than a mere footpath; there is no need to suppose that passage by foot became any more difficult at that time than it had been both before and after the time over which the Abbot's Way was in use. Following this trackway, built around 2000 bc, there are no further trackways in the raised bog peat until a further change in environment led to renewed flooding of the Levels in Bronze Age times, in response to which further trackways were built.

Many other interesting details of the activities of Neolithic man may be established with the aid of pollen analysis. Amongst these are the evolution of farming practices in the area. In all of the pollen diagrams thus far produced from the Levels there is a notable decline of Elm pollen. This appears to be synchronous over the area, and is associated with the first increase in the representation of those plants we assume to be associated with early agriculture. These are plants of open or disturbed ground, plants we now call 'weeds'.

Returning to the pollen diagram from Chilton track 1 the fall in values of elm (*Ulmus*) pollen begins at about 60 cm and reaches minimum values around 45 cm. Associated with this fall, the representation of 'weed' pollen, namely Sorrel (*Rumex acetosa*), nettle (*Urtica*), plantain (*Plantago lanceolata*), mugwort (*Artemisia*) and spores of bracken (*Pteridium*), increases. The effect of these changes is summarised in the composite diagram contained in fig. 1.3, in which the basis of the pollen sum is a total of dry land trees, shrubs, those herbaceous plants characteristic of open ground, together with Bracken spores. In this, the disturbance of the vegetation of adjacent dry land areas may be monitored without the overwhelming influence of local pollen types. Such changes would indicate the clearance of forest areas to create open plots on which agriculture could begin. The extent of this clearance is evident; the values of tree pollen fall in relation to the others, in particular values of elm pollen, a plant of fertile soil.

This fall in Elm pollen may be due to its clearance from the area; it may have been realised that the soil on which it characteristically grows is both fertile and easy to work and therefore once the trees have been removed an

fig. 1·2

fig. 1·3

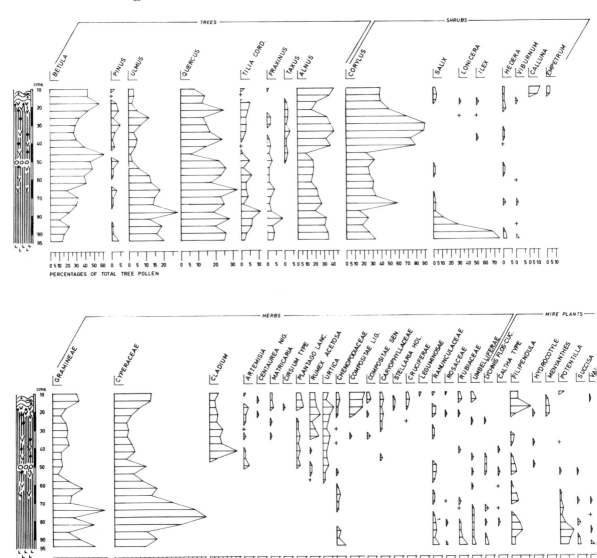

amenable area is available. Alternatively the flowering of the tree may have been prevented by frequent and regular pollarding, a practice which provides young elm shoots about every eight years from individual trees. These may be used as fodder for over-wintering stock, a practice in common use in parts of rural Scandinavia until quite recently. In any event, both clearance and pollarding result in a lowering of the pollen production from the tree. The practice of total clearance is consistent with a marked increase in the pollen representation of plants from open habitats ('weeds') and has been termed *Landnam* by the Danish botanist Iversen. If the tree is used for fodder, then there would not be this

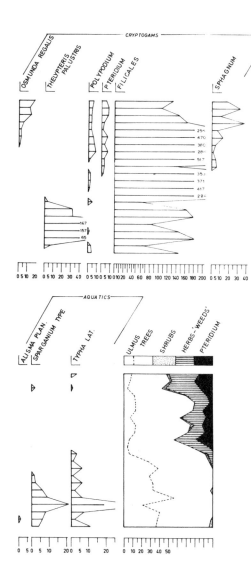

Fig. 1·2 Pollen diagram from the Chilton 1 Trackway, *opposite* shows the three principal types of vegetation encountered on the Levels. From 95 cm to 65 cm there is a reed-swamp (vertical lines on the peat stratigraphy column at far left of the diagram), indicated by much aquatic pollen; at 65 cm wood remains (denoted by V in the peat stratigraphy) and the pollen of *Betula* (Birch) and *Cladium* (Saw-toothed sedge) increase, indicating the development of the Fen-wood with a shallowing of the water. From 15 cm to the top of the profile there is Raised bog peat (wavy horizontal lines) with an increase in pollen from the shrubs *Calluna* (ling) and *Empetrum* (Crowberry) and in spores from the Cryptogam *Sphagnum*. The track itself is shown by open circles at 50 cm, and has been dated to 2800 bc. The composite diagram, *immediately left,* shows how tree pollen, in particular *Ulmus* (Elm), decreases and weed pollen, together with Bracken spores, increases, indicating forest clearance.

increase. At the Chilton site there is a marked increase in 'weed' pollen which would indicate a more decisive clearance of established woodland, and there is also a fall in the representation of pollen from ash (*Fraxinus*) and lime (*Tilia*). It would seem from this that the early agriculture was mainly arable, but so far there have been no finds of pollen grains from cereals. Large amounts of plantain (*Plantago lanceolata*) pollen indicative of areas of grassland and therefore a more pastoral economy, do not appear until later.

In the Chilton diagram, the representation of hazel (*Corylus*) pollen increases at about 50 cm; this increase is a feature common to all diagrams from the **fig. 1·2**

Levels, suggesting some interference with the natural community. There are a large number of long, straight hazel poles used in some trackways, resembling poles obtained today by coppicing the hazel trees. This involves cutting back established trees whereupon a large number of straight stems develop from the original stool. This practice may be repeated and the original stool survives for a long time in spite of this. Such opening of the original forest cover by coppicing would encourage increased flowering of the hazel tree and so account for the increased pollen representation. It is possible that Neolithic man, in addition to being the first to practise agriculture, was also the first to develop silviculture, both in the management of elm trees to produce fodder and of hazel trees to produce sturdy, straight poles for a number of possible uses.

A further aspect of developing land-use at this time involves the determination of the areas in which clearance activities were actually taking place. It is known that there is a clear fall-off in the concentration of any one pollen type in the air as one moves away from its source of production and that the fall takes place over a relatively short distance from the source, beyond which point the values remain low and more or less constant. When present at these low levels it is called the regional pollen rain, representing pollen from plants growing at some distance from the site. Any significant change in pollen production produces a more marked change in representation close to its site of production than it does further away. The latter only produces small, often indiscernible changes in the regional pollen rain. From the Chilton Moor diagram, we can **fig. 1·2** see that the changes are large; the tree pollen falls as a consequence of a large increase in the pollen of 'weeds'. The agricultural activity therefore appears to be close at hand. The light, sandy soils of the adjacent Burtle bed would easily be worked, and so ideal for the primitive techniques of early agriculturalists.

The study of the magnitude of this effect may be broadened to include all sites over the Levels in an attempt to localise areas of more intense agriculture. In fig. 1·3 summary diagrams similar to that already considered from the Chilton **fig. 1·3** area are arranged along two base lines. One of these runs from the Wedmore Ridge in the north to the Poldens in the south; the other roughly east–west from Westhay to Burtle. Considering the Westhay–Burtle transect first of all, it would seem that, although there are characteristics of agricultural activity in all of the diagrams, its intensity in each varies. Those with the highest disturbance indicate the proximity of intense farming practices. Similarly the influence may be detected from the Wedmore–Polden transect. Taken together, they suggest that although the Westhay area was not one in intensive use, the Burtle area and a smaller outcrop of sand, close to the Poldens by the Sweet and Viper's tracks, show significant shifts in pollen representation which would indicate that these sandy ridges were scenes of clearance and intense agricultural activity.

The development of this arrangement of pollen diagrams along transects has shown how the botanical evidence may be further used to localise, within a large area, sites of possible archaeological significance. This is made possible

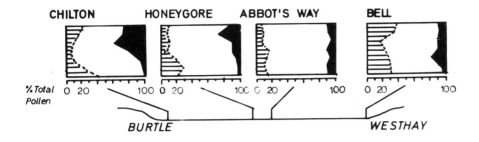

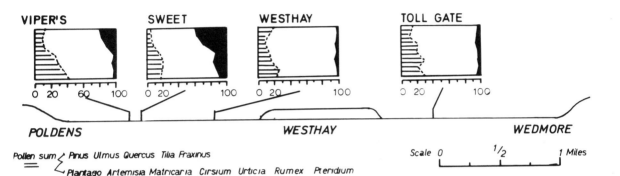

Fig. 1·3 Diagram showing the relationship of pollen profiles from selected sites to the islands of dry land within the Levels. Each diagram shows *Ulmus* (elm) (hatched lines), total trees (white) and weeds (black), and is drawn to show the relationship between closed forest and the changes which follow should this forest be cleared. In this way the greater the degree of increase in weed pollen, the greater is the intensity of local clearance activity. Those pollen diagrams from around the island of Westhay (Abbot's Way, Bell, Westhay, Tollgate) show only a small increase, indicating little clearance there, while those from near Burtle (Chilton, Honeygore) and approaching the Poldens (Sweet, Viper's) show large changes, indicating local activity.

in the Somerset Levels because of the great extent of peat deposits from which the evidence may be gained and the relationship of this to outcrops of dry land on which prehistoric people were thought to be exerting their influence on the natural vegetation.

The totality of the evidence of Man's past behaviour in the Levels therefore is a sum of the data obtained from both archaeological and palaeobotanical sources. These draw widely upon related disciplines for such aspects as absolute dating by radio-carbon, processes of exploitation in the recent past, and the conservation techniques for the fragile material that has been preserved for over four thousand years. The investigations continue while this evidence still survives modern commercial exploitation of the peat, in the belief, expressed by others, that the material recovered from even one waterlogged site may give more information than that from hundreds of poorly preserved sites.

Bibliography 1

J. M. Coles and F. A. Hibbert, 'Prehistoric Roads and Tracks in Somerset, England: 1. Neolithic', *Proc. Prehist. Soc.* **34**, 1968, 238–58 (description and illustration of Abbot's Way and Bell Track at Westhay, with discussion of vegetational history of the Levels).

J. M. Coles, F. A. Hibbert and C. F. Clements, 'Prehistoric Roads and Tracks in Somerset, England: 2. Neolithic', *Proc. Prehist. Soc.* **36**, 1970, 125–51 (complete record of third-millennium bc tracks and stray finds in Levels and uplands, now augmented by more recent work, cf fig. 1·1.).

J. M. Coles, 'Late Bronze Age Activity in the Somerset Levels', *Ant. J.* **52**, 1972, 269–75 (summary with map of late prehistoric finds from the Levels).

H. S. L. Dewar and H. Godwin, 'Archaeological Discoveries in the Raised Bogs of the Somerset Levels, England', *Proc. Prehist. Soc.* **29**, 1963, 17–49 (details of finds from the Levels, with pollen diagrams).

M. Williams, *The Draining of the Somerset Levels* (Cambridge University Press, 1970) (useful source for medieval exploitation of the Levels, and full documentation of flooding).

Acknowledgements
Much of the work on which this chapter is based has been generously supported by the Crowther-Beynon Fund of the University Museum of Archaeology and Ethnology, Cambridge, and by the Maltwood Fund for Archaeological Research in Somerset.

2 Settlement, Farming and Environment in South West England to *c.* 1000 BC

Roger Mercer

An attempt is made here to bring together the cultural and 'environmental' information that we have at our disposal concerning the south western peninsula of England (the present-day counties of Devon and Cornwall) during early pre-history up to *c* 1000 BC. The conjunction of these two groups of evidence will have the effect of presenting to us the steady encroachment of Man upon his natural environment during prehistory. This process was achieved almost entirely by means of stabilised food production, arable or stock-producing, which we can broadly term farming. The significance of an understanding of the position of farming within any prehistoric society and of the technology of its actual processes lies in the insights that it gives us into the development of population, economy and life-styles *across* the artificially erected divisions of the Three Age System (the conventional Stone, Bronze and Iron Ages). These factors, taken together with a study of the negative reaction of man to climatic changes which dominated the landscape and ecology around him, may lead us eventually to the proposition of more regionalised and less 'artificial' ideas about our remote past.

The Nature of the Evidence

The evidence available for our study divides itself into three categories:

1 Evidence that has now become an integral and visible part of our present-day landscape. This includes the boundary banks and lynchets of field systems, enclosures for stock-rearing, farm boundaries, farm settlements, drove roads and other structures that survive as upstanding field monuments or as shadows and colour differentiations on photographs of the landscape taken from the air. It is a tragic irony that, particularly during the last twenty years after survival for several thousand years, precisely this evidence in many parts of our country is being erased forever, often without adequate record, by our own quest for food through modern farming techniques.

2 Artefactual evidence. This includes the many objects made by man to carry out the processes of agriculture which in themselves are the principal evidence available to us for technological innovation. This category will include the 'negative impressions' of these tools and objects, such as plough and spade marks, where these are preserved beneath the soil and have been recovered by skilful excavation.

3 Environmental evidence. This category includes the inorganic and organic materials of the ecology and geomorphology of the prehistoric environment which have survived, either through such processes as carbonisation, fossilisation and waterlogging or because of their own intrinsic high survival value. It includes the bones of wild and domesticated animals, carbonised seeds, nuts and wood fragments, fossilised pollen grains, shells of land and sea mollusca, and indeed the deposits of soil themselves which, where they have accumulated through such processes as sand blows, peat formation and podsolisation, can point to changing environmental factors.

There are various limitations to this evidence which ought to be discussed before we proceed. From the point of view of visible structures built during the course of prehistoric agricultural activity, the problem always exists of the establishment of contemporaneity of one 'structure' to another within one apparent system. A seemingly logical layout of fields visible as low banks on a hillside may be one period of clearance and farming but can also be a gradual development over a long period of time without all parts of the system being in use at once. Estimates of output and population will be seriously affected by these differences and only selective excavation over the whole area of a field system can hope to solve this problem. The same problem arises in establishing the contemporaneity of a settlement with a nearby field system or stock enclosures.

Certain limitations also exist with the artefactual evidence. Only those artefacts manufactured in stone, metal or baked clay will survive in normal circumstances (on the acid and abrasive soils which predominate in south west England, bone objects will not survive as they do elsewhere, and even pottery will often slowly erode away). For this reason a plough manufactured entirely of wood will leave no perceptible vestige to the archaeologist and even a small share made of stone may in its apparent isolation be interpreted as a stone axe. It should be borne in mind that we cannot be certain of the exact function of many tools.

The interpretation and evaluation of environmental evidence is a matter of great complexity and the writer will only attempt to make one or two points which he sees to be of outstanding importance. As we have said, bone and shells will seldom survive in the acid soils which prevail in south west England. Pollen grains on the other hand generally find this environment most hospitable, and peat and other waterlogged soils are the best contexts for their preservation. For this reason in south west England we have come to rely perhaps unduly upon pollen analysis for our glimpses of natural environment throughout pre-history. Two principal areas of peat formation, one inside and one just outside our chosen area, have been closely studied from the point of view of pollen analysis. They are Dartmoor and the Somerset Levels (*above* pp. 12–26). It will be upon these two vertical chronometers, where some equation has been drawn between environmental change and time, that we shall depend for much of the skeleton of this essay. First, however, it should be emphasised that the different types of environmental evidence (pollen analysis, shell analysis, bone studies and charcoal identification) differ markedly in their qualities.

Bones and charcoal are essentially the remains of materials *brought* on to an archaeological site by its prehistoric inhabitants as dead animals and wood for building or fuel. They are therefore basically selected evidence, showing in the case of bone largely what was domesticated or hunted rather than what animals actually existed in any area. Similarly with charcoals, they are an expression of what woods were used for building and burning rather than of all the trees that grew nearby. Pollen grains and snail shells are, however, rather different in that they are predominantly a natural selection of all the species in the area which happen to have become incorporated in the particular column of soil being excavated. They are therefore likely to give a far sharper insight into the totality of the content of the prehistoric environment. Pollen, however, will reflect a situation over a fairly wide area, as the grains can be blown considerable distances, whereas snail species will tend to reflect very local conditions. Thus on the site of a prehistoric forest clearing, the pollen grains recovered might indicate a predominantly forested environment while the snails will reflect to a greater extent the clearing itself by the absence of shade-loving species.

Chronology

The radio-carbon dating technique which enables any organic substance containing carbon to be dated absolutely within a standard deviation of a number of years has, of course, revolutionised, over the last twenty years or so, our whole approach to the relation of prehistoric 'events' to absolute time. Recent work on dating the successive tree rings of very long-lived trees in California and Nevada (in particular the Bristlecone Pine with a life-span of up to 4000 years) has resulted in a 'revaluation' of so-called 'carbon years'. There still remains much work to be done to clarify to what extent this 'revaluation' should take place. In this essay, however, 'calibrated' or revalued dates have been calculated by the author on the basis of a recently published 'conversion table' to give at least an order of magnitude to our new view of the timescale of prehistory in south west England. All carbon dates, however, carry with them a standard deviation (expressed, for example, ± 100), and it is important to remember that this gives only a 2:3 chance that the true date will fall *anywhere* within the bracket so indicated. All C14 dates used in this paper are listed in Table 1 **table 1** in their 'uncalibrated' and 'calibrated' forms and will be referred to in the text by their laboratory numbers.

A form of 'relative-absolute' dating has emerged, based upon the evidence of pollen analysis, which shows widespread climatic changes taking place gradually at certain junctures in prehistory. Through time, variations in pollen spectra will indicate changes in the contemporary flora brought about either by Man's interference or by climatic fluctuation. These changes can be formalised in relative chronological terms and are known as climatic Zones. It has proved possible by the use of radio-carbon dating to 'date' within a fairly broad bracket these climatic events. Our concern with Man's effective incursion upon

Table 1 Radio-carbon 'dates' for the SW from sites quoted in the text
(*see* p. 29 for explanatory note)

Lab. No.	Site	5568 ± 30 ½ life bc	Bristlecone Calibrated BC
Q-672	Westward Ho!	4635 ± 130	*c* 5500
BM-181	Church Hill, Findon	3390 ± 150	4340
BM-130	Hembury Fort	3150 ± 150	3950
BM-136	Hembury Fort	3240 ± 150	3990
BM-138	Hembury Fort	3330 ± 150	4030 or 4110 or 4220
BM-823	Carn Brea	2611 ± 47	3395
BM-824	Carn Brea	2747 ± 60	3510
BM-825	Carn Brea	3049 ± 64	3740
BM-149	Hazard Hill	2970 ± 150	3700
BM-150	Hazard Hill	2750 ± 150	3510
BM-214	High Peak	2680 ± 150	3670
BM-356	South Street Long Barrow	2810 ± 130	3530 or 3590 3640
Q-308	Westhay Trackway	850 ± 110	1070
Q-52	Meare Heath Trackway	900/890 ± 110	1120

the environment will commence at the junction of Zone VI and Zone VIIa, on Dartmoor a time of climatic change towards the warmer and wetter conditions of Zone VII. This change is dated by carbon 14 analysis elsewhere in Britain to a broad period ending just before 5000 BC.

At this period and for the following millennium a thinly scattered population of 'hunter-gatherers' occupied the south western peninsula. It seems from purely archaeological evidence that they can be divided into two cultural groups. On the coastlands, a series of flint scatters characterised by non-geometric microliths and a very few flint scrapers have been linked with the British 'Sauveterrian' and the type-site at Peacock's Farm, Shippea Hill in the Cambridgeshire Fens. These coastal people used beach pebble tools extensively as hammers, perhaps for the manufacture of bone tools and again perhaps as 'limpet scoops', the classic tool-form associated with 'strand-looper' populations in maritime Europe. Living beside their permanent food source, the sea, fishing and gathering shell fish, these men and women probably developed one of the best passive adaptations to their environment possible in Britain at this time. Because of subsequent immersion of coastlines in the south west peninsula few of the sites of the middens and settlements of these littoral hunters have ever been located. The main published example is a midden closely associated with a submerged forest at Westward Ho! near Bideford, Devon. Sealed within this midden were a series of flint tools and waste material related to the other coastal sites of which we have already spoken. Amongst the stumps of the submerged forest, consisting largely of oak and elm trees, nineteenth-century workers claim to have observed sharpened stakes set upright in the forest bed. The midden itself must have been located at approximately sea level during its period of use. Its contents presented a clear picture of a community living by gathering oysters, mussels, limpets and winkles from the rocks and pools of the beach in the intertidal zone. No evidence of fishing was present. Nuts and fruit-stones bore witness to the assiduous gathering of wild nuts, berries and fruits, while pig, wild boar, red and fallow deer and hedgehog bones must indicate the extent of the community's hunting activities. The pollen spectra from above and within the midden reveal a forest environment dominated very strongly by oak, elm and hazel. The slight appearance of *Plantago lanceolata*, a weed which develops in forest clearings, may possibly indicate that some forest clearance, if only for a living platform, had, however, taken place. Radio-carbon dating of the peat immediately on top of the midden produced a date towards the end of the sixth millennium BC (Q-672). This date would fall at the junction of Zone VI and Zone VIIa when warmer wetter conditions were probably introducing dense forests to all parts of the peninsula.

It should not be imagined that this way of life was doomed to failure with the first arrival of farming economy in the area. At Gwithian, near Hayle in Cornwall (Site HU), at a date probably in the fourth millennium BC, the flint implements of these littoral hunters which must have been still lying on the surface were picked up by new people who seem to have been farmers and reworked to produce the new tool types that were becoming widespread in southern Britain. Particularly in Cornwall at sites like Harlyn Bay, we can see these coastal midden settlements persisting into the second and first millennia BC; while assimilating many new influences, they probably find their ethnic origins in our 'strand-loopers' of the fifth and sixth millennia.

If the role of the coastal element of this early population was largely passive in response to a difficult environment, recent work has indicated that this is possibly not the case with reference to the population of the interior. These people are represented by many flint tool and waste scatters on the granite moorlands, perhaps the classic example being the assemblage from Dozmary Pool, near the Jamaica Inn on Bodmin Moor. Archaeologically speaking, this assemblage has been contrasted with the 'British Sauveterrian' groups mentioned above and compared ultimately with sites such as Thatcham in Berkshire. The flint industry is characterised by a heavy element, together with burin and end scrapers on blades and non-geometric microliths. By virtue of its accent on heavy flint equipment, this industry has classically been regarded in archaeological thought as denoting a more aggressive attitude towards the forest environment. (In fairness, it should be emphasised that the most important element of this heavy equipment, the flake axe, is absent from the assemblage collected at

Dozmary Pool.) This interpretation of the nature of these early hunter groups on the granite uplands of the south west may well be at least partially true.

The analysis of pollen grains from a peat exposure 457 m above O.D. not far from the Black Lane Brook at the head of the Plym Valley on Dartmoor has revealed a phase possibly representing forest recession during late Zone VI. This phenomenon is represented by a sudden and rapid rise in grass and bracken pollens denoting the creation of open spaces. The disappearance of *Calluna* (Ling) is put forward as an indicator that this clearance might have been produced by fire. A similar situation was detected in an exposure at Gawler Bottom near Postbridge on the East Dart River 389 m above O.D., a location where microlithic flint assemblages have been encountered. This recession in the forest is in clear opposition to the general trend throughout this period (sixth and early fifth millennia) for the forest to increase in density, with oak and elm predominating. On the lower (latter) site, recovery was quickly made and the grass and bracken pollens soon disappear, but on the higher site sufficient clearance was made for a permanent setback in forest development to be created.

The difficulty with this evidence lies in our inability at present *definitely* to link these vegetational changes with the archaeology of the hunter communities we know to have existed in the locality at the period. Nevertheless widespread fires were altering Dartmoor's vegetation at a time when hunter communities were roving over the area (and the finding of Portland chert in the flint assemblages of these people must illustrate the kind of distances that they covered). The burning down of cover to flush out game or to clear areas for settlement sites is a distinct possibility and may represent in south west Britain the first step in the process of Man's domination of his natural environment.

On Bodmin Moor the afforestation probably never achieved the overall cover that seems to have been the case on Dartmoor; but it is likely that, in both areas, a hunting economy remained dominant well into the fourth and even into the third millennium BC.

Throughout Britain between approximately 4200 and 3700 BC (as indicated by radio-carbon dating) farmers who had been arriving on our coasts by boat bringing their animals and seed corn with them begin, over a wide area and on a scale which is impressive even at the distance from which we study it, to clear away tracts of the forest in preparation for crop husbandry. This massive disturbance of the natural environment is plainly attested in the pollen and molluscan spectra from peats and other soils all over the British Isles. It is revealed frequently in a sudden and dramatic decline in the pollen deposition of elm, and a corresponding rise in the pollen of 'weeds of cultivation', grasses and ultimately, cereals. In the south west of England the record in the peats of the Somerset Levels shows this change (*above* p. 21) but there is no such **fig. 1·2** massive disturbance on the peats of Dartmoor. There only a minimal clearance is apparent with a rapid subsequent forest regeneration. Nevertheless, there was a very real, if dispersed, settlement of the south western peninsula by these immigrant farmers. With the widespread encroachment into the forests which

Pl. 1a Two brushwood footpaths, the Honeygore track running over the Honeycat track which comes in from the lower left. The wood used is almost exclusively birch, some tree stems but mostly branches. The date of the tracks is 2800 bc. The scale totals one metre, and the depth of the tracks beneath the present surface is about two metres.

Pl. 1b The Abbot's Way, a heavy corduroy road of 2000 bc. The wooden planks and split stems are of alder, and the vertical pegs are of birch. The scale totals six feet; a modern drainage channel has removed the track in the foreground. Parts of this track have been preserved in the University Museum of Archaeology and Ethnology, Cambridge, and in Bristol City Museum.

Pl. 1c The line of the Abbot's Way from the islands of Westhay westwards towards Burtle. The targets, and intermediate posts, show the positions where the track has been seen by excavation or borings. The distance between the near and far targets is about one kilometre, and the curving nature of the track is evident.

Pl. 1d A heavy construction at Westhay, on the Bell track terminal. The track itself lies to the left, but here the conditions must have been extremely wet and unstable. Bundles of brushwood have been dumped and the heavy timbers laid on top of this foundation. The result was a form of bridging structure allowing access from the track proper to the dry land of Westhay in the immediate foreground. The date of this construction is about 2300 bc. The scale totals six feet.

Pl. 1e Fragment of the Bell mattress track at Westhay. Constructed of alternate layers of ashwood bearers and hazel, birch and yew twigs, the track represents an attempt to bridge a particularly wet area in the late 3rd millennium bc. The scale totals one foot.

Pl. 2a The Neolithic cultivated surface at Carn Brea revealed in a machine cut strip across the hillside. The piles of stones dispersed in the open cultivated area are clearly visible. A saddle quern is visible in the stone pile nearest but one to the camera.

Pl. 2b Excavations at Gwithian, West Cornwall. The pattern of thin, dark marks in the sand was created in the later 2nd millennium bc by cross-ploughing with a light wooden ard, perhaps with a stone tip on its share. In order to obtain this photograph, not only have all the later, overlying layers representing phases of occupation and wind-deposited sand been removed but the ploughsoil immediately above the ard-marks has been excavated too. Evidence such as this is invaluable in studying early agriculture and although similar examples have been recorded elsewhere, Gwithian remains one of the best because of its impeccable stratification and excellent preservation.

Pl. 3a Oblique air photograph, looking east, of Knoll Down, Damerham, Hants. The area, shown dotted on fig. 3·4 is only about one two hundredth of the total of that plan. It shows a boundary ditch superseding 'Celtic' fields, as well as a variety of other complex relationships. The boundary ditch extends from right of centre at the bottom of the picture to top left. The more distant section is preserved as an earthwork and is scheduled as an Ancient Monument. The ditch bisects or intrudes upon the interiors of at least six 'Celtic'

fields, part of a block arranged off an axis on the near side of the prominent 'knuckle' in the ditch in the far section. Roughly rectangular ditched enclosures, probably of a settlement and conforming axially to the fields, show as soils marks in the area to the right of the knuckle. The curve in the ditch on the near side of the 'knuckle', clearly deliberate, is emphasised by the soil mark of a narrow ditch across its chord, suggesting either a 'marking out' feature, not here followed, or a different phase of the boundary arrangements.

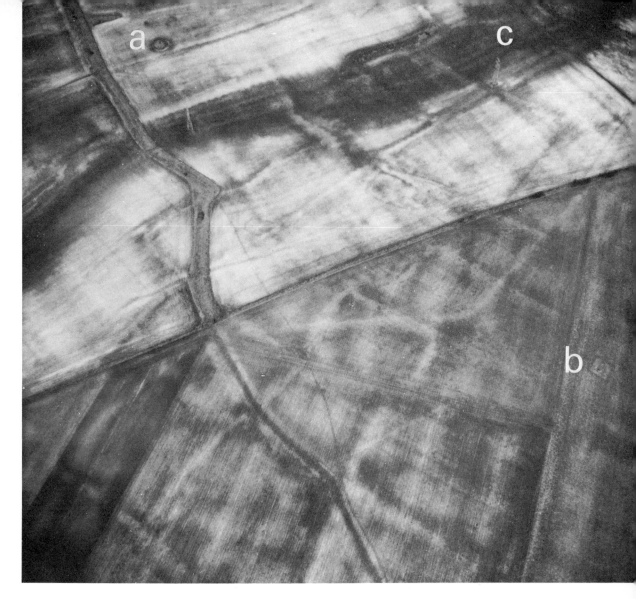

Complex additions and alterations to such boundaries have been demonstrated elsewhere by excavation and fieldwork.

It is not known whether the ditched boundaries were used, in the same way as before, in the Roman period but there were marked changes and innovations between the Conquest and the end of the fourth century. Quite a new sort of large enclosure is marked by the 94-acre enclosure on Rockbourne Down dated to the fourth century AD. The 'Soldiers' Ring', which is undated and much smaller but has a comparable shape and unusual ditch structure, could be of similar date.

The ditched circle at (a), likely to be a barrow of the second millennium BC, is *probably* at a junction of 'Celtic' field sides. It is one of a number requiring close examination since they could be on, and therefore subsequent to, 'Celtic' fields, providing information on their early date. The ditched square at (b) is of a size and shape consistent with its being an Iron Age barrow, within two or three centuries before the Roman invasion. It probably lies on 'Celtic' fields, like a group 70 km to the west in Dorset.

Right of centre, near the top of the picture, at (c), is a rectangular block of parallel 'strips' marked by alternate light and dark lines. These could be the remnant of a larger area of medieval ridge and furrow overlying the 'Celtic' fields or represent a category of ditched 'strips' so far unexplained, possibly Romano-British (p. 48). (SU 0819/10/342 in the National Monuments Record. Crown Copyright.)

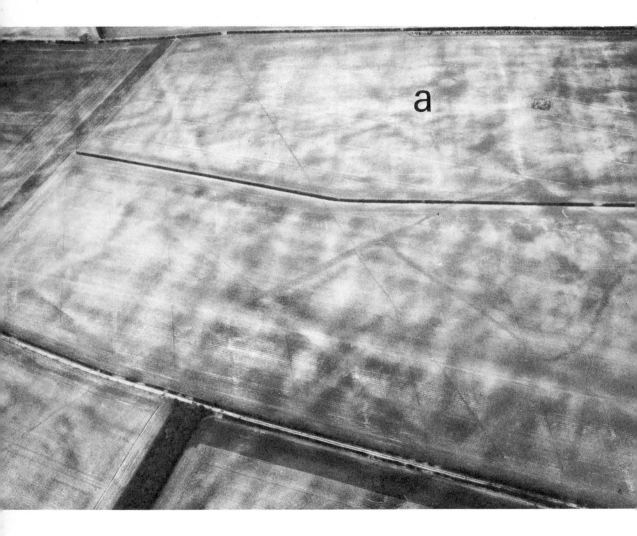

Pl. 3b Oblique air photograph, looking west, showing soil marks of 'Celtic' fields and a settlement, 5 km north east of the hill-fort of Danebury, Hants. The settlement, at map reference SU 353400, is indicated by an enclosure of 2·5 hectares with three straight sides and a fourth curved. The shape is repeated in numbers of other settlements. Romano-British pottery has been found on the surface but an earlier origin is possible. Two of the sides, one extended by a ditch meeting the left edge of the Plate just below the centre, correspond with the axes of the 'Celtic' field block which surrounds it. A block of fields on a different axis can be seen meeting the 'settlement' block of fields in the top left quarter of the picture. Here, therefore, it is conceivable that we have the boundary between two farming territories. There is a ring ditch, probably of a Bronze Age barrow, at (a). A thin dark line, almost straight, extending from top left of centre to a point just left of the bottom right hand corner, is so far undated. (SU 3539/3/77 in the National Monuments Record. Crown Copyright.)

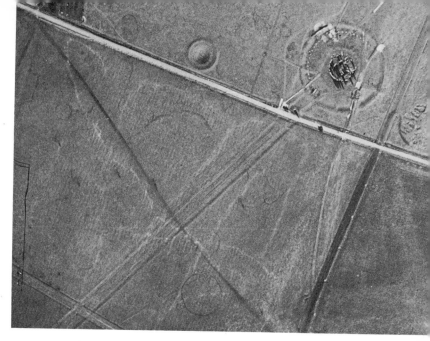

Pl. 3c Vertical air photograph of Stonehenge and its Avenue, north to top, taken in 1922 by the R. A. F. The scale may be taken from the diameter of the earthwork ring around Stonehenge, about 100 m across. This ring had the ditch outside the bank whereas the majority of 'henge' monuments are defined by a circular bank with inner ditch. This emphasises one of the difficulties of interpreting remains on the basis of their forms. (Compare pl. 3d where a large group of ringworks with ditch outside bank remains totally unexplained.)

The Avenue is as straight and regular as any Roman road, although 2000 years older. It has been surveyed and built with precision along an axis that corresponds with sunrise on Midsummer's Day. The area around it was never put down to 'Celtic' fields, as can be seen by the lack of any lynchet formation against the Avenue ditches (*see* p. 45). (SU 1242/14A in National Monuments Record, O. G. S. Crawford collection.)

Pl. 3d Oblique air photograph of part of South Haven Peninsula, Studland, Dorset, with slight earthen circles, each some 15 m to 35 m in diameter, whose origin is totally unknown and whose date, even after intensive investigation, can only be bracketed somewhere between 700 BC and AD 1700.

The form of some of the individual circles here is similar to that of the Stonehenge earthwork, to certain 'pond' barrows or to Iron Age hut circles. Documented activity in the parish includes fishing and the production of salt. For various reasons not one of these possibilities can be accepted.

The almost lunar aspect of this landscape is a reminder that here there has been no obliterative activity such as ploughing which, after a year or two, can totally destroy such relatively slight remains.

Pl. 3e The coastal plateau extends behind a defensive rampart, 2·5 km long, on the inland brow of the 'swine-backed' Bindon Hill, Dorset, to make an enclosure which, in Iron Age times, probably reached nearly 200 hectares. An extension of the rampart covered the approach to Lulworth Cove, the harbour almost certainly associated with these works. Excavation around the entrance through the main rampart produced little but poor quality native pottery not closely dateable, possibly around 400 BC, but the scale of the works suggests an importance, perhaps, like Hengistbury, a 'cross-Channel port', still to be proved. The size of the enclosed area, now largely under grass and not receptive to aerial photography, is such that only chance disclosure can produce further information. Looking east (Crown Copyright.)

Pl. 3f This air photograph shows cropmarks of ditched enclosures, presumed to be Iron Age, at Pimperne, Dorset, over some 2 hectares (5 acres). The ditches crossing the space between inner and outer enclosure clearly divide it into compartments, perhaps for sorting stock. The incurving entrance could have assisted stock herding. A similar pattern is suggested on at least two sites in Hampshire. There are similarities with features of both Little Woodbury and 'banjo' type sites. Compare fig. 3·2 where ditches springing from the 'banjo' entrances curve *outwards* to form a quite separate large enclosure. The interior size and entrance by themselves recall the enclosures with antennae ditches like Little Woodbury, Wilts., or Gussage All Saints, 12 km away in Dorset.

The enclosures are not isolated. A long prehistoric ditch meanders past in the bottom right of the picture. Small barrows, not visible, north of this indicate that there was ancient pasture here. By contrast a massive 'Celtic' field lynchet springs from the apex in the outer enclosure in the top right quarter of the picture. Other large enclosures lie close on the east.

dominated the landscape, the demand immediately arose for edge tools—that is, axes, the vital component in any large-scale assault on the forest. The response to this demand seems to have been made at the very earliest stages of development. In Sussex, carbon dating indicates that as early as *c* 4340 BC the flint mine complex at Church Hill, Findon, was in operation (BM-181). Flint, of course, does not occur naturally in Cornwall or Devon (apart from at Beer in the very east of Devon) and the importation of flint axes seems to have been restricted. The demand in Cornwall, at any rate, was such as to promote the exploitation of selected quarry sites, yielding hard volcanic rocks of predictable fracture in working, known as 'greenstones', which eventually were to 'export' (by whatever mechanism) their products all over southern England. The demand which led to the origin of these 'factories' must have developed, initially at least, locally. At least four of the quarries were active right at the very beginning of the farming colonisation, significantly, perhaps, well dispersed throughout Cornwall: the St Ives area; Ballstone Down, Callington; the Camborne area; and Kenidjack Castle, West Penwith, or perhaps Terras Mill near St Austell. (A convenient form of shorthand is used to identify the various sources of the utilised rocks: the above four are, in geological and archaeological literature, respectively Group IIA, IVA, XVI and XVII.)

With the aid of these raw material resources, the immigrant farmers built their houses and cleared the timber and bracken to create their fields. So far archaeologists have located five of the dwelling sites of these farmers: Hembury Fort, north west of Honiton; High Peak, south west of Sidmouth; Hazard Hill, north west of Totnes; Haldon Hill, about 8 kms south of Exeter; and Carn Brea, 4 kms south west of Redruth in Cornwall. The material which has been recovered from all of these sites leaves us in little doubt that we are dealing here with similar expressions of the culture which appeared in the whole of southern England at this period. Radio-carbon dates (BM-130, BM-136, BM-138, BM-149, BM-150, BM-214) suggest that these settlements probably existed sometime between *c* 4000 and 35000 BC (Table 1). This is the period bracketing in general the decline of elm and the increase of 'weeds' in the pollen record. It seems reasonable to combine the information from our five south western sites to produce a unitary picture of what seems to be a closely related phenomenon. **table 1**

Hunting was of some importance as a source of food to these farming groups, and red and roe deer appear to have been their principal quarry. They bred cattle firstly and then sheep or goats and pigs, and in their clearings they grew possibly einkorn and emmer and bread wheat. There is no direct evidence yet in the south west of the cultivation of barley at this period or the domestication of the dog, although both are known elsewhere in Britain at this period in a similar cultural context. At Hazard Hill the area of settlement was characterised by a series of areas where working had taken place and rubbish had been buried, but no structures were apparent. At both Haldon and Hembury, however, 'houses' of a sub-rectangular form were recovered although, by the appearance of their remains, these can have been no more than the flimsiest of huts.

At Hembury the occupation was at least partially enclosed by an interrupted ditch after the fashion of the 'causewayed camps' which seem to develop at a very slightly later date in southern England. At High Peak, three 'darkened areas' where the majority of the early Neolithic finds occurred may indicate occupation areas and a shallow ditch may again indicate some kind of enclosure.

From all these sites pottery is recovered, the earliest to be seen in south west England. Some of it is very rough, crude and locally made; but other pottery of fine texture also appears to have been made in south Cornwall in the area of the Lizard peninsula and exported throughout the area, adding another facet to the complex pattern of the movement of goods, pottery and axe raw material over the area. The flint industry of these farmers is quite distinctive, with a certain microlithic element perhaps indicating some inter-marriage or other contact with the native population of hunters. The leaf-shaped arrowhead, however, is an introduction or innovation and the end scraper and thumbnail scraper become very common. Add to these the stone axes we have spoken of already and we have a fairly full picture of the material equipment of these people as it survives to us in the archaeological record.

The writer himself is at present in the process of re-examining the important site at Carn Brea near Redruth, Cornwall. Here it seems possible that we are in the presence of an enclosed settlement of some degree of permanence. Structures which at present are difficult to interpret occupy areas of the interior and much occupation débris occurs which conforms closely to that already briefly described above from other sites of this group. At present little is known of the environmental background to this site but one can perhaps view it as an enclosed settlement built on a rocky hill protruding from the oak forest which dominated the area. The enclosure is delineated by a wall built of massive granite blocks which tempts one to suspect that a fairly permanent and settled occupation is indicated.

Upon what economy was this settled way of life based? Extension of the excavated area on to the gentle southern slopes of the site has revealed that, spread evenly over the hill slope, is a layer of organic soil which contains, in so far as they are diagnostic, artefacts relating only to the early farming settle-ment on the enclosed summit. The organic soil partially covers rough piles of stones which rest directly on the natural 'rabb'. The surface of the rabb rises slightly beneath many of these piles of stones which do not conform to any **pl. 2a** real pattern or scheme.

My interpretation is that these piles of stones represent the first clearance of rocks and stones from the surface in order to create small patches of cleared ground in which spade cultivation could be started. In Wiltshire, beneath a long barrow at South Street near Avebury, marks in the surface of the chalk gouged out by the tip of a prehistoric ard bear witness to cross-ploughing prior to the probable planting of seed corn. These have been radio-carbon dated (BM-356) to the time bracket 3660–3400 BC and are probably roughly contemporary with the settlement of Carn Brea (BM-823, BM-824 and BM-826). But although the ard may have been already in use on the lighter stone-free soils of Wessex it seems likely that, at any rate on the granite, spade digging would have remained the only feasible method of cultivation in the south west for a long period. Certainly the reasonable use of an animal-drawn ard would not have been possible in the uneven and roughly cleared patches that have been uncovered at Carn Brea.

fig. 2·1

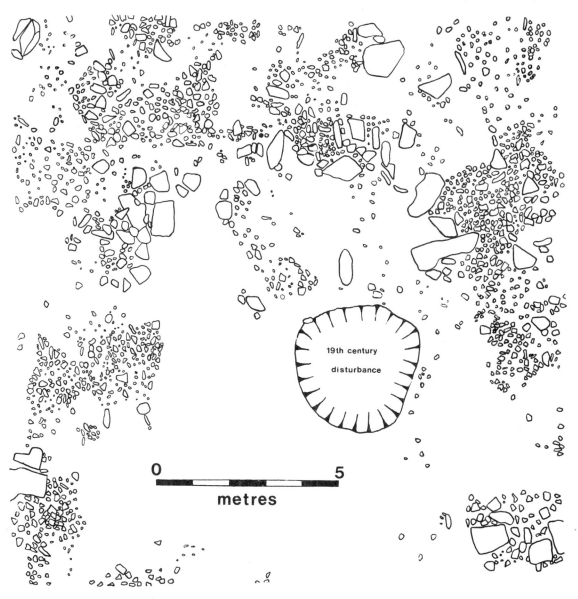

19th century

disturbance

0   5

metres

Fig. 2·1 On the gentle slope of Carn Brea near Camborne, Cornwall, below the site of an enclosed Neolithic village, signs of widespread stone disturbance were detected by excavation. An area of soil is shown here cleared of stones which have been thrown into piles preparatory to spade and hoe cultivation.

The clearance of the stones must have been preceded by the destruction of an area of forest both to provide building materials and to clear the land for cultivation. Over forty complete or fragmentary greenstone axes have now been found on the hill at Carn Brea, the vast majority being from the nearby Group XVI source, near Camborne but not yet pinpointed exactly. Carn Brea itself may also have been a 'distribution centre' for the dispersal of these axes out towards the east. The production from these quarries, not so much in Cornwall where the actual factory sites are either unknown or no longer visible, but in the Lake District and elsewhere where one can actually see thousands of spoilt roughouts lying on the screes below the rock exposures, must have been prodigious. At the Grime's Graves flint mine complex in Norfolk calculations following recent excavations by the writer indicate that the whole complex, during its admittedly long life, must have produced something in the order of several million axes. The excavator of a massive flint mine complex at Rijkholt near Maastricht in Holland has calculated that production there must have approached 400,000 flint axes per year. These figures help to give some idea of the intensity and rapidity of man's offensive against the forest of which we can perhaps see a microcosm at Carn Brea.

The extreme uniformity of the cultural content of these five sites so far known from south west England and their very small number might indicate that the incursion of farming communities into this region at this early period was either short-lived or relatively unsuccessful. We have seen that very little reaction to this settlement is to be seen in the pollen record as it has been studied in the peats of Dartmoor. Presumably the granite moorlands above 305 metres remained forested or partially so and continued to furnish terrain for hunting communities whose flint assemblages, sometimes with exotic 'farmer' tools included, are scattered over the moor. At Carn Brea the massive number of flint arrowheads present on the site might well indicate that hunting was of far greater importance than usually was the case with the farmer immigrants and contact with the native hunters would have probably been inevitable. At Gwithian in a turfline representing a considerable passage of time (Layer 8), two small sherds of pottery and a leaf-shaped arrowhead typical of the early farming communities are found together with a flint industry usually associated with the littoral hunter-fisher element. The date of this association is not known but presumably lies somewhere close to the middle of the third millennium BC. As some of the distinctive features of the Hembury-style pottery (round bases and perforated lugs) are seen to be carried through into the pottery of the post-2500 BC period, it is likely that a small and archaeologically barely perceptible population of these earliest farmers persisted in the south west throughout this long period.

What happened in the middle period of the third millennium is not, at present, at all clear. But certainly once again we are faced with a further massive assault on the wooded areas, and for the first time, widespread settlement and cultivation of the granite moorlands. Significantly perhaps, some axe factories seem to function only from the mid-third millennium onwards, and these are perhaps a response to this development (Groups IA in the West Penwith area, III and IIIA from the Mounts Bay area). Interestingly, an axe of Group IA was found within Layer 8 at Gwithian. At this period immigrants using the distinctive 'Beaker' pottery were beginning to arrive in Britain from various points along the Continental seaboard. But there is very little evidence of any substantial incursion by these groups of people into the south west peninsula of the country (Layer 7 at Gwithian is an exception). Instead, another pottery tradition which seems to develop is probably to be linked to some extent with the complex continuum of pottery cultures developing in southern Britain at this period.

It is at this period, probably at the turn of the second millennium BC, that the first evidence for the use of an ard for ploughing appears in south west **pl. 2b** England. At Gwithian (Layer 5) marks resulting from successive ploughings in the sandy soil were recovered during Professor Charles Thomas' excavations at **pl. 2a** this vitally important site. Several years' ploughings seem to be involved, the land during this period almost certainly being manured with domestic refuse and seaweed. The possibility exists of differential manuring in response to the needs of different crops. The awkward headlands of the fields where the plough could not be turned had been dug by hand with a wooden heart-shaped shovel similar in form to that still used by preference by any Cornish labourer today. The ard used in this ploughing seems to have been tipped with stone as a broken greenstone fragment was found jammed into one of the furrows. The ploughing has resulted in the formation of substantial positive and negative lynchets which, in conjunction with ditches and a wall (or linear stone pile), formed the boundaries of the ploughed areas. These ditches were presumably dug to keep livestock off the crop and we know from faunal remains that cattle, sheep and pigs were kept on the settlement. Two sub-rectangular houses seem to have been associated with this farming activity. This settlement after a long period of exploitation was abandoned and sand blows were permitted to cover the field surfaces. After a period, however, re-occupation took place (Layer 3). Stone hoes were still used for cultivating the ground and, to judge from the grinding querns found on the site, a cereal crop was grown. Cattle, sheep and pigs were kept and perhaps also horses. Two bronze pins and a mould for a bronze socketed axe which occur in this layer would indicated a desertion in this phase of occupation not before 1000 BC. This sequence at Gwithian forms the key to our appreciation of this period of south west prehistory and provides a firm basis for chronology.

On Dartmoor the first glimpse we have of this new phase is the building of the stone row, now tragically buried by china clay waste, at Cholwichtown, 9·5 kms north east of Plymouth. This stone row, despite a lack of firm dating evidence, was probably built some time at the end of the third millennium BC in a clearing in oak forest. We also know from pollen and soil analysis that cereal pollen was present in the clearing at an earlier stage but it had reverted

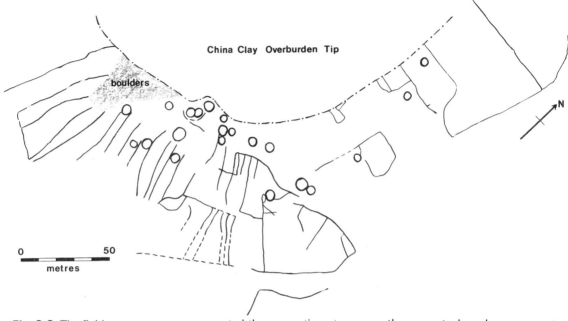

Fig. 2·2 The field system
associated with the Middle
Bronze Age hut circle village at
Stannon Down, St Breward,
Cornwall. The overburden tip
from china clay workings, which
prompted the excavation at
Stannon Down, probably covers a
further area of cultivation. The
narrow 'fields' to the south west
of the site contrast sharply with
the open stock enclosure areas to
the north east. The stock-rearing
areas are carefully separated by
walls and by the village itself
from the crop-bearing area.

to heather heathland by the time the row was built. On Bodmin, as we have
seen, the forest cover was never so complete but, at a phase culturally equivalent
to Gwithian Layers 8 and 7, clearance or cutting had taken place to such an
extent as to create, at least at Stannon Down on the western edge of the moor,
an area available for cultivation. Here, excavation by the writer exposed a layer
of organic cultivated soil (Stannon Phase 1). It lay beneath the foundation of
the huts of a village built on the site (Phase 2) at a period equivalent to Gwithian Layers 5–3. Walls dividing the Phase 1 cultivated surface were recovered
in a very ruined state (having been 'ploughed out' by the activities of the Phase
2 farmers). We do not know the extent of the Phase 1 cultivation at Stannon
but a badly chipped greenstone axe found in the base of the layer of soil may
point to some clearance so cultivation seems likely. A stone hoe found beneath
one of the hut circle walls may point to the technique used. No settlement
site was found, however, which could be linked with the Phase 1 cultivation.

The Phase 2 village was associated with a system of long narrow plots or
fields delineated by walls which were largely the result of stone clearance. The   **fig. 2·2**
field system can only have been about two acres in extent—an area totally inadequate for the support, as a principal food source, of a village the size of
the Stannon hut circle group. One would visualise instead these plots as 'gardens'

in which subsidiary food supplies were grown, possibly cereals or legumes. Despite the amount of stone clearance that had taken place, large boulders still lying within the plots would have neutralised any attempt to use a plough or ard of any kind. It seems most likely that spade cultivation continued to hold sway for some time on these 'granite' sites. Careful excavation of the dug drains which occurred within some of the huts revealed the marks of a spade which seems likely to be readily comparable with that in use at the same period at Gwithian.

The principal food source in this village community would appear to have been the large-scale breeding and herding of stock, possibly cattle. Large corrals with walls, unlike the field walls, carefully built to resist the rubbing and butting of the animals are distributed all over the moor. Three are closely associated with the Stannon village. Pollen evidence from the peat deposit which eventually covers this whole landscape confirms this picture of an economy orientated very strongly away from cereal cultivation (although some cereal pollen grains do occur). On Dartmoor, pollen evidence for the period points to increasing clearance with the cumulative effect of soil leaching and animal grazing preventing forest regeneration. It is against this background that the formation of blanket peat began. Cereal pollen grains indicate the preservation of permanent arable areas on the moor at this time. In a settlement somewhat similar to Stannon at Horridge Common, a bronze palstave found in one of the enclosed fields would be conventionally dated to the fourteenth to twelfth centuries BC, a date with which the Stannon evidence accords well.

Ethnically the content of this stock breeding population has become extremely complex. The flint assemblage, as in earlier times, perhaps betrays some elements of the hunter communities who had dominated the moorlands for so long. The pottery tradition, as we have said, perhaps reveals contacts with the southern British 'Late Neolithic', as do certain aspects of the flint industry and a shale bead found lying on the paved floor of one of the huts at Stannon. Some features of the pottery may hark back to the first farmers in the south west who had arrived at the end of the fifth millennium.

Eventually the settlement at Stannon was deserted. Before the hut walls had begun to collapse a smear of black peat was already forming on the field surfaces. This peat formation heralds a period of climatic deterioration throughout south west Britain. The same formation is seen on Dartmoor. Radio-carbon dating has not yet given us a date for this deterioration and once again we have to turn to the Somerset Levels for a clue. Here also conditions were becoming increasingly waterlogged and, as a response to this, wooden trackways were once again being built across the marshes. Dates for these trackways begin (Westhay trackway, Q-308, and Meare Heath trackway, Q-52) *c* 1100 BC. The parallels between Stannon Phase 2 and Gwithian Layers 5 and 3 here receive some confirmation as both settlements are seen to draw to a close at roughly the same time.

We have seen in this necessarily brief survey the first weak attempts by man to burn down the forest which surrounded him, possibly as an aid to the hunting which was his sole source of food. With the arrival *c* 4000 BC of the first farmers from the continent of Europe, a deliberate mobilisation of raw materials produced a rapid and massive clearance of forest for cultivation, though progress at this phase was probably not as fast in the south west as on the more hospitable soils of central Wessex. After a long pause a major reactivation of clearance *c* 2400–2000 BC took control of the moorlands and other areas. With this phase comes the first detected use of the ard in south west Britain. On the lighter soils, such as at Gwithian, arable farming was probably of considerable importance while, on the more difficult environment of the granite uplands, stock-raising flourished. On the moorlands the onset of a cooler and wetter climatic phase around the turn of the first millennium BC, and possibly also the cumulative effects of over-exploitation of the poor soils, brought the intensive farming of the uplands to an end, at least for several centuries. Whether this desertion was common to the whole peninsula, or whether farming went on in the sheltered valleys leaving only the moorlands deserted, can only be determined by more and more intensive fieldwork to locate the sites relating to the first half of the first millennium BC which have so far eluded us.

Bibliography 2

Radio-Carbon Dating

Basic Principles: E. H. Willis, 'Radio-Carbon Dating' in D. Brothwell and E. Higgs (eds.), *Science in Archaeology* (2nd ed., 1969), 46–57.

Tree-ring Correlation: H. E. Suess in *12th Nobel Symposium* (1970), *see* pp. 303–309.

W. F. Libby, *Phil. Trans. Roy. Soc.* **269A**, 1970, 1–22.

C. Renfrew, 'The Tree Ring Calibration of Radio-Carbon; an archaeological evaluation', *Proc. Prehist. Soc.* **36**, 1970, 280–311.

H. McKerrell, 'Some Aspects of the Accuracy of Carbon-14 Dating', *Scot. Archaeol. Forum* **3**, 1971, 73–84.

Pollen Analysis

Zone VIIA/VIIB transition: H. Godwin, *The History of the British Flora*, 1956.
    A. G. Smith in D. Walker and R. G. West (eds.), *Studies in the Vegetational History of the British Isles* 1970, 81–96.

Zone VI/VIIB forest clearance: I. G. Simmons, 'Environment and Early Man on Dartmoor, Devon, England', *Proc. Prehist. Soc.* **35**, 1969, 203–19.
    'Evidence for British Mesolithic Vegetation Changes', in P. J. Ucko and G. W. Dimbleby (eds.), *The Domestication and Exploitation of Plants and Animals*, 1969, 113–19. *See also*: F. E. Zeuner, *Dating the Past* (4th ed., 1964), 57–67, 92–5.
    G. W. Dimbleby, 'Pollen Analysis as an Aid to the Dating of Prehistoric Monuments', *Proc. Prehist. Soc.* **20**, 1954, 231–6.

Molluscan Evidence

Zone VIIA/VIIB transition: J. G. Evans, 'Habitat change on the calcareous soils of Britain: the impact of Neolithic Man', in D. D. A. Simpson (ed.), *Economy and Settlement in Neolithic and Early Bronze Age Britain and Europe*, 1971, 27–73.
    'Interpretation of Land Snail Faunas', *Univ. London Inst. Archaeol. Bull* **8–9**, 1970, 109–16.
    'Land and Freshwater Mollusca in Archaeology—chronological aspects', *World Archaeology* **1**, 1969, 170–83.

Plant Remains

J. M. Renfrew, 'The Archaeological Evidence for the Domestication of Plants: methods and problems', in Ucko and Dimbleby (eds.), *above*, 149–72.

Bones
I. W. Cornwall, *Bones for the Archaeologist*, 1956, Chap. 16, 'Study and Interpretation'.

Agriculture
H. C. Bowen, *Ancient Fields*, 1961.

P. J. Fowler, 'Early Prehistoric Agriculture in Western Europe: some archaeological evidence', in D. D. A. Simpson (ed.), *above*, 153–82.

and J. G. Evans, 'Plough-marks, Lynchets and Early Fields', *Antiquity* **41**, 1967, 289–301.

'Trade'
Stone Axes in SW England: E. D. Evens *et al.*, 'Fourth Report of the Sub-Committee of the South Western group of Museums and Art Galleries (England) on the Petrological Identification of Stone Axes', *Proc. Prehist. Soc.* **28**, 1962, 209–66.

On Carn Brea as a distribution centre, *see* J. V. S. Megaw, 'The Neolithic in the South West of England; a reply and some further comments', *Cornish Archaeol.* **2**, 1963, 4–8.

Pottery distribution from the Lizard Peninsula: D. P. S. Peacock, 'Archaeology, Science and the Lizard', *The Lizard* **4**, 1969, 3–5.
'Neolithic Pottery Production in Cornwall', *Antiquity* **43**, 1969, 145–9.

British Sauveterrian Groups
J. G. D. Clark, 'A Microlithic Industry from the Cambridgeshire Fenland and Other Industries of Sauveterrian affinities in Britain', *Proc. Prehist. Soc.* **21**, 1955, 3–20.

Sites (arranged alphabetically by site name)
Carn Brea: T. C. Peter, 'The Exploration of Carn Brea', *J. Roy. Inst. Cornwall* **12**, 1896, 92–102.
R. Burnard, 'The Exploration of Carn Brea', *Trans. Plymouth Inst. & Devon & Cornwall Nat. Hist. Soc.* 1895–96, 1–23.
R. J. Mercer, 'The Neolithic Settlement of Carn Brea: Interim Reports, 1970, 1971, 1972, *Cornish Archaeol.* **9**, 1970, 53–62; **10**, 1971, 93; **11**, 1972, 5–8.
Cholwichtown: G. Eogan and I. G. Simmons, 'The Excavation of a Stone Alignment and Circle at Cholwichtown, Lee Moor, Devonshire, England', *Proc. Prehist. Soc.* **30**, 1964, 25–38.
Dozmary Pool: G. J. Wainwright, 'Three Microlithic Industries from South West England and their Affinities', *Proc. Prehist. Soc.* **26**, 1960, 193–201.

Gwithian: A. C. Thomas, *Gwithian—Ten Years' Work* (1958).

'The Palaeolithic and Mesolithic Periods in Cornwall', *Proc. W. Cornwall Fld. Club* **2**, 1957–8, 5–12.

'Bronze Age Spade Marks at Gwithian, Cornwall', in A. Gailey and A. Fenton (eds.), *The Spade in Atlantic and Northern Europe*, 1970, 10–17.

J. V. S. Megaw *et al.*, 'The Bronze Age settlement at Gwithian, Cornwall', *Proc. W. Cornwall Fld. Club* **2**, 1961, 200–15.

Haldon Hill: E. H. Willock, 'A Neolithic Site on Haldon', *Proc. Devon Archaeol. Explor. Soc.* **2**, 1936, 244–263; and **3**, 1937, 33–43.

Hazard Hill: C. Houlder, 'Excavation of a Neolithic Settlement on Hazard Hill, Totnes', *Proc. Devon Archaeol. Explor. Soc.* **21**, 1963, 2–27.

Hembury: D. Liddell, Reports on the Excavations of Hembury Fort, Devon, 1930–2, 1934–5, *Proc. Devon Archaeol. Explor. Soc.* **1** and **2**, 1930, 1931, 1932, 1935, 39–64, 90–113, 162–90, 135–65.

High Peak: S. H. M. Pollard, 'Neolithic and Dark Age Settlements on High Peak, Sidmouth, Devon', *Proc. Devon Archaeol. Explor. Soc.* **23**, 1966, 35–59.

Horridge Down: A. Fox and D. Britton, 'A Continental Palstave from the Ancient Field System on Horridge Common, Dartmoor', *Proc. Prehist. Soc.* **35**, 1969, 220–8.

Stannon Down: R. J. Mercer, 'The Excavation of a Bronze Age Hut Circle Settlement, Stannon Down', *Cornish Archaeol.* **9**, 1970, 17–46.

Westward Ho!: D. M. Churchill and J. J. Wymer, 'The Kitchen Midden Site at Westward Ho!, Devon, England: ecology, age and relation to changes in land and sea level', *Proc. Prehist. Soc.* **31**, 1965, 74–84.

Acknowledgement

I am much indebted to Andrew Brown, School of Botany, Cambridge, for information about prehistoric environment on Bodmin Moor.

3 Pattern and Interpretation: a view of the Wessex landscape from Neolithic to Roman times

Collin Bowen

Unevenly distributed in a vast spread over four thousand or more square kilometres of Dorset, Wiltshire and Hampshire are the remains of banks, ditches, mounds and pits representing the successive activity of Man from about 3000 BC to AD 500. This evidence is now mostly seen only on air photographs. Difficulties of interpretation abound and the most obvious must be mentioned straight away. These vestiges generally survive only in areas which have not been intensely developed in later times. They are further limited by the fact that obliterative destruction was already taking place even before the Roman period. A study of overall settlement pattern is therefore impossible before the Saxon period, simply because the total evidence is not available; but what we do have is still almost overwhelming in its bulk and contains within it repetitions of shapes, conjunctions and relationships which can only be called pattern. It will be the purpose of this essay to consider the nature of the remains, difficulties in interpretation and, finally, assumptions, testable hypotheses, that can serve until proved wrong or modified. Its broad theme will be that from early in the second millennium BC land was being surveyed, segregated and laid out on a large scale for various purposes in a way which reflects notable control and competence.

The evidence lies in a consideration of all the known remains and this is only made possible by the existence of overall air photographs. The theme is extremely difficult to illustrate. It requires maps not yet made or impossible to display in a book such as this. Individual air photographs such as those used in Plates 3a and 3b can give some idea of the complexity to be investigated and demonstrate detail, but large series taken at different times are needed not only to cover sufficient ground but also to provide complementary information, since different features can appear in different years, at different times of the year and, indeed, at different times of day. And before maps can be made it is necessary to have carried out intensive fieldwork and also most highly desirable to have investigated select sites and points of relationship by excavation. Since, however, excavation will never be carried out on any but a relatively small proportion of the remains, it is important to consider what answerable problems are presented by a conspectus of the whole and where they can best be further investigated.

pl. 3a
pl. 3b

What we see in Wessex, after allowing for medieval and later alteration, is concerned with peace and war, life and death, pomp and squalor over some three thousand years, from the middle of the third millennium BC to the break-up of the Roman establishment in the fifth century AD. Surviving earthworks are often set in much larger areas of flattened remains showing, usually, as spread rubble from banks and mounds or dark infill of ditches when the soil is bare and, in crop, as darker lines of corn growing more vigorously over ditches and other holes in the ground. The area, especially between the R. Stour in Dorset (flowing south through Blandford), the R. Meon in Hampshire near the Sussex border, and, to the north, the escarpment of the Chalk, is particularly important because it is one of those very rare regions where remains of fields and boundary ditches and other features are so extensive as to provide a series of physical links or determinable relationships. If jargon were allowed, it would be called a situation allowing of both horizontal and vertical stratigraphy.

The remains of 'ritual' or 'funerary' monuments are largely dealt with in Chapter 4. Secular activities were, however, very much concerned with religious attitudes and this is frequently reflected in the disposition of surviving features. Thus, certain Bronze Age burial grounds, like that on Snail Down, near Tidworth, Wiltshire, were eventually enclosed by banks which were clearly intended to segregate the area for grazing, and so combined respect for the barrows with practical use. The tendency to have large nuclear burial grounds, not infrequently associated with ritual monuments of considerable size, reflects an impressive organisation of parts of the landscape. Substantial areas of ground were bespoken at an early time, since it is rare for barrows to be found on land that was used for purposes demonstrably other than ritual. The arrangement of *cursus* monuments, in particular, shows an intention to impose ritual control over very considerable single areas. The Dorset Cursus, the largest known, is about 75 m wide and some 10 km long over its two sections and is associated with long and round barrows, the latter frequently in large concentrations. The cursus maintains almost straight alignments *across* the grain of the country involving three streams and the ridges dividing them. Its date is **fig. 3.1** probably about 2500 BC. The inference is that there was a powerful hierarchy and competent surveyors to lay it out, that the country along that strip was cleared of obstructive vegetation, and that movement north to south was severely impeded by its presence.

The power and technical competence to lay out monuments on a large scale, directly and indirectly affecting land use, is seen also at Stonehenge. Here is **pl. 3c** technical ability reflected in a remarkable manner not only by the architectural detail of the stones and the engineering ability implicit in their erection, but also in the survey and setting out of the Avenue. The air photograph shows a long section of this to be as straight and true as any Roman road. The lack of any lynchet formation against it shows that no prehistoric agriculture was ever practised around it. In view of the fact that 'Celtic' fields are found in most other comparable situations the segregation of this and a large adjacent

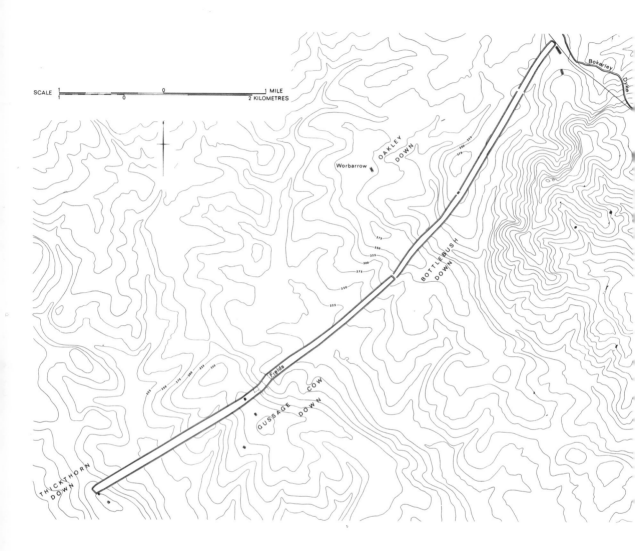

Fig. 3·1 *The Dorset Cursus* demonstrates, by the fact of its existence, that in the 3rd millennium BC, it was possible to conceive, survey and construct a monument with massive bank and ditch in an almost straight line for a total, in its two sections, of 10·4 km across a series of valleys and ridges between points that were not intervisible. The route was either already clear of trees or was cleared deliberately. Some 80 hectares were thereby segregated for ritual usages and it seems likely that north–south movement was effectively blocked for its entire length. This planned land-use and the technical ability to lay out long lines in broken country should be borne in mind by the reader when he considers the alignment of 'Celtic' fields in fig 3·3.

Factors involved in planning the Cursus include the incorporation of a long barrow in its north bank about 3 km from the east end. Although the barrow is not quite in line with the Cursus bank an intention from the outset to incorporate it is strongly suggested by its alignment which is virtually at right angles to all the other long barrows in the area. Compare fig. 3·4 where a long mound, usually called a long barrow, is incorporated in a prehistoric but otherwise not closely dated boundary bank of the Grim's Ditch complex. Based on plan by R.C.H.M. (England).

area might be shown someday to have a bearing on the chronology of religious observance at Stonehenge, involving the possible uses of this ground for periodic concentrations of population. It is not only technical competence and sheer power that is involved. The alignment of the Avenue, as is well known, extending the axis of Stonehenge itself, points to the rising sun on Midsummer's Day. The achievement of this alignment is remarkable and demonstrates clearly a fusion of practical purpose, in fixing the Calendar, with undoubted religious observance. It encourages speculation that many other alignments might have been connected with religious observance while having a practical use. In the ritual sphere, long barrows have the most obvious capacity to 'point'. Long barrows 'point' to either end of the Dorset *cursus*, for instance. We shall return to this when considering the arrangement of early 'Celtic' field blocks.   **fig. 3·1**

Before indulging in such detail it may help very briefly to specify some recognisable forms of secular features. 'Celtic' fields are the most widespread. They are rectangular plots varying in size from $\frac{1}{4}$ acre to over 1 acre, defined by lynchets or banks or, very occasionally, by walls. The fields are usually more   **pl. 3b** obvious than the settlements from which they were farmed. These settlements may be marked by ditched enclosures, though in all periods there are settlements without such enclosures and they are correspondingly difficult to identify. 'Celtic' field sides are always straight unless there is a specific reason. One of the reasons is that they may lie against (or on, if disused) the bounds of enclosures which were not arable fields. Tracks may be marked by flanking ditches or lynchets and are usually about 6 m across. Wide tracks about 12 m across were presumably drove tracks. Very broad ways, up to *c* 30 m across, are associated in some instances with Romano-British settlement. Long ditches are interpreted according to their context rather than their form. If they appear to bond with a widespread system, skirt round barrows presumably used as markers), and possibly link with hill-forts, then they can be thought of as 'ranch boundaries' in use from a very arbitrary *c* 1500 BC to 300 BC, any connection with hill-forts possibly relating to a late phase of their use. They may run quite straight or be serpentine. The difference may relate to the existence of vanished obstacles but has never been seriously investigated. They frequently cut across 'Celtic' fields but also, on occasion, bound them. The term 'ranch boundary' can reasonably be taken to reflect in some sense an original purpose just as, indeed, 'Celtic' fields can be seen from associated lynchet formation to be arable fields. Certain other features are less easily seen in functional terms.

Certain small roughly circular enclosures with long-necked entrances, like short sections of track, are now usually called 'banjos' or 'banjo enclosures'.   **fig. 3·2** The proportions might not always be apt but there are also, not infrequently, traces of ditches springing from the outer ends of the entrances suggesting the keys of a banjo. Something like 40 of these enclosures are now known in Wessex generally confined within the same bounds, the Rivers Stour and Meon, that bound the ranch boundary system but a direct link with proven 'ranch boundaries' of the early prehistoric system is not known to the writer. They may

appear singly or in pairs and there is a growing awareness that they were probably associated with adjacent enclosures not always recognised. The form of
their entrance suggests a use for some form of 'processing' stock. 'Banjos' are,
in fact, the most clearly recognisable elements in, to use a medical term, a
syndrome or collection of symptoms. By themselves, they remain fairly constant
in shape, though occasionally an internal variation, such as the presence of pits,
suggests a use, at some phase, not connected with segregation of stock. The
associated earthworks may vary in form but almost always include ditches
bounding relatively large spaces and, not infrequently, late Iron Age and   **fig. 3·2**
Romano-British settlement. Another form of Iron Age enclosure, two or three
times the size of the typical 'banjo' and well known since its excavation in the
1930's, is represented by Little Woodbury, near Salisbury, a site so much discussed that nothing more will be said of it here except to say that the antennae
ditches splaying outwards from the entrance to form a funnel as wide as the
enclosure itself represents a function not yet satisfactorily settled, but one that
will be much discussed in coming years when the results of Dr Wainwright's
total excavation of such a site in 1972 at Gussage All Saints, Dorset, become
available. A further form of complex enclosure, not yet excavated, is shown
in pl. 3f.   **pl. 3f**

Interpretation is bedevilled both by lack of excavation and by the problems
of excavation. Much of what we see on air photographs represents superimposed
patterns, a palimpsest, and, with little doubt, excludes elements that will be
found only under excavation. Not one hundredth of the known remains will
ever be excavated. When a palimpset is concerned, even when excavation is
contemplated, it is helpful if major elements of the pattern can be recognised
and related to sites where the forms are clearer. Here lies the importance of
looking for 'type-sites'. Identical form will rarely, if ever, be found but rough
analogy of character and its repetition in different circumstances, can be one
of the useful bases for considering function and, of course, range of date. It
is possible to take a relatively modern example of this. Water-meadows, representing a system of controlled flooding first recorded some 350 years ago, consist
of elaborate patterns of ridges with ditches or 'carriages' running lengthwise
along them carrying water that eventually overflows into the gulleys between
the ridges. Many of these ridges were probably built by ploughing in much
the same way as ridge and furrow in the arable fields. Limited but detailed
excavation of a small section might produce quite the wrong answer yet consideration of a whole series would provide both a rough guide to their true
nature and, by association, a very rough idea of their date.

The prospect of putting this theory to use on remains also defined by long
'strips' is now emerging. In parts of Dorset and Hampshire there occasionally
appear on air photographs single small blocks of apparently ditched strips of
rather varying form, characterised particularly by their appearance in single
blocks in areas otherwise containing 'Celtic' fields. Probably cognate examples
are well known in the Fens, so a Romano-British date is suspected. All we

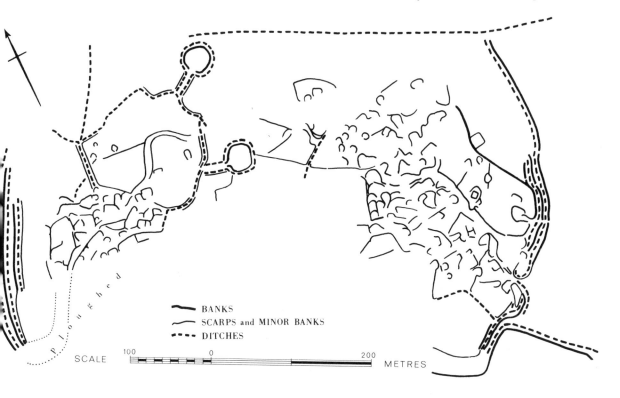

BANKS

SCARPS and MINOR BANKS

DITCHES

SCALE   100   0   200   METRES

Fig. 3·2 Diagram of Iron Age and Romano-British earthworks at Hamshill Ditches, Wiltshire by D. J. Bonney based on a plan by R.C.H.M. (England). In the top left quarter are two 'banjo' enclosures, clearly seen to be elements of a complex, their entrances opening into an enclosure of some 2 hectares, here partly overlaid by later building platforms. This is a pattern that recurs. A variation also found has the ditches curving back to encircle the 'banjo'. The pattern thus made recalls the situation at Pimperne (pl. 3f) and although the proportions and detail vary it appears that similar activities, probably to do with stock, are reflected.

can be safe in assuming for the moment is that repetition provides a pattern likely to be associated with a particular economic activity in one period. It is the repetition which gives most hope.

A single site might totally defy interpretation or dating, as has the group of some sixty earthwork circles, none less than 17 m across, on Studland Heath just south of the Poole Harbour entrance in Dorset. Here the circles have superficial affinities with pond barrows and hut-platforms, but are certainly neither. They have been investigated by all reasonable means without establishing a satisfactory answer as to date or function, and an appeal in *Antiquity* (**37**, 1963, 220–3) produced no acceptable suggestions. An air photograph illustrated here **pl. 3d** repeats the appeal.

Even when patterns emerge over substantial areas there are difficulties which, though fairly obvious, need comment. It is clear that there are regional differences even within the three counties which largely concern us here. These differences do not coincide with any known Iron Age tribal boundaries. It is possible that some relate to topographical differences. For instance, the 'ranch boundaries' might be regarded as unsuitable to the broken country west of the R. Stour or to the steep slopes of the South Downs in Sussex. Some features, and this appears to apply to the hill-forts which edge Salisbury Plain, require nearer proximity to better sources of water than is provided by relatively arid blocks of downland. The other side of this coin is that new sites, even hill-forts, are constantly emerging and it is unsafe to base arguments on distribution alone until there is reasonable certainty about its limits. The writer confesses to having made a monumental error in respect of curious boundary features, akin in many ways to 'ranch-boundaries', which at one time were thought to exist only in the river valleys of east Britain from the Thames to the Forth. These are the 'pit-alignments', lines of close-set pits, square or round, about 2 m across which divide up large blocks of land. The little excavation carried out on these ten years ago suggested a post-Iron Age date and this was unwisely linked to their preponderant eastern distribution to suggest early Saxon origins. Their distribution is now known to include even ground high in the Cotswolds and excavation has demonstrated a late Iron Age and early Roman date. Although the attribution was wrong, it can be noted that the features themselves demonstrate a widespread carving up of the land in an interesting and curious technique known only in this particular period.

Before looking again at the broad patterns that might be thought to emerge from all this, a little thought can be given to numbers. So far as sites go, we are just beginning to count and a vast amount of work lies ahead. It is vitally important to get ranges of date and to connect works with dated settlements adequately excavated. There are other indications that the population, at least in the Iron Age, is greater than once thought. One such indication of this occurred as the incidental result of experiment in the mid-1960's whereby it was sought to show that corn could be stored underground over a British winter, substantiating the theory that this was one of the major uses to which Iron Age pits were put. The possibility was proved but at the same time it was found that pits had a storage capacity some nine times as great as had been supposed in the famous Little Woodbury report, on which calculations of population and arable acreages were based. Even when allowing for other factors it seemed that the population and arable must have been at least three times as great as those supposed. This makes more plausible the concept that hill-forts were to some extent a by-product of population pressures on land.

The present agreement that deep pits are generally for storage and not for living in as 'pit-dwellings' removes a further reason for looking on the native Britons as unorganised semi-troglodytes. The scatters of pits once encouraged the idea of low, untidy standards in sharp contrast with the regimentation of Roman patterns and ways of life. There is little doubt that much of the pre-Roman and, indeed, native Romano-British ways were squalid but the evidence of patterns we are considering suggests elements of high organisation for 2000 years before the Roman invasion. A recent book described Bronze Age fields as 'higgledy-piggledy'. It is becoming apparent that substantial blocks were just the opposite. We have mentioned regular arrangement and hinted at an occasional possible connection with long barrows. Neolithic long barrows are sometimes found incorporated in 'Celtic' field groups. In south east Dorset there are three examples which form sides of 'Celtic' fields. Since long barrows are massive earthworks they cannot have been altered to fit the 'Celtic' field pattern. This sounds of little significance until it is remembered that blocks of 'Celtic' fields are frequently arranged in rectangular fashion according to axes that pre- **fig. 3·3** determine their alignment whatever the situation of the ground. This arrangement is carried out with the sort of accuracy already noted for the Neolithic Dorset *cursus*—a very approximately straight line over broken country. Now, the relationship of 'Celtic' fields to specific long barrows has never been determined by excavation so there is no knowledge of *how soon* after the building (or use) of any long barrow the 'Celtic' fields were laid out.

Whatever the relationship with long barrows, and this will certainly be very variable, the point that seems to be established is the priority of the 'Celtic' field system as a whole over the ranch boundary system. It was once thought that ranch boundaries represented the earliest organisation of the landscape. It now seems that deliberate allotment was generally marked, at an earlier date, by the apportionment of land to arable agriculture (though it must always be remembered that some 'Celtic' fields originated as late as in the Roman period). Just how much earlier needs to be tested by excavation in many places. The 'ranch boundaries' still betoken a remarkable carving up of the landscape. Evidence of excavation and fieldwork on Martin Down in Hampshire points to **fig. 3·4** an almost certain Middle Bronze Age date, say 1200 BC, for 'Celtic' fields crossed obliquely by a ranch boundary of possibly the same rough period. However this may be, there is in the 8 km east from Bokerley dyke a pattern of ranch boundaries which certainly crosses 'Celtic' fields in a number of places and **pl. 3a** would appear to be connected with lines radiating from Whitsbury hill-fort. The hill-fort is presumably at least 600 years later than some of these boundaries but its apparently nodal position is repeated in many other areas. The best preserved is around Sidbury, west of Tidworth. Here, again, four ranch boundaries stem from the hill-fort and in seven different parts of an adjacent 70 km² region they cross well-formed axially aligned blocks of 'Celtic' fields. A long barrow and another long mound, possibly a long barrow, are embodied in the 'Celtic' field blocks. At Quarley hill-fort, as Professor Hawkes showed long ago, ranch boundaries meet *at* the hill-fort but the hill-fort defences lie physically over them indicating their prior existence. Something even more dramatic than the first slighting of 'Celtic' fields was now taking place: a reorganisation based upon power in citadels. Whether this derives from the spontaneous pressures of population, as already suggested here, or from other causes to do with immigration or threats from abroad must remain an open question until large programmes of investigation are achieved.

The implications of the widespread incidence of the 'banjo' syndrome, 'banjo' enclosures and hybrid forms linked to other enclosures and probably in most instances, to settlements, are not yet clearly seen. A tentative view might be that they represent a new element in the organisation of stock on a scale that invites thoughts of an organised trade. As Strabo tells us 'hides' were one of the commodities on Britain's export list before the Romans came. Investigation of the organisation of Channel ports in the Iron Age has been curiously neg-   **pl. 3e** lected. Associations so far recognised strongly suggest an extension of the use of 'banjos' into the Roman period. There is no known connection with hill-forts or with ranch boundaries other than a general distributional coincidence. Who organised these things, how the patterns were disseminated or enforced, is still a matter for speculation but it seems reasonable to assume that this is the third of the orderly impositions of an economically inspired pattern on the landscape in the pre-Roman period. Amongst it all were the aristocrats known to us from classical sources. There is no doubt that they were connected with hill-forts and, in the writer's view, it is still very probable that they also occupied certain other settlements, notably those of Little Woodbury type. The strands are there. They need to be woven.

In a Roman view the 'foundation of so great exploits' that built the Roman empire were 'accomplished by the eminent merit of a few citizens' (Sallust in M. Grant, *Roman Readings*, 1967, 123). The eminent merit of a few may account for so much that we have considered in prehistoric Britain, too, but the evidence is accumulating for substantial and growing populations. The level of order,

Fig. 3·3 These 'Celtic' fields in Central Dorset are arranged on a rough north west–south east axis which continues across ridge and valley unaltered by whatever direction the ground may face. It is suggested that this axis was laid out as a planning operation since it cuts across a stream and a narrow flood plain that was clearly never cultivated. Such planned segregation of land for a particular use and its apparent connection with a selected axis surveyed over broken country may be compared with fig. 3·1.

The area illustrated shows only part of 800 hectares or so wherein 'Celtic' fields were virtually continuous, some in blocks on different alignments.

'Celtic' fields are frequently arranged in blocks according to such axes. These blocks of fields are often seen to be crossed by ditched boundaries (*cf.* pl. 3a) some dated to 1000 BC or earlier. There is, therefore, a strong suggestion of planned land allocation, before the construction of those ditched boundaries, in the Middle Bronze Age at the least. This was a period when round barrows were being laid out in deliberate relationship to long barrows so all relationships of 'Celtic' fields to long barrows, which are monuments which have a massively marked axis (*cf.* fig. 3·4) similarly require close examination. See p. 51. Plan after part of R.C.H.M. plan of Celtic field group 45 (Cheselbourne area) in *Central Dorset*.

KINGCOMBE

stream

——— 'CELTIC' FIELDS   ● ROUND BARROW   *NORTH to top of plan*

SCALE

1000   0   2000 FEET

100   0   800 METRES

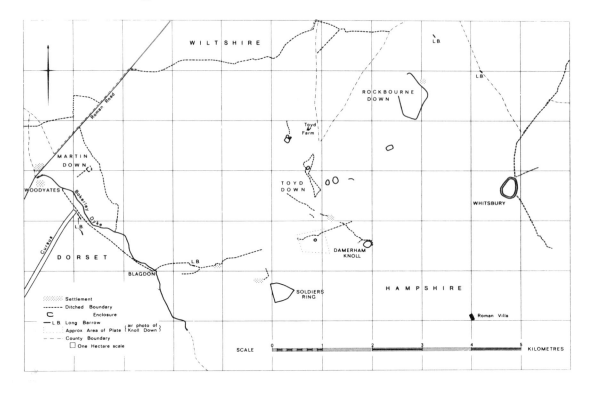

Fig. 3·4 This diagram shows the pattern of boundary banks and ditches so far recognised in five south west Hampshire parishes between Bokerly Dyke and Whitsbury hill-fort. Some other select features are shown. No attempt has been made to plot the 'Celtic' fields which once covered most of the area. It is a one hundredth part of a complex which once covered most of the Chalk between the Rivers Stour in Dorset and Meon in Hampshire.

There is no doubt that the pattern shown is very incomplete and it is likely that the whole area was eventually broken up into large enclosures. Three boundaries can be seen to meet at Whitsbury. A fourth now ends 3 km west of it but on a line which, if extended, would also meet the others at Whitsbury. This suggests a control from Whitsbury in the Iron Age but some of the boundaries are at least 500 years earlier than the earliest date for Whitsbury which, at a guess, could be 500 BC. In the west it is clear that Bokerly Dyke, a late Roman boundary of defensive proportions, closely follows and may lie over or have replaced elements of the prehistoric system. The west boundary position itself seems likely to be connected with the presumably sacred properties suggested by the ending of the Dorset Cursus and the long barrows 'pointing' in to it. Since the County boundary follows Bokerly Dyke we have here an example of a boundary line still in use (and surviving even the 1974 re-organisation of local government) though established, in some sense, more than 4000 years ago.

Innumerable points both to broad themes and to individual complexity need endless attention. Boundary ditches cross 'Celtic' fields on both Martin and Knoll Downs in a way which suggests that some of the fields, at least, ceased to be regarded as arable ground. This is illustrated in pl. 3a, an aerial photograph of the small trapezoidal area enclosed by dotted lines on the diagram, where the ditch itself is complex and lies by a probable settlement perhaps associated with the fields. In the north east there is a long barrow on the county boundary between Wilts. and Hants. In this another prehistoric boundary? Notice also the 'long barrow' incorporated in the boundary on Tidpit Common, south west of the diagram. The linear features themselves vary in size and nature. A recent excavation by the South Wessex Archaeological Association across the 'ditch' north of Soldier's Ring showed this to be a shallow hollow. It was used as a track to the Romano-British settlement south west of it but might have existed as a boundary before this.

political and economic, that is suggested needs to be set side by side with the certain sophistication of Stonehenge, and the ability to record astronomic alignments without, so far as we know, a written language. It also needs to be considered against the effort and population reflected in the first large-scale and regular allotment of land. If, as has recently been suggested, the ice once covered much of Britain south of the Thames, then the achievement of Man's first spring-clean in clearing erratics so effectively is indeed formidable. Where were they swept to?, Long barrows and lynchets offer a good place to look. Ability in some ways could have been higher in the pre-Roman period than later, as Fred Hoyle has suggested. It is important to remember that it was no less. The Romano-Britons were the same people as the Ancient Britons. They achieved much in the way of order long before the Romans. 'To bring order out of chaos is a process of civilisation' (Lord Clark). Even if we cannot accord 'civilisation' to the peoples of the period, doing great works as long before the Romans as we are after them, the aphorism may help us to look up to, rather than down on them.

Bibliography 3

Ordnance Survey map at 1:25,000, *Celtic earthworks of Salisbury Plain*, Old Sarum Sheet (1937: the only one to be published of six projected sheets. One other, for the area north east of Amesbury, was prepared but not published. The scheme was the work of Dr O. G. S. Crawford.)

C. M. Piggott, 'The Grim's ditch complex in Cranborne Chase', *Antiquity* **18**, 1944, 65–71, with note by Dr O. G. S. Crawford, p. 71. This deals with the area covered by fig. 3·4.

A. H. Pitt-Rivers, *Excavations in Cranborne Chase IV* (1898), (Martin Down excavation).

H. C. Bowen, *Ancient Fields* (1961). Considers the relationship of 'ranch boundaries' and 'Celtic' fields on Martin Down. (The book also has a useful bibliography.)

C. F. C. Hawkes, 'Excavation of Quarley hill-fort', *Proc. Hants. Fld. Club* **14**, 1936, 136–94, proves that the hill-fort overlay a junction of 'ranch-boundaries'.

H. C. Bowen and P. J. Fowler 'Romano-British Rural Settlement in Dorset and Wiltshire', in C. Thomas (ed.), *Rural Settlement in Roman Britain* (CBA Research Report No. 7, 1966), 43–67.

B. Perry, 'Iron Age Enclosures and Settlements on the Hampshire Chalklands', *Archaeol. J.* **126**, 1970, 29–43.

R. C. H. M. volumes on *Dorset* show plans of Bindon Hill (Vol. II), the Pimperne Down enclosure (Vol. IV) and the Cursus (Vol. V). For hill-forts, they give pointers to control in the pre-Roman Iron Age and, in what they seem to take over, in the organisational sense, the earlier periods.

D. J. Bonney, 'Hamshill Ditches', *Wilts. Arch. Mag*, **62**, 1967, 118–20.

H. C. Bowen and P. D. Wood, 'Experimental storage of corn underground and its implications for Iron Age Settlements', *Univ. London Inst. Archaeol. Bull* **7**, 1968, 1–14.

4 Religion and Settlement in Wessex, 3000–1700 bc

Geoffrey Wainwright

In recent years the orientation of excavation work in the rural areas of Wessex has been governed by the necessity of rescuing as many sites as possible from destructive modern agricultural processes and the construction of roads and buildings. With a few exceptions where monuments have been investigated preparatory to their display for the public, the emphasis of the work has been placed on rescuing sites rather than conducting investigations to solve particular problems, save where it has been possible to create an ordered programme of investigation out of the destruction.

To some degree this has coloured our knowledge of prehistoric settlement in Wessex, for some aspects have received more attention than others. For example, our knowledge of the sepulchral practices of the period has been greatly enriched by the concentration of effort on the burial mounds, most of which have been damaged by agricultural operations, so that much evidence obtained from modern excavations will eventually be available to set alongside the mass of material obtained from less controlled work in the nineteenth century. This concentration on sepulchral aspects, however necessary at the time, has resulted in many centuries of our prehistory being represented solely by graves and objects obtained from them. More recently some aspects of the rescue programme have been re-directed, thus redressing the balance, but much work remains to be done in the field of domestic settlement, environment, economy and social organisation.

The majority of the recorded sites of the third and early second millennia in southern England are those represented by banks and ditches, or occasionally stones, which are now in many cases degraded after millennia of ploughing. The structures and buildings that were of timber have not survived as visible remains, leaving an enormous vacuum in our knowledge and consequent assessment of this era. On the whole, the remains are clustered on the chalklands—the Marlborough Downs, Salisbury Plain, Cranborne Chase and the Dorset Downs. They are represented by the burial mounds, both long and round, some circular earthwork enclosures of variable type which have been grouped as causewayed camps and henge monuments, together with some sparse evidence for industrial activity represented by the flint mines. Very few domestic sites are known and these are represented by clusters of shallow pits, whose ultimate use was for the disposal of rubbish, or simply by scatters of stone tools on the surface of ploughed fields. Similarly, the artefacts found are not very impressive and consist of fragmentary pots, bone and flint cutting and scraping implements and some polished axes of flint and stone. The exotic objects of copper, bronze and occasionally gold, which began to appear in the area towards the end of the period with which we are concerned, were few in number and must have been restricted to a minority amongst a population who were still using stone for their implements. This essay is not concerned with the material remains of the period but rather with assessing the results of recent field research on those earthworks and structures that have survived, the advances in attempts to determine the environment of the time, and with efforts that have been made to evaluate problems of social organisation and demography for the third and first part of the second millennia bc.

A very few burials in the third millennium bc were made beneath round barrows, the normal covering mound being the earthen long barrow, an elongated mound of earth and chalk rubble with flanking quarry ditches. Some are less than 30 m long, others are almost 170 m, and a small group are larger still. Inhumed burials were deposited, apparently one at a time, beneath the often broader easterly ends and had sometimes been housed in structures of turf or timber. The long barrow structure, however, was largely conditioned by local geology and a variant is represented by long barrows or cairns covering stone chambers, to which there would have been periodic access. Rather less than 200 earthen long barrows and approximately 130 stone tombs are known in southern England, our present knowledge of them being based on the relatively intensive excavation of a small series of monuments. The length of time during which these tombs were being built and used can now be reckoned as in excess of 1000 years, the carbon-14 dates for the earthen long barrows ranging from 3415 bc for Lambourn in Berkshire and 3240 bc for the Horslip Barrow near Avebury, Wiltshire, to 2460 bc and 2370 bc for the Giants Hill barrow in Lincolnshire, whilst the stone tomb of Waylands Smithy in Berkshire has a date of 2820 bc. The ceramic evidence from the West Kennet stone **table 2** tomb suggests that it was open for not less than 1000 years and that the remains of 20 adults, one youth and at least 12 children and adults found within it had been re-buried after temporary storage in an ossuary. The numbers of individuals in earthen long barrow burials vary considerably from a single inhumation to 53 or 57 at Fussell's Lodge, with an average of 10. The stone tombs that have been excavated give an average of about 15 burials. Quite clearly, not more than three or four persons died each year who merited burial in a formal tomb, a calculation which is based on the probably false assumption that the Neolithic population remained static throughout the third millennium. Allowing for an approximately exponential increase of the population on account of improved farming techniques, Professor R. J. C. Atkinson has arrived at a population for the last century of the third millennium in lowland England of between 70 and 140. The tombs may well have been used for the burial of

Table 2 Alphabetical list of radio-carbon determinations quoted in the text (all dates bc)

ington Walls				Mount Pleasant		
enclosure	1977 ± 90	(BM-398)		*Timber Structure*	1961 ± 89	(BM-663)
	2015 ± 90	(BM-399)			1991 ± 72	(BM-666)
	2050 ± 90	(BM-400)			2038 ± 84	(BM-667)
hern Circle	1950 ± 90	(BM-395)		*Main Enclosure*	2108 ± 71	(BM-792)
	2000 ± 90	(BM-396)			2098 ± 54	(BM-793)
	1900 ± 90	(BM-397)		*Stone Cove*	1680 ± 60	(BM-668)
hern Circle	1955 ± 140	(NPL-240)		*Palisade*	1687 ± 63	(BM-662)
Farm Down	2010 ± 110	(NPL-77)			1695 ± 43	(BM-665)
on Down	2530 ± 150	(BM-190)		Silbury I	2145 ± 95	(I-4136)
ts Hill, Long Barrow	2460 ± 150	(BM-191)		South Street Barrow	2810 ± 130	(BM-356)
	2370 ± 150	(BM-192)		Stonehenge		
bury	3330 ± 150	(BM-138)		*Phase I*	2180 ± 105	(I-2328)
lip Barrow	3240 ± 150	(BM-180)			1848 ± 275	(C-602)
bourne Barrow	3415 ± 180	(GX-1178)		*Phase II/IIIA*	1720 ± 150	(BM-46)
degai	2790 ± 150	(NPL-220)			1620 ± 110	(I-2384)
den	1988 ± 48	(BM-557)		*Phase IIIB/IIIC*	1240 ± 105	(I-2445)
				Waylands Smithy	2820 ± 130	(I-2328)
				Windmill Hill,		
				Enclosure	2580 ± 150	(BM-74)
				Woodhenge, Ditch	1867 ± 74	(BM-677)
					1805 ± 54	(BM-678)

In Table 2, and throughout the text of p. 4, the radio-carbon dates are alibrated, *cf.* p. 11 and Table 1.

selected members of the population only, however, and the majority of the dead were perhaps disposed of in a way which has left no archaeological trace.

A similar conclusion results from a study of the round barrows, which were built when the funerary rite of collective inhumation was succeeded by that of single burials under round mounds. Although a few round barrows were constructed in northern and eastern England during the third millennium bc, the single-grave tradition did not become established until around 2000 bc, the earliest dates of 2145 and 2010 bc having been obtained respectively from Silbury Hill and Earls Farm Down near Avebury. A detailed study of the distribution of such burial mounds in a limited region—the Ridgeway area of south-east Dorset (45 square miles), has revealed 233 barrows on the Ridgeway itself and a further 205 on the slopes related to the top of the ridge. The average barrow density is 10 per square mile, which compares with 10 barrows per square mile and 25 per square mile around the ritual centres of Avebury and **pl. 4a** Stonehenge respectively. These figures seem high when compared with those **pl. 4b** of two barrows per square mile for the Berkshire Downs, but if one accepts that most of the barrows were built in the second millennium bc, then an average of only one burial mound was built in the whole Ridgeway area every two years. This either indicates a very small population or more probably that the majority of the population did not have graves indicated by a 'tumulus'.

This selection procedure hints at some social stratification in the society and the emergence of a class whose status entitled them to a formal tomb. The grouping of the long barrows in clusters of two or three suggests that each group may have been located within its own individual territory. The only centres to have been recognised that could have co-ordinated social, religious and economic activities within these territories in the third millennium are the so-called Causewayed Enclosures. Some 16 or 17 such centres have been identified in southern England, their distribution being concentrated in the counties of Dorset, Wiltshire and Sussex. Most are on hills or downland but an elevated situation does not seem to have been essential. Reasonably reliable plans are available for only 11 of these enclosures, which comprise from one to three rings of causewayed ditches with internal banks. The majority of the enclosures are between three and seven acres in extent, although Maiden Castle in Dorset, **pl. 4c** Hambledon Hill in Dorset, and Windmill Hill in Wiltshire enclose between 17 and **pl. 4d** 21 acres. Regrettably very little excavation has been undertaken in the interior of these enclosures so that little or nothing is known of their internal structures. It does seem apparent that portions of the banks were pushed into the ditches to cover quantities of meat, pot-sherds, flint tools and *debitage*, and the interpretation of these causewayed enclosures has normally revolved around various views regarding the significance of this refuse. Interpretations of such refuse are necessarily subjective and incapable of proof. Current suggestions range from the remains of communal feasts ceremonially buried during periodic gatherings to scraped-up settlement debris which was buried because of the supposed magic powers of its fertilising properties. The evidence of radio-carbon dating indicates that the enclosures were constructed from the late fourth millennium, as at Hembury in Devon with its date of 3330 bc, to the middle of the third millennium as at Windmill Hill with its date of 2580 bc, although the evidence from the latter site is of continued use well into the second millennium.

The evidence from the causewayed enclosures is therefore unclear as to whether they were cult centres, rally points for the population of a fairly wide area, or whether there was any permanent occupation within their banks and ditches. Nevertheless, it is possible to suggest that they were focal points for territories or regions. Each of the major territorial groups of long barrows is accompanied by a causewayed enclosure (three in the case of the Marlborough Downs), with an average of 20 long barrows in each 'territory' (Dorset Downs, Cranborne Chase, West Salisbury Plain, East Salisbury Plain and the Marlborough Downs). It seems possible that each region served by a causewayed camp was populated by a tribal unit, possibly with a centralised power base, as such is indicated by other evidence for social stratification within the society and the emergence of a special class. It is therefore particularly interesting that these same focal areas persist into the second millennium, albeit in a rather different form from *c* 2000 bc. At this time were constructed a series of large enclosures, surrounded by great continuous earthworks with internal ditches, which relate closely to the earlier territories and to the causewayed enclosures which they probably superseded. These enclosures are Durrington Walls in Wiltshire, Marden in the Vale of Pewsey, Mount Pleasant near Dorchester and Avebury in Wiltshire.

Since 1966 excavations have been undertaken at Durrington, Marden and Mount Pleasant and much information obtained regarding their date of construction and internal features. It has been established that the three enclosures, which are 30 acres, 35 acres and 12 acres respectively in area, are all associated **fig. 4·1** with a distinctive ceramic style known as 'Grooved Ware' and that they all surrounded circular buildings of timber which had their roofs supported on concentric rings of posts. The Marden, Mount Pleasant and Durrington Walls enclosures were constructed around 2000 bc and probably replaced the causewayed enclosures of Knap Hill, Maiden Castle and Robin Hood's Ball respectively. Within the Durrington Walls enclosure at least two large circular buildings were constructed between 2000 and 1900 bc, the larger of which was 38·90 m in diameter and had its roof supported on five concentric rings of timber uprights. The plan of the building suggests that it had an outward sloping roof and a **fig. 4·2** high ridge surrounding an open central court which contained a free-standing ring of timber uprights. Assuming a roof-pitch of 25° and an eaves height of about 3 m for the outer wall, such a building would have had a maximum height of about 10·5 m. Similar buildings have been excavated at Marden and at Mount Pleasant which were also constructed around 2000 bc. In addition, **pl. 4e** closely comparable structures have been excavated at Woodhenge close to Durrington and at the Sanctuary at Overton in Wiltshire. Excavations in 1970 at Woodhenge indicated that the timber structure was probably built between 1850 **pl. 4f** and 1800 bc, much later than the excavated buildings within the main Durrington Walls enclosure.

It is rewarding to consider the effort expended on the construction of these enclosures and their attendant buildings. The estimated man-hours for the construction of the Durrington Walls enclosure are 900,000, involving the extracting of 1,750,000 cu ft of chalk rubble with antler picks, baskets and ropes. It has been estimated that the construction of the Avebury enclosure would **pl. 4a** have required 1,500,000 man-hours. There is reason to believe that the Avebury earthwork was also constructed between 2000 and 1800 bc and was associated in some way with the Windmill Hill causewayed enclosure, which 500 years earlier had required 120,000 man-hours for its construction. On this basis we are perhaps entitled to think in terms of a population increase and a more developed social hierarchy which could ensure such organisation of labour. In addition, the construction of the timber buildings would have presented formidable logistical problems. For the large structure at Durrington Walls over 260 tons of oak timber would have been required. In excess of 1000 m of timbers of varying diameters would have been required for the upright posts in the structure and lengths totalling 1500 m for purlins, ring-beams and rafters.

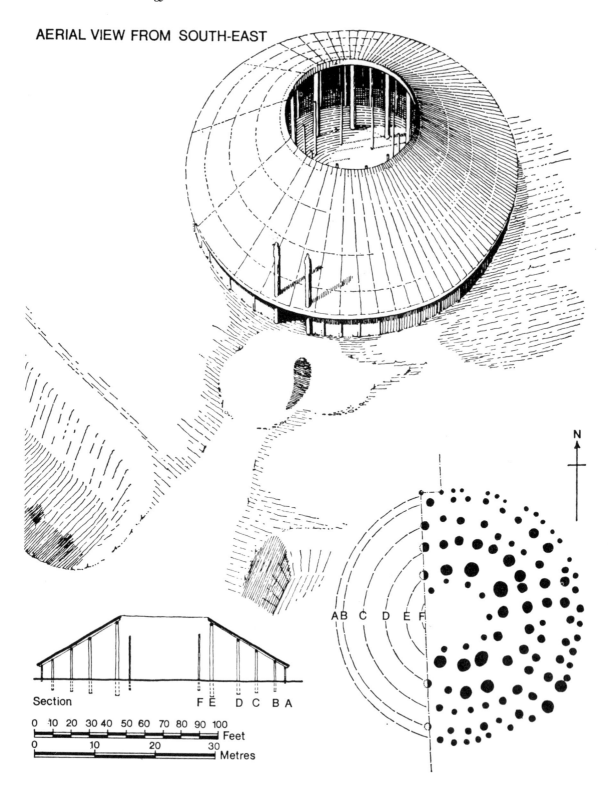

AERIAL VIEW FROM SOUTH-EAST

Section   F E D C B A

0 10 20 30 40 50 60 70 80 90 100
                                    Feet
0   10   20   30
                                    Metres

A B C   D E F

N

Fig. 4·1 A tentative reconstruction of the post-hole structure (the Southern Circle), dated to 2000–1900 bc, which was excavated at Durrington Walls, Wilts, in 1967. The structural posts were of oak and it was fronted by a platform of chalk blocks on which much debris had been deposited.

The timber would have been obtained in 3·5 hectares (8·75 acres) of natural deciduous oak forest and the building would probably have survived for the best part of 200 years.

Throughout the period when these burial mounds, enclosures and buildings were under construction the land would have been cultivated, domestic stock maintained and industry .and trade developed, but little is known of the early manifestations of land use and social interaction. In recent years Dr J. G. Evans has employed with considerable success the techniques of molluscan analysis and soil studies in respect of fossil land surfaces buried beneath earthworks on calcareous soils. His preliminary conclusions are that certain areas of Britain, which are now open downland or agricultural land, once supported forest cover and that clearance in these areas began in the late fourth or early third millennia bc. It seems likely that this forest clearance was brought about by early farming communities, possibly on a system of shifting cultivation. Subsequent land-use indicating arable or pastoral farming is indicated by disturbance of the fossil soil profiles to varying degrees and plough-marks, or more correctly ard-marks, have been recorded under the long burial mound at South Street near Avebury. At South Street, the buried soil was disturbed by cultivation through its entire depth and ard-marks were visible on the subsoil surface, from which charcoal gave a radio-carbon date of 2810 bc. These are the earliest examples of criss-cross ard-marks in Britain and were probably produced by a crook-ard, the simplest type of plough.

Additional evidence for agriculture and for stock-breeding has come almost entirely from the ditches of the causewayed enclosures. Information on cereals has been obtained from imprints on pottery. Barley accounts for 11% of all the impressions and the remainder are varieties of wheat, Emmer or Einkorn and Breadwheat. Spelt has occurred as a carbonised grain from Hembury, flax and apple pips from Windmill Hill, and hazel nut and marine shells from various sites. Amongst the stock, a large breed of domestic cattle was dominant, followed by sheep, goats and pigs. Wild animal bones form a small percentage of the whole. Towards the end of the third millennium some change can be seen in the pattern of stock-breeding and is exemplified by collections of fauna from the ditches of the large enclosures that were constructed between 2000 and 1800 bc. At Durrington Walls, pig comprises 63% of the total, cattle 26% and sheep 2% with very few remains of wild animals. Remarkably, no grain impressions have been recorded on any of the very distinctive pottery that was produced at this time and the available evidence suggests an economy which in its pastoral aspect was based primarily on the breeding of pigs, an animal which is valuable only to the settled farmer.

Industrial activity, though not necessarily full-time, is indicated by the flint mines. The Easton Down mines in Wiltshire cover *c* 40 acres, the flint being obtained by digging vertical shafts down to a seam of suitable flint nodules some 3–4 m below ground level. The extracted flint was then manufactured into roughed-out axes on the surface. A radio-carbon date from Easton Down   **table 2** indicates that the complex was operating by the middle of the third millennium and its products may have been traded over great distances, as were the axes of igneous stones which originated in factories to the west and north of Wessex. Not only stone axes were objects of trade, for Dr D. Peacock by employing petrological analysis has demonstrated that a distinctive style of fine pottery was probably a trade product dispersed from specialist workshops in the Lizard area of Cornwall early in the third millennium bc. A second specialist pottery source may have been amongst the outcrops of Jurassic Limestone in the Bath–Frome area of east Somerset—the products occurring within a radius of 20–30 miles from the presumed area of origin.

The development of agriculture in lowland England during the third millennium involved increases in population and social complexity which can be deduced from a study of the character and distribution of the burial mounds, enclosures and buildings as well as from the evidence for developing industrial activities and trade contacts. The social complexity is nowhere more clearly demonstrated than in the development of ceremonialism. In general, ceremonial or cult centres appear to be a normal step in the development of human cultures. They appear at or shortly after the development of economically efficient agricultural techniques, for these bring with them the need to manipulate the system of supernatural controls required by an agricultural economic base. In Britain these ceremonial centres are represented by structures of a wholly insular type which are referred to generically as 'Henge Monuments'. They comprise a bank and ditch, the latter normally being internal, surrounding a roughly circular area within which may be settings of stones, timber uprights, pits or burials. The diameters of these enclosures are extremely variable but average around 80 m. On the basis of a single radio-carbon date from Llandegai in Caernarvonshire, these sites were being constructed by *c* 2800 bc, although the main emphasis of the dating evidence is for a development from 2000 bc until *c* 1700 bc. In the heart of Wessex is Stonehenge which was originally constructed   **pl. 4b** shortly before 2000 bc as a circle of 56 pits (Aubrey Holes) arranged in a circle within a bank with an external ditch and one monolith (the Heel Stone) outside the single entrance. In its second phase Stonehenge was a double ring of bluestones brought from north Pembrokeshire with four outlying stones (the Station Stones) which were replaced between 1720 and 1620 bc by the sarsen structure

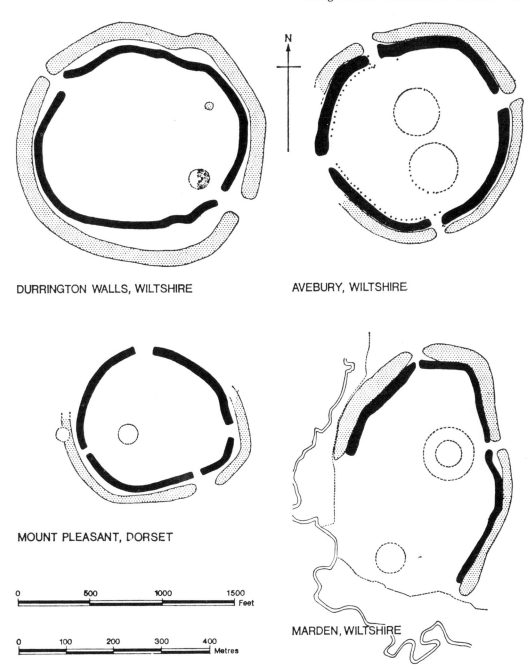

Fig. 4·2 Comparative plans of four earthwork enclosures in Wessex which were raised between 2000 and 1800 bc. The enclosures of Durrington Walls, Marden and Mount Pleasant have been shown to surround large circular timber buildings associated with pottery of the Grooved Ware ceramic tradition. Similar pottery has been recorded at Avebury but comparable timber structures have not yet been found.

of Stonehenge III consisting of an outer lintelled ring and an inner horseshoe of detached archways or trilithons. Final modifications to the structure took place as late as 1240 bc. Professor G. Hawkins has suggested that in its earliest phases the alignments between various stones and post-holes were designed to indicate the extreme positions of the rising and setting points of the sun and moon and were also arranged to predict eclipses. Professor Hawkins claimed that a 56-year cycle of eclipses existed which could be forecast by a system of moving stones round the Aubrey Holes at regular intervals. The two main arguments against this theory are that the Aubrey Holes appear to have been filled in again almost as soon as they were dug and would not therefore have been permanent markers and that no 56-year cycle of lunar eclipses can be shown to have existed. There seems little doubt that the eclipse-predicting functions so far suggested for Stonehenge are highly implausible and that a ritualistic purpose seems the more likely.

More common than henge monuments are circles of standing stones which are distributed mainly in north and west Britain where suitable rocks were readily available for their construction, an easterly extension of the distribution occurring in Dorset and Wiltshire. Such circles can occur within henge enclosures, as at Avebury, be free-standing with no bank and ditch, as at Stanton Drew in Somerset, or even occur under a burial mound. The circles may or may not surround a central burial but even when the latter is present it may be argued whether the primary purpose of the circle was sepulchral or whether the burial was of a dedicatory nature. Related to these stone circles are rings of posts which may be interpreted in part as a reflection of a lowland environment where stone was not readily available for building. Professor A. Thom has published studies of the metrical and astronomical properties of prehistoric stone circles in Britain and deduced from them a knowledge of geometry and the use of a unit of measurement, christened the 'megalithic yard', which he suggested was standardised throughout the country. Professor Thom also argued that stone circles and their outliers were sometimes built with astronomical observation as one of their main functions.

In 1971 Professor Thom extended these astronomical findings to include a number of linear arrangements in Scotland which he suggested had been devised for the observation and record of the complex movements of the moon including a very small perturbation of the lunar orbit, a knowledge of which would have facilitated the prediction of eclipses. These conclusions, if correct, indicate a degree of intellectual activity which is completely at variance with what we know of the material culture of the time. Intellectual endeavour need not be synonymous with technological advance, but Professor Thom's arguments can be questioned not on the basis of astronomical theory and survey techniques but on the basic unreliability of the circles and alignments themselves as evidence. The dangerous assumptions are adopted throughout that all the elements visible on an unexcavated site need be contemporary and that the modern distribution of stones in the settings bears a significant relation to the original layout. Furthermore, the possibility of timber elements in the structures is disregarded. Nor is the numerical evidence for the megalithic yard of 2·72 feet conclusive: the unit has a striking resemblance to the human pace which is normally accurate for survey work to within 2% or 3%.

The reasons why henge monuments in general are thought to have ceremonial use are, firstly, the presence of an external bank, secondly the presence within certain externally embanked enclosures of stone structures which have a presumed ritual significance and, thirdly, the absence of occupation debris. In retrospect there seems little doubt that the presence of stone settings within some externally embanked enclosures has led to the probably false assumption that all late Neolithic enclosures with an external bank had a ritual purpose; and in the case of the Durrington–Marden–Mount Pleasant enclosures it is possible to argue that this was not the case.

As recently as 1971, having directed excavations at those three large monuments, I was not prepared to regard large enclosures with external banks as serving a utilitarian purpose but rather viewed them as boundaries surrounding a sacred area. Partially as a result of some excavations in 1972 at an Iron Age farm near Gussage All Saints in Dorset, a three acre settlement surrounded by a boundary ditch and external bank, I would not now regard the late Neolithic earthworks as anything other than secular. In certain situations, for example in areas where stock is to be confined, an internal ditch is a positive advantage and such enclosures occur for example amongst the pastoral settlements of the Iron Age in Wessex (*above* p. 47).

A characteristic peculiar to these buildings and their surrounding earthworks is the great quantity of human refuse—sherds, stone and bone artefacts and animal bones. In this respect these sites differ from those with an overtly ritual function and superficially this should be strong evidence for a domestic usage. Other interpretations, however, are possible. Sherds of the same vessels occurred both inside and outside the large building at Durrington and were also found widely distributed within that building. Such a distribution could have occurred either as a result of keeping the building clean or it could have resulted from the deliberate breaking and distribution of sherds from vessels as a ritual act. Unfortunately it is not normally possible to distinguish on arbitrary grounds between domestic refuse and ceremonial refuse and the resolution of the problem is a subjective matter.

It may be suggested therefore that a reconsideration of those points concerning the character of the earthworks and the quantity of refuse could result in secular interpretations being placed on the enclosures and structures under discussion. There is, however, a further aspect to be considered which in the past has been termed *lithicisation*.

At a high level in the ditch surrounding the timber building at Mount Pleasant occurred a thick layer of black ash, fresh chips of sarsen, stone mauls and large numbers of Beaker sherds. From it a radio-carbon date of 1680 bc was obtained. This consistent deposit is related to the construction of a stone cove with three outliers which replaced the timber building at about this time. Similarly, at the Sanctuary on Overton Hill, the multi-phase timber building was replaced in Phase 4 by two concentric stone circles which were connected with the West Kennet Avenue. A crouched burial associated with a Beaker decorated with 'barbed-wire' ornament is thought to be contemporary and dates of *c* 1600 bc for Beakers of this type have been obtained on the continent. In addition, Phase II/IIIA of Stonehenge which comprised the erection of a double circle of 82 Bluestones from north Pembrokeshire is associated with a radio-carbon date of 1620 bc.

There is therefore some indication of a period in Wessex between 1700 and 1600 bc when certain of the timber buildings at Mount Pleasant, The Sanctuary and possibly Stonehenge, were replaced by stone settings of a ritualistic nature. In this connection we can also tentatively include Avebury where excavation may yet reveal timber structures pre-dating the stone settings. The transmutation of timber structures into stone is not a rare phenomenon in the third and second millennia BC. It has been invoked, for example, to explain relationships between megalithic tombs and earthen long barrows, and has been demonstrated at several stone circles, notably Croft Moraig in Perthshire. Its relevance in the present context is that the process should indicate some special function for the multi-ring buildings under discussion, which made it necessary for their ruins to be permanently indicated by stone settings. For this reason alone a purely domestic use for the buildings seems unlikely and a pre-eminent function within a secular context seems the explanation best suited to the arguments which have been outlined. It can be suggested that in earthworks of the Durrington–Marden–Mount Pleasant class we are seeing secular centres dominated by large public buildings which were accompanied, as at Durrington and Marden, by less massive structures for which a more purely domestic use might be deduced. This conclusion is supported by the character of the earthworks, their material associations including a consistent ceramic style, their siting in relation to contemporary earthworks and their development in relation to the earlier causewayed enclosures and later hill-forts.

These developments in the third and early second millennia in Wessex can be explained as the result of the arrival in the area of an economically viable system of agriculture which resulted in territorial divisions and a population increase, a developed social stratification within the society, and an increase in social complexity which is most apparent in the development of ceremonialism. The persistence of the territorial patterns from causewayed enclosure to continuously embanked area in the second millennium can best be seen in the Maiden Castle–Mount Pleasant region in Dorset as a result of extensive excavations at these two sites, 4 km apart across a shallow valley.   table 3

In the late fourth or early third millennium the focus is at Maiden Castle with a causewayed enclosure, the ditches of which had silted up before the long mound was built across its western earthworks. There was some settlement on Mount Pleasant hill in the third millennium but from about 2000 bc the

Table 3 The relationship suggested between Maiden Castle and Mount Pleasant
near Dorchester, Dorset

	Maiden Castle	Mount Pleasant
3000 bc	A causewayed enclosure around a knoll of a hill some 17–18 acres in extent **pl 4c**	
	A bank barrow 600 m long built over the silted ditches of the enclosure	Sporadic occupation
2000 bc		Multi-ring timber structure on top of hill **pl 4e**
		Earthwork enclosure of 12 acres
		Palisade enclosure of 11 acres
1500 bc		Bronze Age occupation
1000 bc	Successive Iron Age Hill-forts	

focus moved to that site with the construction of a multi-ring timber building 38 m in diameter sited within its own ditch. While this building was standing, 12 acres of the hill-top was enclosed *c* 2000 bc by a ditch and external bank. This earthwork was succeeded in 1700 bc by the construction of a palisade around 11 acres of the hill-top. It can be calculated that the palisade was formed of oak posts 9 m long and 40–50 cms in diameter standing side by side in a continuous palisade trench and that this timber wall probably stood some 6 m high above ground level. To obtain such a large quantity of good quality posts no less than 90 acres of oak forest would have to be exploited. In addition to the raw materials needed for this stockade, a large labour force would have been necessary to select the trees, to fell them and to lop the branches, to drag them from the valley to the crest of the hill and finally to erect them in the required positions, all this after a foundation trench 3 m deep, 1·20 cm wide and 750 m long had been excavated into the solid chalk with antler picks. Subsequent occupation on the hill-top is represented by rubbish in ditches and hollows down to *c* 1000 bc. Shortly after this time the first earthwork defences were built on Maiden Castle (a ditch 16 m wide and 6 m deep surrounding 16 acres), to which the focus of settlement appears to have moved with only intermittent occupation on Mount Pleasant hill. In AD 43 the final Iron Age hill-fort was sacked by Vespasian's Legion, following which the inhabitants were moved into the valley and finally into the Roman town of Dorchester.

One could deduce from this sequence a hypothetical picture of increasing centralisation of power in the third and second millennia bc, culminating in the immensely strong timber fortifications in *c* 1700 bc and the movement back to Maiden Castle in the first millennium. This persistence of territorial and focal patterns can be paralleled elsewhere in Wessex and evidence for it has already been quoted, but nowhere is it as clear or as prolonged as in Dorset. It is this conservatism of social, economic, cultural and ceremonial traditions which is becoming more apparent as techniques of analysis and excavation are extended and developed and as emphasis is placed on early land use within the emerging territorial areas in Wessex.

Bibliography 4

P. Ashbee, *The Earthen Long Barrow in Britain*, 1970.

R.C.H.M., *Inventory of the Historical Monuments in the County of Dorset*, II, *South-East, Pt 3*, 1970.

S. Piggot, 1962, *The West Kennet Long Barrow: Excavations 1955–56*, 1962.

D. D. A. Simpson (ed.), *Economy and Settlement in Neolithic and Early Bronze Age Britain and Europe*, 1971.

A. Thom, *Megalithic Sites in Britain*, 1967.

      Megalithic Lunar Observatories, 1971.

G. J. Wainwright and I. H. Longworth, *Durrington Walls: Excavations 1966–1968* (Reports of the Research Committee of the Society of Antiquaries of London XXXIX, 1971).

5 The Brochs of Scotland

Euan MacKie

The Scottish brochs are among the most striking of all the prehistoric monuments of Europe which have survived to modern times. Perched on tiny sea and loch islands, or on the remote rocky shores and rugged terrain of the highlands and islands of Scotland, they take on for foreign visitors the aura of the country in which they stand—mysterious and dreamlike—and seem to belong to the unfathomable past of the most northerly and remote parts of the British Isles. Their peculiarly Scottish name—like wags, weems, wheelhouses and the others—also seems to set them apart from the rest of British archaeology and to reinforce the impression of northern oddness. Yet, strange as they appear, the brochs, like the other structures mentioned, will fit quite easily into the general pattern of British prehistory and become markedly less strange with closer acquaintance.

Brochs should have a particular interest for all concerned with Britain's past for one important general reason. Apart from Stonehenge they appear to be the only really advanced architectural creation of prehistoric and early historic times which was invented entirely within Britain, instead of being imported here from elsewhere. Nearly every other major class of stone building from Neolithic times onwards—chambered cairns, hill-forts, Roman forts and buildings, early stone castles and Romanesque and Gothic cathedrals—was developed first on the continent of Europe and then introduced to the British Isles. Yet no structures remotely similar to a broch are known outside Scotland so it seems that this building—which may fairly be claimed as Man's greatest architectural achievement in drystone masonry—was developed wholly in Scotland. This gives the broch an interest and importance for the history of buildings which is out of all proportion to the superficial impression given by its restricted distribution and short period of use when set against the European background.

Some 510 known and suspected brochs are thickly scattered in what is known as the Atlantic province of Scotland, that rugged highland and island maritime zone which includes the west coastal strip north of the Firth of Clyde, the Western Isles, the counties of Caithness and Sutherland and the Orkney and Shetland Isles. Their distribution is most dense in the Orkney Isles and in Caithness (23 and 35 known and 81 and 114 suspected sites in each zone respectively). However Sutherland, Shetland and the Isle of Skye also have large numbers, though there are far fewer in Mull and the Outer Isles. There are also a handful round the Firths of Forth and Tay, in the east central mainland and far from the main concentrations.

This wide distribution, the clear boundaries of the broch zone, the striking architectural uniqueness of the structures and the general similarity of all brochs everywhere, have for years obliged all investigators to face certain basic questions. What were the brochs used for? Why are they so uniform? Why do they appear to have sprung into existence fully formed, like Athena from the head of Zeus, with no obvious ancestors? Do they represent the castles of an intrusive conquering minority (like Norman mottes in England) or the refuges of an agricultural population (like the fortified log cabins of the early settlers in America)? How far does the structural uniformity of the brochs throughout Atlantic Scotland reflect a cultural and political uniformity in the resident Iron Age population? Was there a specialist class of broch engineers who travelled round building the towers for each community—or could anyone put one up? What were the social conditions into which they emerged? No clear answers are yet available to some of these questions but much light has been thrown on many of the others by the work of the last twenty-five years.

Several brochs are sufficiently well-preserved to give an accurate idea of the original appearance of at least some of them. These include Mousa in Shetland, Dun Dornadilla in Sutherland, Dun Troddan and Dun Telve in western Inverness-shire and Dun Carloway in the island of Lewis. Together they give a reasonably complete picture of the architecture of a typical broch. **pl. 5a**
pl. 5b

Essentially these brochs are drystone tower-forts, circular in plan with a wall base which is massive and thick in proportion to the enclosed area. The overall diameters of the five just mentioned vary from 14·8 m (Dun Carloway) to 18·3 m (Dun Telve). The enclosed circular courts vary in diameter, in the order of the names given above, from 5·8 to 5·2 m, 7·45 m, 8·55 m, 9·84 m and 7·3 m. An effective way of expressing the massiveness of a broch's wall in relation to its total size is to add together the widths of opposing wall-bases and compare the total with the overall diameter. In this way Mousa is seen to be by far the most massively built, with a wall which takes up about 64% of the total diameter: the width of its tiny central court is therefore, conversely, only 36% of this. In the same way Dun Dornadilla's wall occupies 48% of the overall diameter, Dun Troddan's 52$\frac{1}{2}$%. Dun Telve's 46$\frac{1}{2}$% and Dun Carloway's 48%.

In all five brochs the typical hollow-wall construction, unique to this class of monument, is clearly visible. The upper parts of the structures each consist in fact of two concentric walls separated by a narrow gap from 0·6 to 1·5 m wide, and bonded together by horizontal rows of flat stone lintels. Thus the walls contain a series of superimposed galleries linked by an ascending stone stair which usually starts from a chamber at or near ground level and spirals round inside the wall to the top in a clock-wise direction. The function of the wall galleries is likely to be entirely structural, to lighten the thick stone wall and allow it to be built to a great height, probably over 12 m originally in **fig. 5·1;**
pl. 5a 5b
and 5c

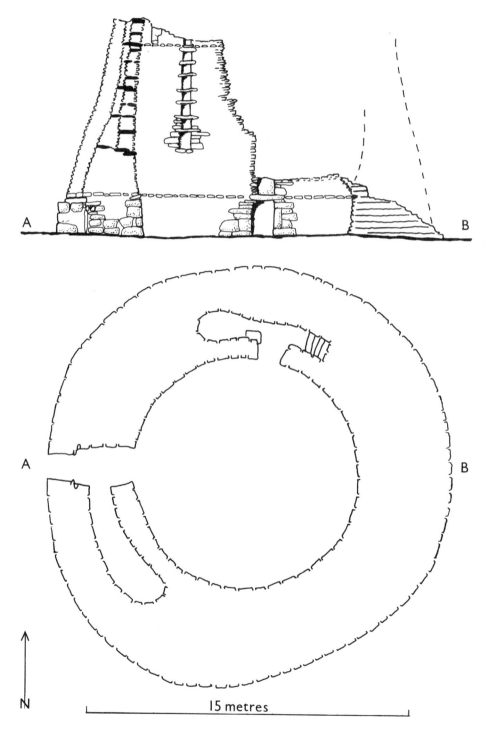

Fig. 5·1 Plan and elevation of the
Dun Telve broch, Inverness-shire
(*cf* pl. 5a), re-drawn from the
original in *Proc. Soc. Ant. Scot.*
50, 1915–16, 244–5.

four of the five brochs being described and perhaps to over 15 m in the case of Mousa. This view is confirmed by the fact that the sides of the galleries are often built with no attempt at smoothness—many of the stones project into the open space—and by the fact that the ascending stair makes the galleries difficult to reach. The stair has to break through each level of gallery and a gap of several feet must be left in each floor of lintels to allow people to walk up the steps. The stairway also effectively walls off the sections of galleries in front of the person ascending, making them inaccessible. There can be little doubt that it was the invention of this ingenious double drystone wall which made technically possible the architectural development which led to the broch tower (*below* p. 78).

The entire architecture of these five brochs gives the impression of being designed to create an impregnable refuge, a bolt-hole in which a local community or warrior band could retreat and defy a short attack or siege. Such a siege occurred at the broch of Mousa in Norse times and is described in the *Orkneyinga Saga*. The besiegers had to give up and negotiate. The great height of the wall is the most obvious defence, proof against stones and spears and quite probably against fire-arrows as well if these were used. There were no windows or other openings in the external wall-face apart from the main entrance. Unless the door could be breached the broch could probably be held against anything except a systematic assault by professional soldiers or until the inhabitants were starved out. Should any daring besieger attempt to scale the outside of the tower by means of the rough walling he could probably be dislodged with a well-aimed rock dropped from the top of the tower.

The typical broch entrance is a narrow tunnel, perhaps 1·6 m high and 0·75 m wide at the outside and roofed with flat stone lintels. Usually between 1 and 3 m from the exterior are checks in the walls for the massive wooden door, probably bound with iron, which swung on a pivot stone sunk into the floor. This door was held shut by a wooden drawbar which was run out from a hole in the wall behind the door into a socket in the opposite wall. Quite probably an iron ring handle, fastened to the inside of the door, was used to pull it open. One of these was found in Dun Ardtreck, a broch-like fort in Sky (*below* p. 84), and is remarkably sophisticated technologically. It consists of a flat bar which had been bolted to the door and which curved round the ring to form a simple hinge. The ring itself is made from a rope of four cords, each of several strands of iron wire and 5 mm in diameter. The complete rope is 12 mm in diameter and was twisted into a ring like a small deck quoit 80 mm in diameter: there are no visible joins. The method by which the fine iron bands or wires, some 2 mm wide, were drawn out to form the material with which the iron cords were spun is obscure but clearly reflects great technological skill. (It is also a powerful argument for the fortlet having been built at the behest of some Iron Age chieftain on Skye who could afford and command the resources of the various experts concerned—architects, masons and iron-working craftsmen.)

pls 5e and 5f

pls 5g and 5h

Behind the main door a guard cell often opens from a low doorway in the side of the passage, usually on the right, sometimes on the left side and occasionally on both. These cells were high, corbelled chambers whose ceiling height contrasted with the low openings, often less than a metre high, which led to them. Above the roofing of the entrance passage is usually a chamber, a structural necessity to divert the enormous weight of the high wall from the flat lintel stones. The outermost lintel is much more massive, sometimes triangular, as it has to support the outer wallface. It is likely that the chamber or void above the entrance was continued upwards, to form a series of openings in the inner wallface separated by bracing stone cross-lintels. Such voids can often be seen in other parts of the inside wallface in the well-preserved brochs and are evidently another device to reduce the weight of stone in the upper works of the tower without sacrificing strength. The chamber over the entrance occasionally served another purpose: gaps could be left between the lintels above the part of the passage in front of the main door and spears thrust down through them at attackers.

Around the wall of the central court, at a height of between 1·5 and 3·3 m above the floor, a ledge was built into the wallface. On this seems to have rested a platform upheld by a ring of posts, in effect an upper wooden floor around a central circular space. Holes for the posts for this raised floor have been found in several brochs and, in two, upper ledges or scarcements which supported a roof above it. The broch at Caisteal Grugaig, near Totaig on the south shore of Loch Alsh, Inverness-shire, shows why at least one lower scarcement cannot have been for a lean-to roof, as Sir Lindsay Scott thought. This broch is built on sharply sloping rock but the scarcement, as always, is level. At the downhill end of the court the ledge stands 2·1 m above the rock floor but at the uphill side only 0·7 m, too low for a roof. Several brochs, including Caisteal Grugaig, show door-sized voids leading from the stairway out on to the scarcement and access on to the raised floor must have been in this way.

There is no direct evidence for how these tall towers were roofed. Only two have the upper scarcement preserved, though presumably all had them once. At Dun Telve this ledge is 9 m above the ground and at Mousa 4·05 m. A simple flat wooden roof could have been made from a series of squares of wooden beams, of diminishing size. The corners of the largest square would rest on the stone ledge, those of the next largest would rest on the centres of the beams forming the sides of the first square and so on. In this way the framework for a flat roof could be built and the interstices filled with rafters and covered with turf or thatch. A wide hole in the centre could admit some light into the gloomy well of the interior and perhaps rain to help fill the water tank in the floor. Such a roof, however, would need only four massive short ledges, not the continuous scarcements which are visible. The continuous ledge may mean that a low conical roof was built on it, though for a central light- and rain-hole in this would perhaps not be so easy to arrange.

At Dun Telve a high void leads out on to the upper scarcement from the gallery behind, presumably to allow for repairs to the roof. At Mousa the roof-carrying scarcement has either vanished or it is the upper of the two visible low ones.

The general arrangement of the ground-level features in the 50 or so sites where they are clearly visible illustrates the brochs' capacity for defence, even after the outer door has been breached. In some the main door is much further down the passage than in others, making it harder to bring up a ram against it. The guard cell provides a second line of defence and occasionally, particularly often in Caithness, there is a second massive door behind the first. The narrowness and lowness of the entrance passage would prevent more than one or two attackers advancing down it at a time. If these gained the central court they would be exposed to spears and arrows from the upper wooden floor (assuming bows were used: no arrowpoints have been found). The only method of usefully pressing the attack further would be up the stair and in the majority of brochs the door leading to the foot of this is in the 8 to 10 o'clock segment (in the clockface reference system the main entrance is at 6 o'clock). This means that an attacker crossing to this door—thus moving to the left from the entrance—exposes his unshielded right side to missiles from the upper parts of the broch. Possibly the raising of the scarcement floor, to more than 2·7 m high in some brochs, was partly intended to reduce the amount of cover which the raised floor would provide in these circumstances to someone hostile making for the stair. In many brochs the stair door is also raised a metre or more above the ground making it even harder to get into. It may be supposed that these refinements in defensive capability only came about after brochs had been built for some time, since many do not possess them. In other words, assuming a continuous period of building, the architecture and design of the brochs should have become more efficient and sophisticated with time. It is indeed a study of such details which allows us to infer a typological development in what appears superficially to be a remarkably homogeneous group of buildings, and thereby to deduce where they originated.

One problem needs to be solved first before further progress can be made in understanding the brochs: are the five or six surviving tower-like brochs typical of the other 500 or were most of them much lower? Sir Lindsay Scott argued the latter case forcibly a quarter of a century ago and maintained that the tower brochs were rare aberrations: most, he thought, were not more than 3 m high, 4·6 m at the most, and were in fact only exceptionally massive defended farmhouses. Scott based this belief on the assumption that the scarcement ledge was a roof support (which was later shown to be very unlikely when the Caisteal Grugaig broch was first described) and that therefore the wall had never risen more than about a metre above it. He also believed—and this was before Hamilton's excavations of the 1950's—that the stratigraphy of the broch complex at Jarlshof showed that the wheelhouses there were all earlier than the broch. He was thus able to suggest a sequence of domestic structures which originated in the wooden Iron Age round-houses of southern and south western

England and which were brought to Atlantic Shetland by a migration of people from that area about 50 BC. In the north, according to Scott, the stone wheel-house developed out of this round-house and led finally to the low, thick-walled broch.

Mr Angus Graham argued the contrary view at the same meeting of the Prehistoric Society in 1947. He pointed out that there was already good evidence, from the surveys of the Royal Commission on the Ancient and Historical Monuments of Scotland, that the wheelhouse was certainly *later* than the broch at Mousa and that similar relationships existed at Jarlshof too. The latter was shown conclusively to be so in the excavations of the early 1950's. Graham also showed that the shape and massive structure of the basal storey of the brochs was at variance with the theory of low walls. A low drystone wall between 4·5 and 6·0 m high could easily be built more economically with a much thinner base; the great thickness and circularity of the broch wall base would only make sense if it supported a really great height. The fact that the basal storeys of nearly all other excavated brochs are strikingly similar in general design and proportion to the five tall towers therefore surely argues that all brochs once has tower-like proportions, though doubtless varying in height and diameter.

Joseph Anderson made the same point with documentary evidence in his *Scotland in Pagan Times* (1883). He showed that several brochs were described by seventeenth- and eighteenth-century travellers as being considerably higher than they were in his own time and drew the reasonable conclusion that such dilapidation had been going on ever since the Iron Age. In 1947 Graham reviewed similar data for Dun Troddan and Dun Telve, two well-preserved brochs on the mainland opposite Skye. The same process can still be seen going on. Three brochs in Lewis—Dun Cromore, Dun Baravat and Loch an Duna, all situated on islets in lochs—were described and planned by Capt. F. W. L. Thomas in about 1870 and all were then well over 7·5 m high with several upper wall galleries preserved. The Royal Commission's investigators described them much reduced in 1915. In September 1971 the writer visited them, hoping to make accurate plans (*below* p. 85), and found nothing but ruined stumps whose walls scarcely reach a height of 2·5 to 3·0 m in limited parts of their circuits. The older local people told him that massive looting of these brochs for building stone had occurred within the last forty years and it is obvious that extensive robbing has taken place.

The available evidence is thus on the whole against the theory that the majority of brochs were low and in favour of the view that most were once tall towers. The close similarity in the design of the basal storeys of all brochs indicates that it is arbitrary to separate out the five surviving tall ones simply because they are still high. If these five are still in part tower-like, the other 505 are also very likely to have been so at one time. The whole range of structural and architectural features in brochs only really make sense with this assumption.

The concept of 510 tall drystone towers being built throughout Atlantic Scotland in the first centuries BC and AD is a striking one and eloquent of some powerful social motive behind it. What were these towers used for? As we have seen, the height and design of the brochs must have made them excellent refuges, proof against all but the most systematic siege. Is there any direct evidence for the brochs having been used primarily as forts, inhabited only occasionally, or as permanently garrisoned castles, or as exceptionally well defended farm-houses? As always when precise questions are asked of the brochs, precise answers are made difficult by the dearth of reliable evidence. Of the five brochs which have been stratigraphically excavated—namely, Clickhimin, Jarlshof, Torwoodlee, Dun Mor Vaul and Crosskirk—only the last two were previously undisturbed and had their primary broch floors intact. At Vaul the evidence was exceptionally clear and showed that the tower was first used as a refuge for a large number of people, who evidently returned to their dwellings when the danger had passed.

fig. 5·2

The lowest broch floor level was a thick deposit of gravel, sand and earth containing very large numbers of potsherds and fresh-looking broken animal bones. There was no single hearth but numerous patches of peat ash suggested that several fires were lit in various parts of the court at different times. In spite of the masses of food refuse, this primary broch floor deposit was very clean and light in colour. It contrasted with other occupation layers on the site which were dark grey, having presumably been impregnated with organic refuse. A cess-pit was found in one deep part of the wall gallery which had been used at an early stage in the broch's history, and this explained the cleanliness of the central court. Evidently large numbers of people lived in the broch and were subject to firm discipline over hygiene. Since the evidence suggests that the tower was in use in its first phase for at least 100 years, and very probably as much as 200 or even 250 years, this occupation presumably took place only sporadically and for short periods. The whole of the Vaul evidence fits well with the view that this broch was built as a temporarily occupied refuge for the local community when danger threatened. This is the only direct evidence for the primary use of brochs which is available and, while we cannot automatically assume that all the others were the same, their close structural similarity, and the almost universal close association with farmland, suggests that they were.

Later the Vaul broch was converted to a permanent dwelling for a single family and during this secondary phase of use it was demolished down to a height of about 2 m. Similar direct evidence at several other brochs, mainly in the far north, provides important indirect evidence for their primary function. Many others have outbuildings around them, domestic settlements which seem to have grown up round the towers after they ceased primarily to be fortresses. The occasional stratigraphical excavation, as at Jarlshof and Midhowe, has shown that these outbuildings were put up on top of, or instead of, the original outer defences of the tower. Most may fairly be assumed to have been built

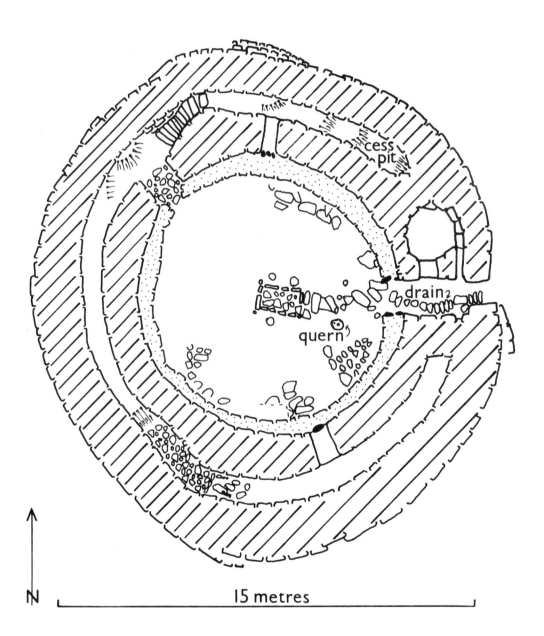

cess
pit

drain

quern

N

15 metres

Fig. 5·2 Plan of the Dun Mor Vaul broch, Tiree, Argyllshire (*cf* pl. 5c) at ground level showing the continuous mural gallery, the mural stair and the entrance passage with guard cell on the right. The water tank and overflow drain are primary features but the rectangular hearth was added later, probably after the broch had ceased to be a communal fort. The relatively slim wall and the large central court, 9·9 m in diameter, is typical of Hebridean brochs and contrasts with many in the far north which are smaller and with thicker walls.

Pl. 4a Avebury, Wiltshire. The
internal stone settings are visible
within the surrounding earthwork
as are the remains of the West
Kennet Avenue which lead to
the Sanctuary on Overton Hill.

Pl. 4b Stonehenge, Wiltshire. The final stage of the structure is shown in this photograph with the ring of Aubrey Holes in the background.

Pl. 4c Maiden Castle, Dorset. The rampart of the earlier Iron Age hill-fort which overlies the causewayed enclosure is clearly visible within the ramparts of the final defences.

Pl. 4d Hambledon Hill, Dorset. The outline of the causewayed enclosure is visible outside the defences of the Iron Age hill-fort.

Pl. 4e Mount Pleasant, Dorset. The foundations of a circular timber building which was constructed around 2000 bc. The structure was surrounded by its own ditch, the entrance through which is in the foreground of the photograph.

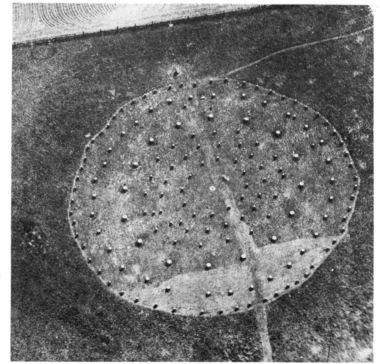

Pl. 4f Woodhenge, Wiltshire. The site of a circular timber building constructed between 1900 and 1800 bc. The positions of the timber uprights are now shown by concrete blocks.

Pl. 5a General view of the Dun Telve solid-based broch, near Glenelg, Inverness-shire. Its situation on flat, open ground is typical of the solid-based brochs of the far north and dissimilar to those of its neighbours on Skye. One third of the tower still stands to about 10 m in height and on the right is a section through the hollow wall—unique to the brochs—showing the superimposed intra-mural galleries. The other openings are the voids, the set on the left being over the internal doorway to the stair inside the wall. The upper scarcement can be seen, 9 m above the ground; it probably supported a flat roof of wood and a doorway to it from an upper gallery is visible. The smooth curve of the outer face of the broch wall is striking. Although the stone used in Dun Telve is similiar to that with which the brochs on neighbouring Skye were built, the skill shown in the drystone masonry here is much greater than in the Skye sites.

Pl. 5b Dun Carloway, a transitional broch on Lewis in the Outer Hebrides. This view again shows the cross section of the partly destroyed, high galleried wall and a set of voids in the inside wallface. The broch is situated on a rock knoll in a characteristically Hebridean position.

Pl. 5c General view of the excavations on the Dun Mor Vaul broch, Tiree, looking down into the interior from a photographic tower mounted on the wallhead. The entrance passage is at the lower left and the secondary wall can be clearly seen built against its inner end. The raised scarcement in the primary wallface is also visible above the secondary wall as is the mural gallery behind. Before excavation started the interior was filled with rubble up to the level of the present wallhead.

Pl. 5d A general view of Dun Ardtreck semibroch, Skye, in its cliff top situation. Behind the fort the cliff falls 21 m sheer to the sea while in front several rock terraces form natural walls. The actual outer wall of the fort runs along the uppermost terraces.

Pl. 5e A view of the entrance passage of the Dun Ardtreck semibroch, Skye, looking outwards after its excavation. The stone lintels which once roofed the passage have gone, probably pulled off when the fortlet was demolished in the Iron Age. The stone checks for the door can be clearly seen and the raised sill of the door to the guard chamber is apparent in the left wall. The door handle was behind the right check.

Pl. 5f The same entrance passage looking inwards.

Pl. 5g The door-handle of Dun Ardtreck as it was found on the floor of the entrance passage and behind the right check. Intense heat has fused it to several stones.

Pl. 5h The Dun Ardtreck door-handle in detail. It consists of two parts, a ring made of iron wires and a flat iron bar one end of which is bent round the ring to form a simple hinge. The bar was nailed or bolted to the main door and the head of one of the bolts, with a square washer, is visible. The ring itself is an iron rope with no visible join, from 76–82 mm in diameter and 12 mm thick. The rope consists of four twisted iron cords each of which is made from several thick wires. Presumably these wires were wrought rather than drawn out. So intense was the heat to which this door-handle was subjected during the destruction of Dun Ardtreck that some stone had actually run and vitrified, solidifying again on to one part of the ring. This can be seen in the photograph next to the long projecting stone.

with stone quarried from the towers themselves. Such clear signs at many broch sites of a change in primary use to undefended or poorly defended open settlements implies that originally they had a quite different function and were non-domestic refuges.

If the brochs were fortifications then they ought to be explicable as part of the general tradition of Iron Age defensive works and—unique and strange-looking as they are to those accustomed to the hill-forts of the lowland areas of Britain—their ancestry might well be traceable back to such hill-forts. The alternative view—which sees the broch as a special creation from nothing by a unique group of people in response to a unique combination of circumstances and environment—has no more to recommend it than all other special creation theories when opposed by evolutionary ones.

By studying the varying sizes and proportions of the brochs, as well as the different designs and arrangements of their architectural features, definite progress can be made in working out how these buildings were developed and improved during the period they were in use. Indeed clear clues to the actual place of invention of the brochs can be detected in this way and this allows one to explore further the whole problem of the origin of the brochs and their builders.

Two basic architectural types of brochs can be seen, one of which has two sub-types, and this classification is the basis of broch typological study. *Ground-galleried brochs* have wall galleries at ground level and a variant of these, *Transitional brochs*, have various combinations of cells and galleries in the basal storey. In *Solid-based brochs*, on the other hand, the hollow, galleried wall is mounted on a massive solid ring of masonry which contains the entrance and usually one or more corbelled cells.

It is possible to plot about 120 brochs on a scatter diagram, to show how the diameters of their central courts and the thickness of their walls vary. This shows fairly clearly that, with some exceptions, it is generally true that the smaller the enclosed area is the more massive is the wall surrounding it. The well known broch of Mousa in Shetland shows the extreme form of this trend: its central court is tiny, only 5·5 m in diameter on average with the wallbase occupying no less than 64% of the overall diameter of 15·2 m. Mousa is also the best preserved of all brochs and, considering its remarkable proportions, this may be only partly due to its remote and isolated situation. It may also be because it is the best built. This gives us a valuable clue to the direction in which broch development took place. If the solid-based broch of Mousa is one of the best designed and built it must surely be one of the latest in the sequence.

It is then interesting to notice that the ground-galleried and transitional brochs are all relatively slender; their wall-bases are all less than 4·5 m and mostly less than 3·9 m thick. On the other hand the solid-based type, although it can be slim-walled, is the only kind of broch to have achieved a really thick and massive wall-base, up to 5·2 m wide in a few cases. Moreover the ground-galleried and transitional forms are concentrated in the Hebrides, where there are only two solid-based brochs (Dun Troddan and Dun Telve), but the latter form is extremely numerous in the northern mainland and in the Orkney and Shetland isles.

This tendency towards a geographical and architectural distinction between thin-walled and thick-walled brochs strongly suggests that they represent the early and late stages of development and improvement in design and efficiency. Mousa implies that the solid-based brochs are the evolved form and that, conversely, the Hebridean ground-galleried brochs are the earliest and most primitive. It is easy to understand why such a development should have taken place. In the Hebrides brochs are usually situated on naturally defensive rocky knolls and other elevations. In Orkney, Caithness and Shetland, on the other hand, they usually had to be sited on flat or undulating ground. The solid base seems a natural adaptation to such conditions, increasing the height and defensive capacity of the broch with an artificial 'knoll' instead of the natural ones which were not to be had. An analysis of siting positions does in fact show that slimmer-walled brochs are more likely to be built on rugged sites and vice versa.

It has been argued in the past, however, and still could be from the evidence of the scatter diagram, that Orkney saw the birth of broch building. The two excavated ground-galleried brochs there, Midhowe and Gurness, both had their basal galleries blocked up with stone at an early stage in their histories, suggesting that this form was unsuited to great height and to the local building material (Old Red sandstone). This clearly shows that the ground-galleried design was early but it could still have been invented either in Orkney or the Hebrides. If the former happened the subsequent development would have been in two directions, to the Hebrides where the larger ground-galleried form was maintained, and to Shetland and the north mainland where the solid-based form was evolved and improved.

Analyses of most of the other structural features of the brochs, and their **table 4** comparison with the basic picture given by the scatter diagram, failed to give any positive lead to which of these two views—involving an Orkney or a Hebridean origin—was most likely. However the data on the design of the entrance passages does give such a lead, and a very clear one.

It is reasonable to assume that the area of the entrance—the focal point of the defence of the broch—could only evolve towards greater efficiency and not away from it. The distance of the door down the passage from the outside varies from about 0·9 m to more than 2·75 m and there are a few brochs with two doors, one behind the other. There can be no doubt that greater depth gives greater protection to the door by making it harder to bring battering rams to bear, or to mount any sort of attack against it: the outer part of the passage is so narrow and low that only one person at a time can go down it. Neither can there be much doubt that the double-door is the most advanced and efficient design. This table of the distribution of the four types of door arrangement shows quite clearly that the most primitive arrangement is com-

Table 4 The design of the entrance passage in sixty-one brochs, analysed in relation to the main areas where brochs occur.

Distance of door-checks down the passage	*Geographical region*					
	Hebrides	Sutherland	Caithness	Orkney	Shetland	total
less than 1·5 m	10 (63%)	3 (18½%)	3 (18½%)	—	—	16 (100%)
between 1·5 & 2·75 m	1 (5½%)	4 (22%)	5 (28%)	6 (33½%)	2 (11%)	18 (100%)
more than 2·75 m	—	2 (14%)	7 (50%)	2 (14%)	3 (22%)	14 (100%)
2 sets of door-checks	—	6 (46%)	5 (39%)	2 (15%)	—	13 (100%)
totals	11	15	20	10	5	61

monest in the Hebrides and the two most advanced forms—the deepest doors and the double doors—are commonest in Caithness and Sutherland. As in many other ways the brochs of Orkney seem to occupy an intermediate position.

This evidence from the entrances must surely mean that the only plausible interpretation is that the design of the brochs evolved from the primary, thin-walled ground-galleried towers of the Western Isles towards the more massive, solid-based forms of the far north (Dun Troddan and Dun Telve are reasonably explained as the late return of the broch design, in more advanced form, to the west). In other words the tower-fort was invented in the Western Isles, probably on Skye where most of them are. Any alternative view, which would involve the broch being taken *to* the west, *must* explain why the design of the entrance passage became less efficient there.

An obvious check on this theory of typological development would be available if one could identify the earlier stone forts from which the brochs must surely have developed. There are in fact a number of stone duns and fortlets scattered all over western Atlantic Scotland, showing various forms of hollow-wall construction. Among these is a group of eleven, closely similar in design and situation, six of which have the same distinctive high, hollow wall as the brochs. However these semibrochs are not built as circular towers but are open-sided and sited on the edges of cliffs and precipices; in plan they are either D-shaped or simple curved walls barring off a promontory. When I re-stated the view in 1965 that these semibrochs should be prototype brochs and not late degenerate derivatives from the towers, none of them had been excavated. Since then two have, Dun Ardtreck on Skye and Dun an Rhiroy on Loch Broom in Wester Ross. Both were dated by carbon-14 and both are likely to have been built in the first or second centuries BC. They are thus at least as old as the brochs and quite possibly slightly older. This view of the status of the semibrochs as prototype brochs was derived from the typological analysis of the towers themselves, outlined earlier, which gave rise to the theory of Hebridean origin. Thus a specific prediction about the semibrochs made by this theory was tested and found to be correct.

Dun Ardtreck stands on an isolated rock knoll the back of which is a sheer **pl. 5d** cliff standing 23 m above the sea. In plan the fortlet is D-shaped, the straight edge being the cliff; the entrance passage is in the centre of the curved, galleried-wall and faces inland. Excavations in 1965 showed that the fort was built on rock which slopes sharply downwards inland and that the galleried wall stands on an artificial, level, rubble platform on this. The outer face of both platform and wall above was continuous and the whole had clearly been built in a single operation. Small fragments of charcoal from the rubble of this platform gave a carbon-14 date of 55 ± 105 bc (GX-1120).

The fortlet was violently destroyed by fire, its wall was then extensively demolished and the ruins were inhabited for a long period as a domestic site. Fragments of Roman pottery were found in the immediately post-destruction levels, confirming the early date of the building of the fort. During the destruction pottery vessels in the interior broke and some of the sherds were partly vitrified; an iron axe and a string of small glass beads were also dropped and a rotary quern was cracked and shattered by the heat. In the entrance passage the wooden door seems to have caught fire and fallen, or been battered, inwards. The draught of air which then rushed up the narrow, tunnel-like entrance (then **pl. 5e** presumably still lintelled) seems to have fanned the charred wood to a red heat **and 5f** and fused the iron door-handle to some stone. This ring handle is a remarkable **pl. 5h** object, the only one of its kind so far known.

If the tower forts were first invented on Skye their development might be visualised in terms of the natural selection of efficient kinds of drystone defence works. The preceding semibrochs are few in number and there are a variety of other gallery-walled fortlets in Argyll and the Western Isles which were quite probably contemporary with them. At this stage the ingenious high, galleried wall does not seem to have offered a decisive advantage to the semibrochs, tied as they were to cliff edges. Then a 'mutation' occurred, which in social terms of course means that someone influential realised that, if this high wall was built in a circle, a totally enclosed, free-standing round tower would result which would be almost impregnable to assault and which could be built almost anywhere, away from cliff-top sites and close to fields and settlements. The subsequent enormous increase in the brochs, both in terms of number and of territory, clearly shows that this 'mutation' in drystone fort-building was exactly suited to the environment into which it emerged. The vast numbers of brochs in Caithness and Orkney are particularly striking in this respect; there are hardly any fortlets there which are suspected, and none which are known, to be earlier than the brochs and otherwise only the few hill-forts in Caithness are likely to antedate them. Such an environment, abundant in farmland, presumably populous yet apparently poorly equipped in fort-building capability, was evidently the ideal one in which the imported broch could be spectacularly successful. The concentration can be remarkable: there are three within half a square mile in some places.

This scheme for the architectural development of the brochs, the deductions about the place where they were invented, and the interpretation of this process in terms of natural selection, raises two important questions. First, what sort of individuals designed and built the brochs, and took their plans to new territories? Second, can anything be inferred about the circumstances in which the broch was actually invented in the Western Isles?

As regards the first problem, the general design of all the known brochs is, despite the differences in detail which have been discussed, so standardised that it is difficult to believe that groups of specialists were not at work supervising their planning and construction. The same is suggested by the clear paths of typological development which have been inferred; the steady evolution of the brochs' design towards greater efficiency suggests that a body of knowledge and experience was being conserved and added to by small groups of skilled men. Such professional dun builders are attested for medieval Ireland.

This view is also supported by the marked differences in the material culture—pottery and other artefacts—which are found in brochs in different regions, even in the same territory. This shows that brochs were used by a variety of local cultures and that there is no single uniform 'broch culture'. The pottery of the Hebridean brochs, for example, is totally dissimilar to the comparable wares in the far north. The two characteristic Hebridean wares, found separated stratigraphically at Vaul, are the 'native' incised pottery and the everted rim cordoned jars with curvilinear ornament. Very little trace of these styles is found in the far north where two other separate ceramic zones can be seen, in the northern islands and in Caithness/Sutherland respectively. There are some artefacts common to the whole broch area, as one would expect, but the firmly local nature of the pottery and some other equipment is clear.

In 1971 further dramatic evidence was found of the existence of a specialist class of broch architects and of the ancient traditions this had inherited. The central courts of 30 excavated or otherwise reasonably well exposed brochs were precisely measured by the writer with a steel tape and a theodolite or alidade. The resulting measurements were subjected to a statistical analysis by Dr G. I. Crawford of the University of Glasgow to discover, first, how accurately the courts were laid out as true circles and secondly, if they were accurate, whether a standard unit of measurement (a 'broch yard') was being used. The methods of survey and analysis we used were similar to those applied by Professor A. Thom to the stone circles and were partly intended as a check on his work (*cf. above* p. 66).

Most of the measured brochs turned out to be very precisely circular inside with mean errors from the 'best fit' circles varying from 93 to 19 mm. The **fig. 5·3** radii of these circles had evidently been measured out with a 'yardstick' of

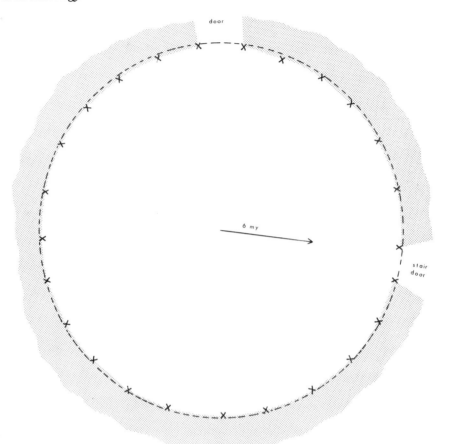

Fig. 5·3 Dun Telve broch, Inverness-shire. The circle which fits the wall-base best has a radius of 4·919 m; 6 megalithic yards is equivalent to 4·974 m. The difference between the radii of the two circles is 55 mm (2·1 in.).

The average variation of the wallface from the best fit circle is 19 mm and this illustrates how precisely the shape of the broch was set out on the ground. On Figs 5·3, 5·4, 5·5 the actual measured points are shown as crosses and

the visible wallface is shaded. The geometrical reconstructions, the radii of the arcs of which are in megalithic yards are superimposed as dashed lines. Scale: 1:100.

0·839 m, 1 cm larger than Thom's 'megalithic yard' or 0·829 m; (this inference has a probability level of 2%). If, however, one makes the reasonable assumption that the builders intended their diameters to be whole numbers of their yardsticks, then the frequently observed discrepancies away from such multiples of 0·839 m, though small, could be explained by supposing that individual measuring rods varied slightly in length (over a range of 8·5 cms) with 0·839 m being the mean.

Moreover a few brochs are not true circles but fit remarkably well round some of the more complex geometrical shapes first identified in the stone circles. Dun Torcuill in North Uist and Dun Borodale on Raasay island, Skye, for example, are both ellipses; the latter, though unexcavated, fits very well round   **fig. 5·**

a flattened ellipse. Ness in Caithness, although one quarter of the wall has been **fig. 5·5**
completely destroyed, appears to fit quite well round a Type A flattened circle.
The Caithness sites in particular, because of the excellent building stone available there, fit the shapes very closely: several are exact circles of exact multiples
of megalithic yards.

The similarity of the unit of length and the geometrical construction found
in the brochs to that in the stone circles of 2000 years earlier is surprising
and exciting. Either the surveying and planning techniques were re-invented
in the Iron Age and by chance closely resembled the earlier ideas, or a continuous tradition was kept alive in a learned order over the eighteen or so inter-
vening centuries. In either case the care and skill with which the designs of

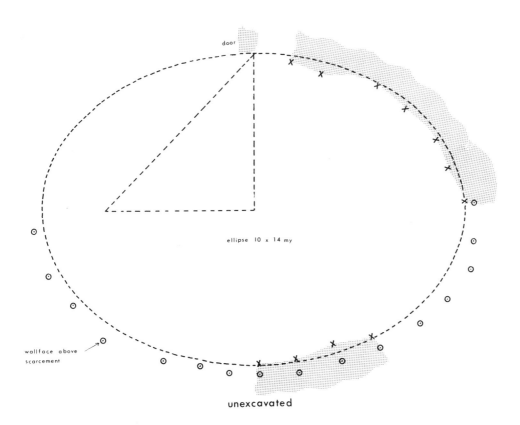

Fig. 5·4 Dun Borodale broch,
Raasay Island, off Skye,
Inverness-shire. This broch is
unexcavated and full of rubble;
the wallface below the level of
the scarcement is visible only in
two fairly short stretches but that
above the ledge for considerably

more. The inner face is obviously,
at the height measured (perhaps
1·5–2 m above the floor), leaning
inwards from the vertical in some
places. Nevertheless the
suggested geometrical
construction—an ellipse with
major and minor axes of 14 and

10 megalithic yards
respectively—fits the lower
wallface extremely well and the
fact that the wall above the
scarcement also follows the
ellipse closely suggests that the
fit is not likely to be accidental.
Scale 1:100

the brochs were laid out on the ground now seem even more remarkable and there can surely be no doubt that a professional class of architects, possibly the direct inheritors of very ancient Neolithic traditions, were responsible for the invention and development of the brochs and supervised their construction.

This brings us to our last question: how did the brochs get invented? What was the nature of the 'mutation' in fort-building techniques which produced such a successful new species? We have seen that the few semibrochs are likely to be the immediately ancestral form but none of these have yet been examined for geometrical constructions or 'broch yards', though it will be no surprise if they produce them.

The possible Neolithic origin of elements of broch architecture reinforces the view that there was much more continuity than has previously been suspected between the Stone, Bronze and Iron Ages in Britain. The brochs, however, show a gigantic leap forward in the quality of their design and in general efficiency, rooted though they are in earlier local structures and perhaps in Scottish Neolithic learning. They surely illustrate the presence of a formidable intellectual power which saw undreamt of possibilities in one minor local fortlet which had evolved a peculiar hollow wall. By adding a single major idea, that of circularity, this was turned into a universally useful, highly successful and adaptable tower-fort. This is the sort of inspiration which could well be the result of the blending of new minds and skills with the local ones.

The presence of guard cells opening off the entrance passages in many brochs may be significant here. Such cells, in the form of round corbelled chambers, are quite unknown in pre-broch forts: only one semibroch, Dun Ardtreck, has a guard chamber and this is quite different—simply a blocked-off part of the lintelled mural gallery. On the other hand guard-chambers are known from hill-forts in Europe, southern England and north Wales: the pair at Dinorben hill-fort, for example, now seem likely to belong to the fourth or third centuries bc from radio-carbon dates. The appearance of guard cells in Atlantic Iron Age forts at the moment when the broch towers mutated out of the semi-brochs could either be an extra bit of local ingenuity or it could signify the arrival of knowledge of fort-building techniques from southern England or Wales.

With this possibility in mind the study of the material culture of the broch builders and dwellers in the Western Isles is rewarding. The Western Isles, more particularly Tiree, Barra and the Uists, are the only place in north Britain where the *Clettraval ware* of the brochs and wheelhouses is found: these vessels are cordoned, everted-rim jars often ornamented with multiple arches or eyebrow motifs. This curvilinear ornament looks like an ultimate northern reflection of some of that on middle Iron Age pottery in eastern and southern England (but not of that of the elaborately decorated 'Glastonbury ware'). This seems to have been confirmed by the discovery at Dun Mor Vaul of what may be a locally made copy of a Wessex Iron Age 'B' bead-rimmed bowl. A number of other south English artefacts appear first in Scotland at about the same time, probably in the first century bc, including bronze spiral finger rings, glass beads of various

Fig. 5·5 Ness broch, Caithness. The inner wallface seems to fit one of Thom's Type A flattened circles extremely closely except at one point. The main circle is almost exactly 9 megalithic yards in diameter and the wallface follows the circle very closely. The flattened sector is an arc of a circle 16 megalithic yards in diameter and here again the wallface follows the theoretical geometrical construction within a few millimetres. The position and shape of the corners in a flattened circle of this type are determined by making them arcs of circles of half the radius of the main one, and the surviving masonry corner again fits the geometry very closely. Two fifths of the interior wallface has been completely destroyed but the characteristic peripheral paving—which is usually found in brochs running round the inside wall in a 2 m wide band—was found in 1972 at one point extending out almost as far as the theoretical position of the wall as determined by the geometrical figure. This paving shows plainly that the isolated stone blocks within this area (shown striped) are part of a secondary wallface. This *may* mean that the part of the apparently original wallface to the right of the main entrance—at

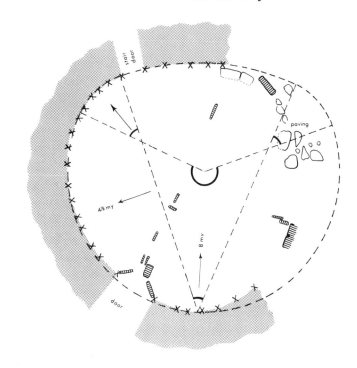

the point where it begins to deviate markedly from the dotted line—is also part of a secondary construction. Nevertheless, nothing was seen during the recent excavations to suggest that the inner wallface to the right of the main entrance —where it veers most sharply away from the suggested geometrical construction—was

not a continuous, primary one, so there may be a better explanation for the curious shape of Ness. A similar situation was found in the Skirza Head broch in 1972; there the secondary wallface blended closely with the primary one and then curved inwards much more sharply. The other striped stones are secondary upright slabs set into the floor. Scale 1:100

kinds, bone dice, possibly long-handled combs, triangular crucibles and flat rotary querns with upright handles. Although it is true that the exact chronology of all these items in the south is not always clear, the time of their appearance in the broch province is now documented at three sites with levels extending back to pre-broch times. The new material evidently appears either with the brochs or shortly before. Also significant must be the fact that many of these objects with southern British links are the same ones that appear throughout the broch province, contrasting in this way with the more localised pottery styles. They might well have spread with the brochs themselves, or shortly before the towers were invented.

There is certainly a good deal of circumstantial evidence in favour of a possibly short phase of contact in the late pre-Roman Iron Age between central and Atlantic Scotland on the one hand and southern England and Wales on the other, a phase which shows itself in the arrival of new objects, ceramic influences and one hill-fort defensive feature. This evidence cannot be dismissed by casting doubt on each item separately or by claims about the old-fashioned nature of diffusionist ideas. It hangs together at present reasonably well, makes much better sense when considered as a whole and provides a background against which the emergence of the brochs takes on a new and clearer aspect. With all its inevitable imperfections, there is independent evidence of the arrival of a few people—surely energetic and influential ones—in Atlantic Scotland from southern England just at the time the brochs appeared. The infusion of new talent and ideas from the south into the old fort-building class of the Western Isles, however it was done, seems just the sort of event which could result in an outburst of inventiveness in drystone fort-building such as that which produced the broch. Thus perhaps were inaugurated three brilliant centuries of spectacular drystone construction, culminating in the wheelhouses, throughout the whole of this farthest northwestern maritime province of Europe.

Bibliography 5

The writer has set out his ideas on the brochs in two papers, 'The Origin and Development of the Broch . . . Cultures of the Scottish Iron Age', in *Proc. Prehist. Soc.* **31**, 1965, 93–146, and 'English Migrants and Scottish Brochs', *Glasgow Archaeol. J.* **2**, 1971, 39–71. The totals of the brochs in various regions are on p. 143 of the former paper; the most up-to-date version of the scatter diagram (*above* p. 81) is fig. 1 of the latter paper. The description of the siege of the broch of Mousa is given in the *Orkneyinga Saga* in the translation of A. B. Taylor (1938), 311–312. The excavation of Dun Ardtreck is described in an interim report (1965) available from the writer; the full report is expected to be in Vol. IV or V of the *Glasgow Archaeol. J.* The door-handle from that site is in the Hunterian Museum of the University of Glasgow.

The gaps in broch entrance lintels, or *meurtrières*, are well seen in the Midhowe broch on Rousay island, Orkney. Sir Lindsay Scott expressed his views in two long papers in the *Proc. Prehist. Soc.* **13**, 1947, 1–36, and *ibid.*, **14**, 1948, 46–125. The broch of Caisteal Grugaig is described in *Proc. Soc. Antiq. Scot.* **83**, 1948–9, 14–19. The paper by Angus Graham, 'Some observations on the brochs' in *Proc. Soc. Antiq. Scot.* **81**, 1946–7, 48–99, includes valuable comments on the roofing of brochs, the function of scarcements, the probable original height of the structures and several other aspects of the broch architecture. His views are also printed at the end of the 1947 paper of Sir Lindsay Scott, mentioned earlier.

One of the earliest useful accounts of the brochs was by Joseph Anderson in his *Scotland in Pagan Times* (1883). A summary of the excavation of Dun Mor Vaul broch is in *Antiquity* **39**, 1965, 266–78: the main report is expected to be produced shortly as a monograph by the University of Glasgow. One of the 'special creation' theories of broch origins was that of B. H. St J. O'Neil in 'The date and purpose of the brochs' in W. D. Simpson (ed.), *The Viking Congress*, 1954, 46–52. He suggested that the towers were built against Belgic and Roman slave-raiders.

Some of the analyses of broch architectural features are in my *Proc. Prehist. Soc.* paper referred to earlier. They are set out in full in my Ph.D thesis '*The origin and development of the broch and wheelhouse building cultures of the Scottish Iron Age*' (University of Glasgow 1972). J. R. C. Hamilton has long been the protagonist of a different view of broch origins and development, set out most recently in his *Excavations at Clickhimin, Shetland* (1968). This sees the brochs originating in Orkney and draws extensive parallels with Early Irish society. The Royal Commission on the Ancient and Historical Monuments of Scotland, in its *Inventory* for Skye, the Outer Hebrides and the Small Isles (1928), tentatively suggested that the many drystone forts with galleried walls on Skye indicated that the broch originated there (introduction). The radio-carbon dating of the semibrochs is described in my *Glasgow Archaeol. J.* paper mentioned earlier and the Scottish Iron Age Carbon-14 dates in general in *Antiquity* **43**, 1969, 15–26. A recent general summary of Scottish Iron Age research is my paper in the *Scot. Hist. Rev.* **49**, 1970, 1–32. The professional dun builders of Medieval Ireland are described by A. Graham in 'Archaeological Gleanings from Dark Age Records' in *Proc. Soc. Antiq. Scot.* **85**, 1950–1, 64–91.

The geometry and metrology of the brochs are to be described by G. I. Crawford and E. W. MacKie in 'Units of length and geometry in Scottish brochs', which it is hoped will be in *Nature*.

The Dinorben hill-fort is published as *Dinorben* by W. Gardner and H. N. Savory (1964); the radio-carbon dates for the hill-fort by H. N. Savory in *Antiquity* **45**, 1971, 251–61. A photograph of the eyebrow-ornamented bowl from Vaul is in *Antiquity* **43**, 1969, Pl.Vc, and the arguments about influence from the south English Iron Age B cultures arriving in the Western Isles are put forward in my paper in the *Glasgow Archaeol. J.* mentioned earlier. D. V. Clarke disagrees with these interpretations, in 'Bone dice and the Scottish Iron Age', *Proc. Prehist. Soc.* **36**, 1970, 214–32, and in 'Small finds in the Atlantic province: problems of approach', *Scot. Archaeol. Forum* **3**, 1971, 22–54.

6 The North-Western Interface

Barri Jones

The division between the Highland and Lowland zones of Britain has been a common link affecting archaeological thinking in the last 40 years. What has perhaps not been fully realised is the limitations of this division in relation to the fluctuating boundary between Roman military and civil control. The fluctuations in this interface are perhaps nowhere more varied than in the north-west of England from the Welsh borderland to the Eden Valley and Carlisle. This chapter attempts to assess current thinking based on discovery and analysis of the Iron Age and Roman countryside of that area within a morphological and chronological framework. At present, while some large areas still form zones in which primary discovery is taking place, others present more detailed material that, properly applied, could have an important bearing on the better known problems of the villa-based economy of southern Britain in the Roman period. Thus the topographical framework is large. The Marches to the south-west and the Cheviots to the north mark the boundaries of the necessarily broad approach involved. Within these limits information from various zones is emerging at different levels; and at the southern end of the Pennines, in Shropshire and the north-east Midlands, fuller information is now available for assessing the overall effect of Romanisation on the countryside.

The great majority of so-called native settlements in this country have been viewed from the morphological standpoint. The element of shape is the only common criterion for which equivalent information is available. Yet the commonest type, particularly in the west of the British Isles, the circular settlement of approximately one acre in size, does not normally respond to such treatment. Amongst the various types in which meaningful morphological distinctions have been discerned, the rath and round of south-west Wales, Cornwall and Devon, have benefited not at all. Yet an estimated thirty thousand sites of this type are known to have existed in Ireland, ranging in date from the Bronze Age to the sixteenth century AD. Their distribution along the western side of this country makes an important contribution to the settlement pattern of western Britain. We thus have a situation in which a predominant variety of site does not lend itself to morphological classification.

Elsewhere, in North Wales for instance, Hogg has distinguished oval and polygonal sites, the latter of two varieties depending on the thickness of the stone walls. While this serves as a morphologically helpful distinction, it has yet to prove of any general chronological or indeed functional significance. Moreover, in its relation solely to stone-built sites it is likely to be of diminished value when translated to the equivalent timber-built structures that are being discovered through aerial photography or other means.

With the pioneer work of Jobey and the surveys of the Royal Commission in Lowland Scotland, the morphological approach has been applied with greater success. This is due in part to a wider variety of sites and a correlated series of excavations across the last decade. In particular Carbon-14 dating of palisaded settlements as early as the sixth or seventh century bc has established their primacy in the development of the defended settlements of the area. On many sites in the Cheviot area the normal sequence seems to be that the palisaded settlement developed into an earth or stone-walled enclosure and sometimes culminated in a multivallate strongpoint. The idea is one that could be applied **pl. 6a** with advantage to several of the small hill-forts of North Wales, like Caer Caradog, Denbighshire. Excavation in the Scottish borderland has shown that a large **pl. 6b** proportion of the non-defended sites developed later than the more massively defended enclosures in the Roman period. These take the form of enclosures with a variety of surrounding ditch forms with internal stone- or timber-built huts. In the Northumberland plain the rectilinear planning of some settlements has in fact led to their confusion with Roman military fortlets, but recent excavations at Rudston in the East Riding suggest that their occurrence may be commoner than currently appreciated. The most recent work by Jobey has revolutionised knowledge of Dumfriesshire and shown that the few well-known hill-forts were accompanied by hundreds of homesteads and settlements in the valleys of the Esk, Ewes Water, the Dryfe Water and the Water of Milk.

At the moment several survey programmes are in progress in the west and north-west. Some are in an embryonic stage of primary discovery, others are concerned with the survey and excavation of known earthworks. South West Wales is well served at the moment with the first complete excavation of a rath, at Walesland in Pembrokeshire, and the establishment of a survey project designed to elucidate a study of raths and cognate sites in Carmarthenshire. By and large, in these areas aerial photography has only a limited contribution to make because of the amount of land permanently given over to pasture. This is not the case in two other regions where it is clear that a revolutionary picture will ultimately emerge from the results of air photographic work allied to selective excavation.

The first of these is the area of the Central March north of Hereford. The intense concentration of hill-forts in the area has long raised the question whether they provided not merely the main defensive strongpoints of the region but also the principal habitation centres. In the writer's view the latter was always unlikely and now an air photographic survey is beginning to show that the fertile plains and valleys running into the fringes of the Welsh highland massif on the west, and the southern extension of the Clee Hills to the east

were heavily populated. Plate 6c gives an idea of the kind of complex site that   **pl. 6c**
is being discovered. It evidently represents the remains of an extensive farm
settlement close to the banks of the River Arrow. The main feature appears to
be a roughly rectangular enclosure with a gate half-way along its south-eastern
side, but the ramifications of the site in the form of ditches extend on
all sides. A neighbouring site also located by aerial photography a few hundred
metres away gives some idea of the density of evidence awaiting discovery.
Further north, in the Severn basin around Shrewsbury, a large spread of settlements has recently been plotted from other aerial surveys, extending from
Oswestry and Wem in the north to Church Stretton and the Severn Gorge.
They begin to form a fairly representative pattern that will be added to across
the next few years and present a picture of the tribal settlement pattern of the
Cornovii. Ultimately they may also provide a clue to the apparent changes in
military occupation of the area. Further north, the predominant pasture of the
Cheshire Plain has largely defeated attempts to locate rural settlement from
the air and on the ground. The line of King Street north of Middlewich has,
however, proved fruitful in this respect. Otherwise the sub-rectangular site
recently excavated at Halton Brow in advance of the construction of Runcorn
New Town forms the only known rural site in north Cheshire, and is of late
second or third century date.

Despite the increasing pace of new discovery, a well-known group of remains
is still in many ways potentially the most interesting of the agricultural sites
in the north-west. They form the settlements known in the Eden Valley of   **fig. 6·1**
Cumberland and Westmorland and in parts of the Cumberland coastal plain.
Because of its location in the hinterland of Hadrian's Wall, this group of sites
is arguably more important in historical terms than that situated to the north
of the Solway, but unlike the latter, the Eden Valley group has not been
explored in unitary fashion, although the evidence is available and growing year
by year from aerial photography.

The best known sites in the Cumberland and Westmorland group, such as
Ewe Close, Crosby Garrett and Waitby, were first systematically recorded in   **fig. 6·2**
the Royal Commission *Inventory* nearly thirty years ago. The sites are justly
well-known, largely because they survive in the form of stone features on marginal land rising to nearly 1000 ft above O.D. It is important to realise, however,
that these known groups of settlement are not isolated phenomena but represent
simply the more durable elements of a pattern that must have extended northwards along the whole of the Eden Valley at considerable density. This is becoming apparent through aerial photography, which although applied only
sporadically and mainly in areas close to known Roman remains has brought
to light numerous agricultural settlements in the area of Brougham and Penrith.
Again aerial photography south of Wigtown on the Cumberland coastal plain
has revealed a startling density of sites in the sandy subsoils of the area around
Wolsty Hall. This was the scene of excavations that constitute almost the only
modern investigation of settlement in the area. Unfortunately, the work stopped

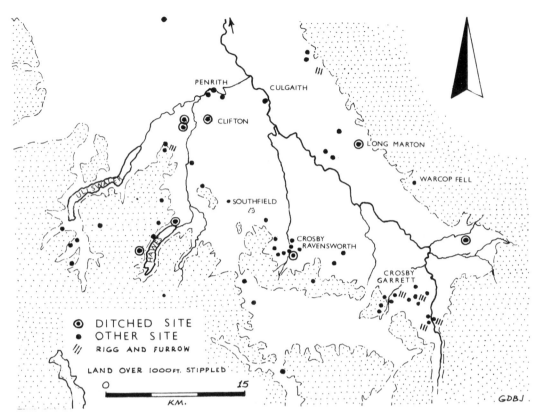

Fig. 6·1 Distribution map of Iron Age/Romano-British settlements in the Upper Eden Valley. The instances of rigg and furrow are those in which association with settlements suggests a pre-medieval date. The Eller Beck complex (p 101) lies 14 km to the south.

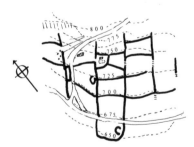

Cold Cam, Helmsley, E. Yorks.

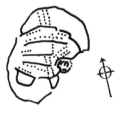

Tamshiel Rig, Roxburghshire

Rippon Tor, Dartmoor

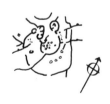

Muriau Gwyddelod, Llanfair

Fig. 6·2 Over many parts of the Highland Zone are visible examples of small farmsteads dating from prehistoric and Roman times, surviving now as low banks, ditches, walls and lines of stones. The four plans above outline some typical sites, with their associated fields and enclosures. The plan opposite shows, at the same scale, one of the best preserved of the settlement complexes.

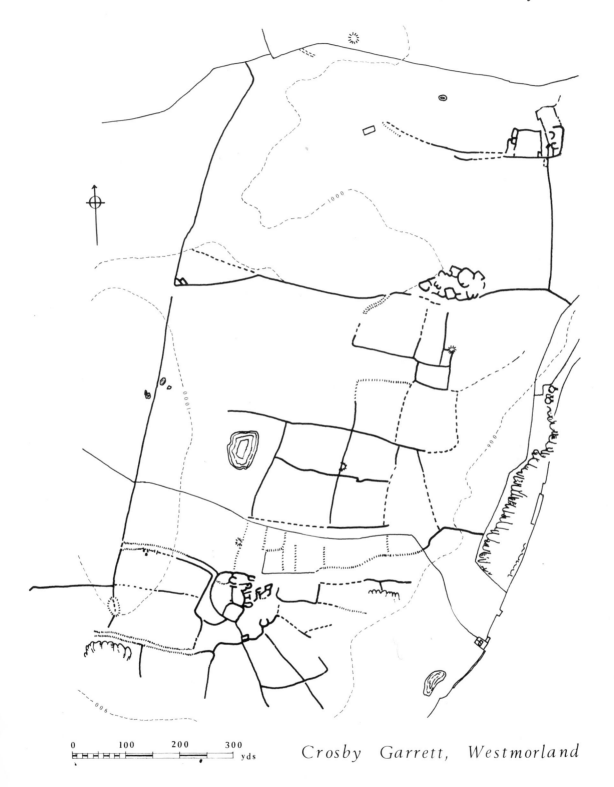

0 100 200 300 yds

Crosby Garrett, Westmorland

short of the complete excavation that would have produced a distinctive picture of the type of site involved, although the excavator, Brian Blake, did succeed in establishing the contemporaneity between the site at Risehow and the fort at Maryport and presented a convincing case for assuming a similar situation around the forts at Old Carlisle and Old Church Brampton. The overall picture is likely to represent a wholly fresh version of a native settlement close to Hadrian's Wall and its hinterland. Recent evidence from a milestone south of Carlisle suggests that the tribe concerned was called the Carvetii. Arguably they formed a sept of the Brigantian confederacy.

, So far the only unitary approach to these sites, which remain almost unexcavated apart from Blake's work, has been by R. A. Webster who recently attempted to present a more refined morphological study of the Westmorland native sites. The basis of the five-fold classification suggested was the distinction between enclosed and agglomerate sites. After the obvious cateogry of hill-forts, the second group is formed by enclosed non-defensive settlements—their non-defensibility relating to unfavourable location. As a development of this category, the third type is composed of an enclosed settlement to which external additions have been made. The two final groups are both agglomerate settlements in which a distinction is made between those with curvilinear walls and those with rectilinear walls. The basic distinction between enclosed and unenclosed types had already been made by Stevens (1966) following the 1902 conclusions of Dymond and Hodgson. However, the sociological deductions drawn by Stevens leap-frogged far beyond the supporting evidence and have not met with acceptance. The morphological development sequence postulated by Webster certainly cannot be accepted without excavation. Once again, one can only question the value of the whole approach. The site of Ewe Close may be treated with greater **pl. 6d** confidence because it lies directly on the line of the Roman road which makes a detour from its basic alignment to serve the settlement. The linking of Ewe Close by means of boundary dykes to other groups of sites in the area, thus establishing contemporaneity of occupation, appears to place the whole group within the Roman period.

In view of the lack of excavation we are forced to turn to other kinds of evidence, notably the overall distribution pattern and to the detail of individual sites. With the material available the advances that can be made stem almost entirely from a further analysis of the associated features belonging to the native farms of southern Westmorland. In particular two major groups are concerned: the sites in the Crosby Ravensworth valley, of which Ewe Close and Burwens form the best known examples, and the more complex sites of Crosby Garrett **fig. 6·1** to the south-east. The distinctive features of both settlements is the extensive system of dykes that are clearly contemporary from their layout with the actual settlements, and themselves form the most cogent reason for treating the farms as roughly contemporary. A plan of the Crosby Ravensworth settlement's features is of considerable interest because it shows that many of the major areas formed by the dyke systems relate to a unit of about 30 acres. The most impor-

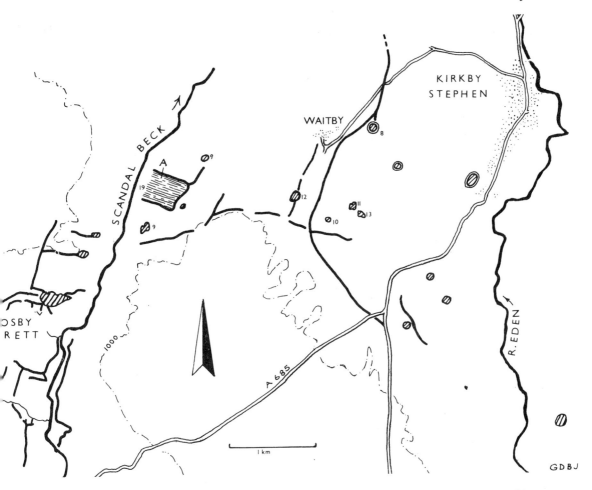

Fig. 6·3 The Waitby dykes. A general plan of the dykes and field systems known in the area comprising Crosby Garrett, Waitby and Kirkby Stephen. The numbers relate to sites in the inventory and are supplemented by new discoveries in the Kirkby Stephen area. Sites with an outer circle represent those defended by a ditch, while hatching represents rigg and furrow.

tant feature to note, however, is the way in which the dykes enclose the sheltered land of the valley slopes up to approximately the 950 ft contour. Presumably we are dealing with an agronomy in which the dykes were primarily for limiting pasturage to the protected areas away from the exposed limestone uplands. The Crosby Ravensworth sites are better known than their more extensive neighbours at Crosby Garrett, although individual plans of the latter have been published; it has, however, not been realised that the Crosby Garrett settlement forms part of a much more extensive and equally well-preserved system extending several miles eastwards to the village of Waitby immediately north of the present town of Kirkby Stephen. This adds up to a total of 8 sq km in which the landscape can be reconsidered in terms of agricultural units subdivided by cross-country dykes that relate sometimes directly to the known sites of the area, as shown in fig. 6.3.

fig. 6·3

The overall area raises a number of important questions that have not been posed in the north before, with the exception of some parts of Jobey's work in the Cheviots. In the sites in the Waitby area we can begin to discern a double pattern of settlement, first in the form of small hilltop enclosures of **pl. 6e** approximately 1 acre, taking advantage of many small, flat-topped hills of the area, and then by more extensive settlements on the lower ground exhibiting a greater incidence of rectilinear planning both in internal layout and associated enclosures. One immediate problem is that many of the sites appear to be di- **pl. 6f** rectly associated with rigg and furrow cultivation. Previously, as noted in the Royal Commission volume on Westmorland, only the site of Askrigg on the fringes of the Eden Valley showed traces of rigg and furrow apparently in direct association with a native site.

Now other evidence is available in the Waitby area; one of the dyke enclosures well away from any medieval or modern settlement exhibits clear evidence of rigg and furrow (marked as A in fig. 6·3). Examination of the area of Waitby **fig. 6·** suggests for a variety of detailed reasons that many of the lynchets and rigg and furrow systems must now be thought of as pre-medieval in date. The hypothesis is one that has previously been questioned. But the whole problem is now being radically altered by results further north where excavations along the line of Hadrian's Wall are producing clear evidence that rigg and furrow cultivation pre-dated some of the fort sites along the line of the wall. This has been most clearly illustrated by the recent excavation at Rudchester by Gillam where rigg and furrow 1·60 m across was located beneath remains of the primary Roman walls, *i.e.* the fort was laid out across cultivated land. The occurrence of this evidence in clear-cut form has now caused a re-appraisal of earlier excavation evidence to show that both Carrawburgh and Haltonchesters illustrate the same phenomenon. Furthermore, recent work at Housesteads fort has indicated that some of the terrace systems in the immediate vicinity of the site are at least contemporary with the Roman occupation. One such system is cut **pl. 6g** by the *vallum* roadway, while a second is cut into by the house platforms of the civil settlement. Both these systems of terraces are linked by terraces common to further groups of field systems. Similarly recent aerial cover near Burwens has produced evidence of strip cultivation east of the known settlement. **pl. 6h**

So far we have only been looking at the area from one particular standpoint, namely a certain method of cultivation. What can be said in terms of overall historical development? Even a superficial survey of the area reveals that a proportion of the settlements take the form of simple hill-top strongpoints, such as Waitby Castle and Croglam Castle in the Kirkby Stephen area. It would appear that such enclosures formed the original foci of settlement in the area and a similar situation may have existed in much of the Drumlin country of Ireland. Interspersed with these hill-top sites, however, are a large number of rectilinear settlements sited in the lower-lying areas. Some few of these, such as Burwens (Crosby Ravensworth), an approximately rectangular enclosure containing a number of well-preserved hut circles interspersed with cattle pens, can be paralleled among the stone-built angular settlements of North Wales, such as Din Lligwy (Anglesey). The majority of these low-lying settlements, however, consist of roughly rectangular enclosures with considerable internal subdivision and traces of a few internal huts. The settlement nucleus is generally associated with a widespread series of large field systems. In terms both of total area involved and of individual field acreage, the Cumberland and Westmorland sites form far larger units on average than do those elsewhere. At Burwens, for instance, the area of 'home fields' reaches approximately 4 acres amidst a possible outlying area of 125 acres, as defined by rivers to the north-east and north-west, and by limestone scree to the south.

There is a tendency to ascribe the rectilinear sites to Roman influence. Support for this at the moment derives from excavation by Lowndes further south at an important group of settlements at Eller Beck in the Lune Valley. There, one site produced evidence of two phases of occupation, in the earlier of which two circular huts formed the basis of the settlement. In the second phase they were partly replaced by means of rectangular enclosures dating from the mid-third to mid-fourth century, a period that corresponds with known rebuilding at the nearby fort at Burrow in Lonsdale. At this particular part of the Eller Beck complex, therefore, a single homestead built in an Iron Age tradition existed in the latter part of the Romano-British period, but was modified apparently to improve agricultural productivity. The excavator suggested that the small rectangular fields around the site supported grain production, while the outlying fields served either as winter grazing for the stock (clearly suggested by the evidence of pens within the settlement), or was subject to cultivation by the hoe. Clearly from the date of the site, there must have been contact between Eller Beck and the nearby fort, and the farmer in question must have contributed to the provisioning of the military site. Indeed, the evidence of pens in the Eller Beck settlement further suggests that meat as well as grain was being supplied to the Roman garrison at this stage.

So far we have been examining evidence almost entirely derived from the location of agricultural sites in the native British tradition, and changes in them within the Roman period. This last section is devoted to describing evidence more directly related to the impact of Roman civilisation through means of military occupation or urbanisation. Villas in the north of Britain are sparse or wholly absent and nothing can be stated about their associated field systems, if any, although a possible survival around the Gargrave site deserves further consideration. Several of the late villas of the Vale of York display interesting developments but these do not directly relate to agricultural changes so far as we know, and any further discussion must turn to other fields of speculation. One such is the evidence of bone remains. Their analysis in excavation reports still tends to be much less than a full statement of the material from both a chronological and stratigraphic standpoint. The topic is thus largely unexplained despite the fact that bone evidence can have widespread implications for the agricultural basis of a settlement. This kind of work can have a number of implications on a relatively simple level. As long ago as 1929, for instance, the results of bone analyses from the two Scottish forts of Mumrills and Newstead were compared. At the former the main source of Roman meat supply was clearly derived from cattle, and other animal remains were few by comparison. In contrast the evidence from native sites in Central Scotland has revealed a great predominance of sheep bones. The same emphasis on cattle consumption by the Roman military garrisons was also obtained at Newstead, where it was thought that there also existed evidence for improved breeding derived from the crossing of native with imported stock. This conclusion must perhaps be regarded with care nowadays to allow for a greater awareness in variations in bone size between male and female livestock.

At Newstead, to examine another aspect, the cattle were mainly slaughtered at an early age; in contrast at Mumrills, further north, all the remains for the short-horned cattle suggest that they had been slaughtered, as were the pigs and sheep on the site, at an adult, well-grown stage. This situation contrasts not only with Newstead but also with native sites of Central Scotland. The implications of general conclusions such as these are of interest to our knowledge of the provisioning of Roman military garrisons. In the Central Scottish fort the garrison did not personally control its own herds but was dependent on a supply of native unimproved stock derived from nearby tribesman. Fortunately we have an almost precise parallel of this situation in the Low Countries. A wooden tablet from Frisia records the sale of grown cattle to a Roman N.C.O., doubtless buying provisions for his garrison.

This is an example, from largely second-century contexts, of bone material that although examined in overall, chronologically undifferentiated terms, nonetheless has an important bearing on the use of the countryside in the military zone, in a way that is normally beyond the capacity of archaeological techniques. It so happens that two sites on the southern edge of the Northern Zone have recently produced large quantities of animal bones from stratified contexts.   **fig. 6**< At Whitchurch in the centre of the Shropshire/Cheshire plain, cattle seem always to have formed an important part of the economy, but during the third and fourth centuries the number of bones shows a gradual increase, indicating that the good quality grazing in the area came to be more and more exploited. During this later period, there was a marked increase in the numbers of both sheep and calf bones. Assuming that lambing occurred from February onwards, it appears that the majority of sheep were slaughtered at the onset of winter, that is at nine to twelve months, while others were killed off at one and a half to two years of age. The rise in the number of calf bones during the last two centuries of the Roman period parallels the rise in the incidence of animals, but is much more dramatic. Calves were often slaughtered at around the age of two months during the later period, presumably to meet the demands of meat consumption. Alternatively they were killed off as young adults, around two years of age. Throughout the Roman period, pigs seem to have been the least important part of the farming stock at the site.

Each square represents a one-hundred animal unit

WHITCHURCH
MEDIOLANUM

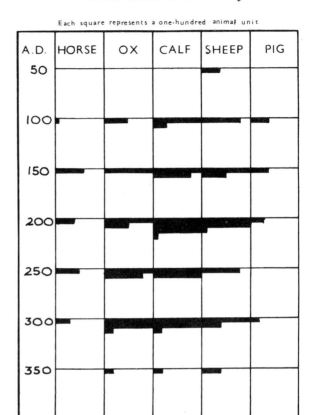

MARGIDUNUM

Period I c.A.D.50-55 to c.A.D.75
Period II c.A.D.75 to c.A.D.150
Period III c.A.D.150 to 250
Period IV c.A.D.250 to early
 fifth century

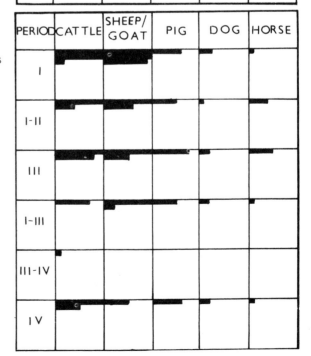

Fig. 6·4 Distribution of animal bones against a chronological basis at Whitchurch and Margidunum.

What does this mean in terms of the surrounding countryside? The virtual absence of red deer combines with the development of cattle raising to suggest that the woodland clearance in this naturally afforested area must have reached considerable proportions. Whether the development of meat production was a response to local or broader needs is arguable, because with the ready availability of brine for curing purposes the area would have been ideally suited to meeting requirements of military bulk meat contracts. A useful cross check for developments in the East Midlands has come from the excavations at Margidunum in Nottinghamshire. There it has been suggested that the animals were kept by a population largely dependent on arable production. Sheeps and goats formed the bulk of the livestock in the first century when the site developed from a military base. Most of these were probably killed for meat at an age of one to two and a half years. In the later periods sheep and goats appear to have died at a later age, thus suggesting that meat production became secondary to wool or milk production. In the period AD 250 to *c* AD 400, the decline in sheep and goats was compensated for by a notable increase in cattle raising. None of the animals died at a very early age; some were killed off at about just under three and a half years, clearly for meat consumption; the majority lived to over five years and were probably kept for breeding or as draught animals. Pigs seem to have been kept as domestic animals, being slaughtered at the end of the main growth period, about three years or younger, the most economic time for slaughter. The complete absence of red deer again attests major clearance of forest cover in the naturally wooded area.

The analysis of the bone remains from the two above mentioned sites shows how such evidence, properly applied, can go some way to answering fundamental questions relating to the Romano-British countryside. When perishables from arable production are involved, however, the problems reach a greater complexity. As we have seen at Margidunum, it was suggested that the early stages in the agricultural life of the settlement were largely related to arable farming. In this country the background to the growing of cereals in the late Bronze Age to Early Iron Age is principally known from the work of Hans Helbaek. He suggests that during the transitional period between the Late Bronze Age and the Early Iron Age the most important development was the change from summer to winter crops and the introduction of spelt, which on many sites began to predominate over emmer and barley during the Early Iron Age. If the carbonised material from a number of southern Iron Age sites in Sussex, Dorset and Somerset is a reliable guide, then spelt can be shown to have superseded other cereals on most sites. Margidunum is again one of the very few sites from the Roman period with positive information. There, spelt again predominated throughout the whole history of the settlement. During the first century AD, emmer predominated over barley, but this position was reversed by the third and fourth centuries. Oats formed a considerable proportion of the cereal crops at Margidunum throughout the fourth century but elsewhere, earlier in the imperial period, appear to have met with mixed results.

Whatever the complexities of the situation at Margidunum, the amount of cereal production must have increased to cater for the feeding of the stock demonstrably wintering on the site. This pattern has been suggested already by Applebaum who postulated large scale winter stalling of cattle. His evidence is based primarily on finds from Thistleton Dyer, Rutland, where in the fourth century two long cow byres were added or adapted to a villa site and found to contain thousands of cattle, sheep and pig bones. Yet there is reason to doubt whether winter stalling was entirely a Roman innovation. Stanwick, the great tribal centre of the northern Brigantes near Scotch Corner, Yorks., has also been claimed to have yielded evidence of the same practice. The whole problem is one where little of the evidence stands up to the generalisations that have been extracted from it. What is needed, and needed urgently, is more fundamental work in this important subject area along the line currently being pursued in Holland by Van Zeist, who has examined charred seed remains ranging in date from 2350 BC to AD 900. The work represents a conspectus of cereal production suggesting that in the Low Countries spelt was largely unused before the Roman period, while a much greater occurrence of bread and club wheats is distinguishable at the same time. Such surveys show just how important can be the results from the collation and study of relevant material from excavated sites. Similar work is now being undertaken in Germany, and a start has been made in this country at Cambridge University. In this aspect it is clear that a study of the ancient countryside in this country is less than half begun. In even more basic ways, in the Pennine area it is hardly begun at all.

Bibliography 6

A. H. A. Hogg, 'Native Settlement in Wales', *Rural Settlement in Roman Britain* (CBA Report No. 7, 1966), 28–38. A general survey of Welsh sites, particularly those of Caernarvonshire and Anglesey.

G. Jobey, 'Homesteads and Settlements of the Frontier Area', *Rural Settlement in Roman Britain* (CBA Report No. 7, 1966), 1–14.
  'A Field Survey in Northumberland', *The Iron Age in Northern Britain* (Edinburgh 1967), 89–109. Two general surveys based on detailed publications appearing across the last decade in *Archaeologia Aeliana*.

G. D. B. Jones, 'Fieldwork and Air Photography in Carmarthenshire', *Carmarthenshire Antiq.* **8**, 1971, 1–40. Survey of Iron Age/Romano-British settlements.

B. Blake, 'Excavations on Native (Iron Age) Sites in Cumberland 1956–58', *Trans. Cumberland Westmorland Antiq. Archaeol. Soc.* **59**, 1960, 1–17.

Royal Commission on Historical Monuments (England), *Westmorland* (1936). The basic account of settlements in the area, though the plans sometimes require caution in interpretation.

R. A. C. Lowndes, 'Celtic Fields, Farmsteads and Burial Mounds in the Lune Valley', *Trans. Cumberland Westmorland Antiq. Archaeol. Soc.* **63**, 1960, 77–89.

Sir G. Macdonald and A. O. Curle, 'The Roman Fort at Mumrills', *Proc. Soc. Antiq. Scotland* **63**, 1928–9, 566–572.

G. D. B. Jones and P. V. Webster, 'Mediolanum: Excavations at Whitchurch', *Archaeol J.* **125**, 1968, 193–254.

M. Todd, 'The Roman Settlement at Margidunum', *Trans. Thoroton Soc.*, 1969, 7–44.

Acknowledgements
For unpublished information from the Central Marches acknowledgement is due to the work of Messrs J. S. Bone, Arnold Baker and G. Toms. The evidence from Cheshire derives from unpublished aerial survey by the author who is particularly indebted to Miss S. Grealey for help with this survey.

7 Roman Settlements in the Nene Valley: the impact of recent archaeology
Christopher Taylor

Perhaps the most important development in British archaeology in the last few years is what has been called 'the quantitative explosion' of archaeological material. From every part of the British Isles has come evidence of previously unknown Neolithic ritual monuments, thousands of Bronze Age and later burial sites, countless settlements of the prehistoric and Roman period, many Roman military establishments, Saxon cemeteries, deserted medieval villages and a host of other kinds of remains of man's activities in the past ten thousand years. We now have perhaps more than ten times the evidence of human activity in the medieval and earlier periods than was known of even 15 years ago and the rate of discovery is still increasing. Much of this new material remains unpublished, largely because the sheer amount of information is beyond our present resources of publication.

This enormous increase in archaeological material has been in part, the result of many more and larger scale excavations by universities and the State, of new techniques developed by scientists and others working in non-archaeological fields, and especially the amount of commercial, agricultural and industrial development which is constantly turning up new archaeological sites. There has also been a remarkable growth of air photography in archaeology again by the State, by the continually expanding work of Dr J. K. S. St Joseph and by a host of other air photographers. In addition there has been the countrywide work of the Archaeological Division of the Ordnance Survey and the much more restricted surveys carried out by the Royal Commissions on Historical and Ancient Monuments of England, Wales and Scotland, and the Archaeological Division of the Ministry of Finance in Northern Ireland. All these individuals and organisations have played a part in making the increase in the amount of new archaeological information available to us.

Far more important than all these, however, has been the contribution of amateur archaeologists, either alone or in groups. The changing social climate and increasing time for recreation during the last 20 years has helped to create a new archaeologically conscious public. Books, magazines, newspapers, television and radio have all popularised the study of the past, while university extra-mural departments, the Workers Education Association, and local education authorities have organised classes and taught archaeology, often to a high academic standard. The result of this has been the formation of large numbers of local archaeological groups and societies and the appearance of almost fanatical individual workers. The excavations, and more important the fieldwork, of these people have been the major source of the vast bulk of the new evidence in British archaeology. The appearance of these amateur archaeologists, their organisation, the staggering results they have achieved and will achieve, together with the implications of their findings for the future, are so important that it is worth looking in detail at some of the work being done.

Many parts of Britain and almost any period from the Mesolithic to the medieval could be used to illustrate the impact of this new archaeological evidence. The one area discussed here has been chosen partly because of the way various organisations and individuals have recovered the new information and partly because of the varied geology and topography of the region. The type of archaeological remains and the period, that of urban and rural settlements in Roman times, were selected because these occupation sites by the virtue of their physical remains are perhaps the easiest ones to discover and therefore in total make the greatest impact. In addition, such sites have a relatively restricted time span and, though by no means all necessarily contemporary, give the best picture of the overall occupation of a landscape that we are likely to obtain between the earliest prehistoric period and medieval times.

The region under examination is the valley and adjacent areas of the River Nene in Northamptonshire, Huntingdonshire and the Soke of Peterborough, from the junction of the two main sources of the Nene at Weedon Bec, west of Northampton, to just east of Peterborough, where the river meets the fens. The overall distance is some 80 kms and a strip of land 13 kms wide centred on the river has been selected. The reason for this rather arbitrary area is that it includes not only the main Nene Valley itself but also the relatively high land on either side and a host of smaller tributary valleys. Within this long, narrow strip of land are immense variations in soil, slope and aspect resulting from its geological and geomorphological history. The River Nene here has cut deeply through the main Jurassic deposits of the East Midlands which take the form of a huge and complex escarpment dipping south eastwards. The result of the massive downcutting of the river and the grading of the tributary streams to it means that a wide range of rock types is exposed throughout the region. These include the Lower Lias Clay, the silts and clays of the Middle Lias, sands, limestones and clays of the Oolitic Series and the Oxford Clay deposits of the Upper Jurassic. In addition, extensive areas of river gravels and alluvium lie in the valley bottoms and much larger areas of glacially derived deposits are spread on the higher land. The latter include a very wide cross-section of materials from heavy clays through to sands and gravels.

These varied rock types and the equally varied soils resulting from them are exposed in a multitude of aspects. There are high plateaux of limestone, Boulder Clay and sands, hill slopes, spurs and valley sides of similar materials, and low-lying level expanses of limestones and gravels. Except on the higher limestone areas copious supplies of water are available from rivers, streams and springs. In addition, exceptionally fine building materials are available from the limestone strata, ironstone from the Northampton Sand deposits and good sands and clays for pottery manufacture. The higher Boulder Clay areas have probably always been well forested, and indeed a large part of the north-east of the region is still wooded today, it being part of the formerly great medieval Rockingham Forest. Within this chosen area, therefore, is a good cross-section of many of the types of natural environments to be found in Lowland Britain.

The known archaeological material for the study of Roman settlements in this region has come from a variety of sources. As in any area, older antiquaries and archaeologists have provided a certain amount of evidence. Here a number of villas, important chance finds as well as the two Roman towns of *Durobrivae*, near Water Newton in Huntingdonshire, and Irchester in Northamptonshire, have been known for many years. The remarkable work of E. T. Artis in the early nineteenth century around *Durobrivae* in the north of the region resulted in the discovery of the important pottery industrial area there (which produced the now well-known Nene Valley Wares) and a host of villas and other sites presumably associated with this industry. Local antiquarians in the late nineteenth and early twentieth centuries, including such notable figures as G. Wyman Abbott in the Peterborough area, also collected important material and evidence of settlement.

This kind of picture, however, can be paralleled almost anywhere in Britain. The remarkable results of the last few years have been produced by all the component parts of modern archaeology. The various organisations of State Archaeology have played an important role here. The Ancient Monuments branch of the Department of the Environment has, with its inevitably limited resources, carried out an immense amount of work in the region, not least a number of important excavations on Roman sites. The Archaeological Division of the Ordnance Survey has recently completed its revision of Northamptonshire and the Soke of Peterborough, including as usual both detailed fieldwork and extensive museum and library research. As a result, its extremely valuable record cards are now very full and up to date. In 1969 the Royal Commission on Historical Monuments (England) published its survey of the archaeological material in the area of development for Peterborough New Town and this too provides a reasonable coverage for most of the extreme north of the region. The problems of dealing with the necessary fieldwork and excavation resulting from the growth of the New Town have devolved upon the Nene Valley Research Committee, a body set up by the Council for British Archaeology. This committee, in spite of inevitable difficulties, has produced and will continue to produce work of the highest value for the study of Roman settlements there.

More recently the Royal Commission on Historical Monuments has commenced work on a survey of archaeological sites along the central section of the Nene Valley and this too is now producing much information from its own fieldwork and air photography. In addition, as with most of Britain, the whole of the Nene Valley has been under careful scrutiny from the air for many years by Dr J. K. St Joseph, and as a result the University of Cambridge Air Photography Library has a large collection of material. There are also two major museums in the region, at Peterborough and Northampton, whose staff have carried out very valuable work.

It is, however, the results of work by amateur archaeologists which have been of far more consequence. Their main concern has been with fieldwork rather than excavation, though the latter has not been entirely neglected. There are five local archaeological groups, three school archaeological societies and a local history society all working in the area as well as a number of individual fieldworkers and excavators. All these engage collectively or alone on various projects and in addition give valuable assistance to the state archaeological organisations operating there. The region even has its own air photographer who not only discovers many new sites but checks them by field examination. The actual fieldwork carried out by these local archaeologists has been greatly aided by the establishment of good relations and close contact with a large number of farmers, landowners, industrial concerns and local authorities, a remarkable achievement in itself. The last are particularly helpful and Northampton Development Corporation now has its own Archaeological Officer, while at Peterborough, not only is there also an Archaeological Officer but the Development Corporation there has been extremely co-operative in ways which were not thought to be possible a few years ago.

While all these local archaeological groups are quite separate organisations, their work is collated by the Federation of Northamptonshire Archaeological Societies, an organisation made up of representatives of the local groups and other interested bodies and supported by the Department of Adult Education of Leicester University. The information collected by the local archaeologists is gathered together by the secretary of the Federation, carefully checked and assessed and then published at least once a year in a *Bulletin*. In fact, the *Bulletin* covers work carried out over the whole of Northamptonshire and the Soke of Peterborough and extends its cover into parts of the adjoining counties as well. Amongst its more recent publications the Federation has produced an illustrated descriptive list of all the air photographs taken over fifteen years by one of its members, together with details of the subsequent fieldwork. There are still considerable difficulties in the collection and assessment of all this material. Much of it is not recorded in a way that can be termed ideal and a great deal of the pottery is either wrongly dated or not dated at all.

On the other hand, some of the local groups are extraordinarily well-organised and trained. Formal field walking expeditions are arranged, magnetometer surveys undertaken, follow-up trial excavations set in motion, and air photographs taken. Just as important, recording is meticulous and reports are written and circulated regularly. Many members are now highly competent in dating pottery, identifying coins etc., and a number of professional archaeologists give freely of their time, expertise and material aid in the form of maps and air photographs. All this practical work is backed up by training courses in field archaeology, lectures and meetings arranged both by the local groups and the Adult Education Department of Leicester University. Individuals too, working in fairly restricted areas, and often with predominantly local history or natural history interests, have been persuaded and encouraged to send in such archaeological discoveries that come to their notice. Many farmers also now report finds to the local archaeologists.

The efforts of all the various organisations to recover archaeological material are 'aided', if that is the correct word, by the continuous discovery and almost immediate destruction of sites of all periods by modern activities. Deep ploughing and other agricultural practices are constantly producing new information all over the region. The river terraces of the Nene are being worked for gravel on an ever increasing scale and ironstone and limestone are being quarried extensively in parts of the area. In addition, Northampton and Peterborough are being rapidly expanded as New Towns, while Wellingborough and Rushden are growing fast. Most villages are increasing in size and new roads and pipe-lines are appearing everywhere. These activities are constantly producing archaeological material of all dates and especially of the Roman period. One valuable source of 'new' evidence, too often ignored in the past, but now being increasingly looked at by professional and amateur archaeologists alike, is that buried in old journals, newspapers and museums. This is laborious work with relatively few rewards but the results have already been notable and a number of actual and potential Roman sites have emerged.

Despite all this work, the basic problem which besets any distributional analysis of archaeological material persists and this needs to be examined in some detail. The difficulty is the extent to which the available evidence is representative of what once existed or, more realistically, what survives to be found. It is clear that, in spite of all the work carried out along the Nene Valley, only a proportion, and perhaps a very small proportion at that, of the total number of sites is known. The survival ratio of settlements can and does vary from place to place and from one type of site to another. Different areas, due to differences in geology and the resulting soils, vary in the extent to which they reveal or conceal evidence, especially if air photography is a basic source of information. While air photography in the Nene Valley itself is eminently suited to discovering settlement sites on the extensive gravel and limestone deposits, it is less useful in the even more widespread areas of clay or heavier glacial deposits. In certain places too vegetation factors have to be considered. Large areas of woodland still exist, especially on the west side of the Nene in Rockingham Forest. This not only precludes air photography but dense undergrowth and thick layers of leaf mould make ground examination difficult if not impossible. Yet such areas certainly contain settlement sites. In addition, the still considerable areas of permanent pasture in many places prevent any archaeological work being carried out at all. Elsewhere, especially on heavier soils, the existence of well-developed medieval ridge and furrow can successfully obscure indications of earlier settlement both from the air and on the ground even when the latter is now permanently arable. Evidence exists along the Nene Valley that deep modern ploughing, as it slowly destroys and flattens this ridge and furrow, is actually producing new settlement sites. Air photographs of specific sites taken over a number of years show the gradual removal of ridge and furrow and the slow emergence of the underlying settlements. The same phenomenon has also been noted on the ground by field-workers. The difficulty is that there is only a relatively short period before the ploughing destroys the occupation sites too. The large urban areas also make discovery of archaeological sites difficult and much evidence has been lost over the last 20 years there in spite of the potential opportunities during development and redevelopment. The fear that archaeological finds might delay or restrict demolition or building is always in the minds of those involved in this kind of work and this results in deliberate concealment of sites.

Finally in this analysis of the nature of the available evidence we must note the problem of the varying amount and distribution of archaeological fieldwork carried out. In spite of the efforts by the organisations and individuals described earlier, the overall distribution of work, as will become clear, is still hopelessly uneven and incomplete. The detailed fieldwork involved in checking *every* field and copse over a long period of time, and the watching of every road re-alignment, building development and mineral extraction, is still far beyond the available resources; nor is it possible to provide the constant air photography needed at all seasons over many years. The blank or apparently sparsely occupied areas on the distribution map are not necessarily to be explained by simple geographical factors such as the existence of heavy soils, or the shortage of water. In almost every case, the explanation is lack of fieldwork and air photography in these particular places.

Before examining results, inadequate as they are, we should look briefly at the problems of chronology and terminology in relation to the specific type of site, Roman settlements, under examination here. The period of the Roman occupation lasted for at least four hundred years, during which time many changes presumably took place both in the nature and distribution of settlement. In plotting on a map all Roman settlements no allowance for these changes can be made in the present state of knowledge. This is unfortunate but the available material, and the somewhat insecure dating of much of the pottery discovered, prevent any precision. Equally difficult is the definition of a settlement. In the Nene Valley settlements range from the two Roman towns through large villages, villas and hamlets down to isolated farmsteads. There are also numerous iron-working sites and a large pottery industrial area. In the present state of knowledge it is difficult to give a precise definition for the majority of the known sites. In the Normangate Field area, west of Peterborough, for example, continuous Roman occupation debris occurs over an area of 60 hectares, far larger than many Roman towns and presumably made up of a large number of separate parts. In the following discussion and on the map this has   **fig. 7·1**

Pl. 6a An air photograph of Northshield Rings, near Peebles, showing a good example of one of the characteristic types of site in the Border country — a small multi-vallate hill-fort.

Pl. 6b Caer Caradog, Cerrig-y-Drudion, Denbighshire, from the north west. Note the hint of an inner palisade similar to those found on sites in the Cheviots.

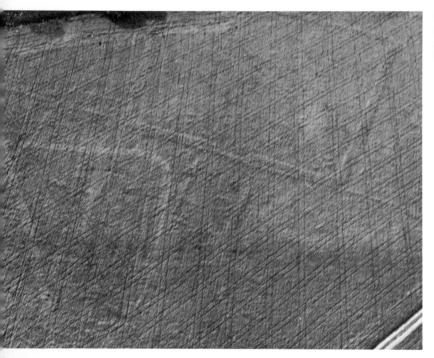

Pl. 6c Newly discovered settlement site close to the River Arrow, north west of Pembridge, Herefordshire.

Pl. 6d Ewe Close, Westmoreland, is one of the best-known and best-preserved of the Romano-British settlements in the North-West.

Pl. 6e An aerial view of Waitby, site No. 13, near Kirkby Stephen, Westmorland. Contrast the irregular layout of the left-hand side of the site, with the rectilinear exterior of the unit to the right-hand side. Waitby, site No. 10, can be seen in the upper right of the photograph and in **Pl. 6f**.

Pl. 6g Housesteads and its
cultivation terraces from the
south east. For discussion *see
page 100.*

Pl. 6h Remains of strip
cultivation east of Burwens,
Crosby Ravensworth,
Westmorland. The field occupying
the centre of the picture shows
clear traces of an ancient strip
cultivation system.

Pl. 7a Cropmarks at Great Billing, east of Northampton. A typical example of one of the many small Roman sites in the area. It was probably only a single farmstead, though there are traces of other features in the same field which may be connected with it.

Pl. 7b Cropmarks at Ashton, near Oundle. The complex pattern seen in this one field is only part of a large Roman settlement, covering some 20 hectares, whose limits have been defined by fieldwork and trial excavation.

Pl. 7c Cropmarks at Thorpe
Achurch, south of Oundle. This
well-known site is certainly of late
Iron Age date, though detailed
fieldwork has shown that some
occupation continued throughout
the Roman period.

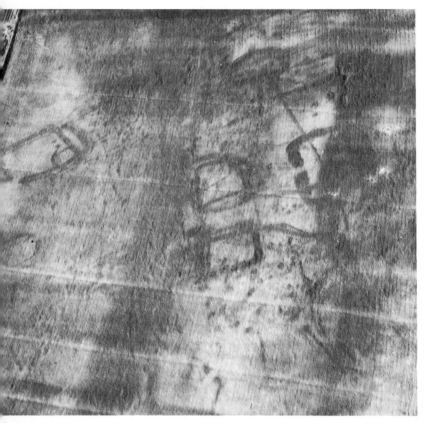

Pl. 7d Cropmarks at Woodford, north of Irthlingborough. This site appears to consist of a series of small farmsteads but no evidence of their date has been discovered. Two certain Roman settlements lie close by, but neither are visible on air photographs and were discovered only by fieldwork.

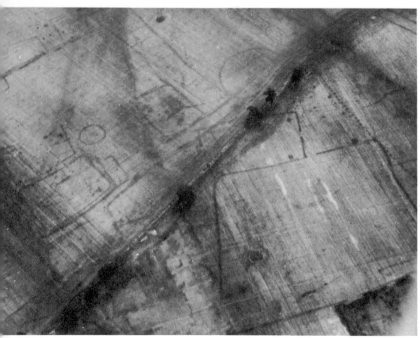

Pl. 7e Cropmarks at Orton Waterville, west of Peterborough. The photograph shows only part of a 30 hectare area of cropmarks, obviously of many periods. It was certainly occupied in the Roman period.

been listed as one single settlement. Likewise in the Middle Nene Valley, near Fotheringhay, there is a Roman 'village' nearly half a kilometre long with buildings lying on either side of a street and with a villa at the southern end. This too is listed as a single site. On the other hand, a scatter of Roman pottery picked up from a ploughed field may be the remains of a small settlement, but unless there is evidence of building materials as well, or the density of pottery is considerable, or there is good evidence from air photographs, such finds have been excluded. Certainly single coins or a few sherds have been ignored, as have the many photographic sites of settlements from which no dating evidence has yet been found. On the accompanying map the use of simple dots to indicate this great variety of settlement type is by no means satisfactory and indeed may be regarded as positively misleading. Any attempt to define, even in broad terms, the differences in type, size and function of the various settlements is, however, virtually impossible. The limited evidence will not allow a meaningful system to be devised. The air photos show to some extent the **pl. 7a–7e** variety of form and size encountered, but no overall pattern can be mapped successfully. This is in itself a measure of the amount of archaeological work which still remains to be done on top of that already achieved.

Within our arbitrary area—80 kms long and 13 kms wide—on the River Nene, the increase in knowledge of Roman settlements in the last few years has been considerable. When the Second Edition of the Ordnance Survey *Map of Roman Britain* was published in 1931, 36 Roman sites were shown in the area under consideration. This is an average density of approximately one settlement every 25 sq kms. By 1956, when the Third Edition of the *Map* was published, some 130 settlements and finds were known, a density of about one settlement or find to every seven square kilometres. By early 1972, 434 definite Roman settlements were known in the area, that is an average density of about one settlement per 2·3 sq kms. This, in numerical terms alone, is the impact of the new work in the Nene Valley. It means that in 16 years 300 new settlements have been found in this relatively small area. This is fairly remarkable by any standards, and yet more detailed analyses of these figures indicate even more important conclusions.

It is obvious from the map showing the settlements as known in 1972 that **fig. 7·1** their distribution is very uneven, with some well-marked concentrations of settlements and some equally well-marked blank areas. Some of the former are apparently obviously explainable, particularly the concentration of sites around *Durobrivae* where the pottery industry was located. But account must be taken of the amount of archaeological work which has been carried out in this area since the early nineteenth century and in particular the ease of discovery of kiln debris and stone wall-footings. There is also much current interest in such sites. This has meant that not only have sites been specifically looked for but also that they are found relatively easily by fieldworkers. In contrast, the area around the Roman town of Irchester, while not devoid of settlement, is apparently sparsely occupied. It is probable that this town never attracted the number

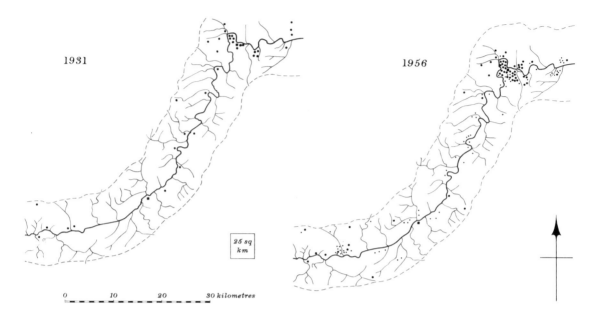

1931

1956

25 sq
km

0   10   20   30 kilometres

of satellite settlements as did *Durobrivae*; but the present picture is due mainly
to the fact that the surrounding area has not been worked over by field archaeologists as intensively as has the *Durobrivae* region.

Other parts of the region which are completely empty of settlement, or have
very little, probably reflect the same lack of fieldwork. The notable scarcity
of occupation along the eastern edge of the region, though the land here is
higher and covered with glacial clays and sands, is most likely to be due to
lack of fieldwork rather than lack of Roman occupation. No local archaeologist
lives in the area and most of the land has never been walked over. The sites
that are known have been discovered mainly by accident. Two, for example,
came from the results of recent road re-alignment, and another when archaeologists were investigating a known deserted medieval village which had been
destroyed by ploughing. Yet large Roman settlements certainly exist there, for
a ground-check in 1971 of the field in which a solitary coffin was discovered
in 1893 revealed occupation debris, including the sites of large buildings, spread
over an area of some five hectares. Similarly air survey of a remote corner
of Huntingdonshire, just within our region, has produced photographs of six
probable Roman settlements, though none has yet been ground-checked so they
are not therefore included in the total number of known sites here.

Likewise the blank area on the distribution map north west of Oundle
is probably due more to a combination of lack of fieldwork, large areas of woodland and permanent pasture than to any real scarcity of Roman settlement in
this Boulder Clay covered region. This is supported by the evidence of identical
land west of Oundle where fairly intensive fieldwork, largely by schoolboys,

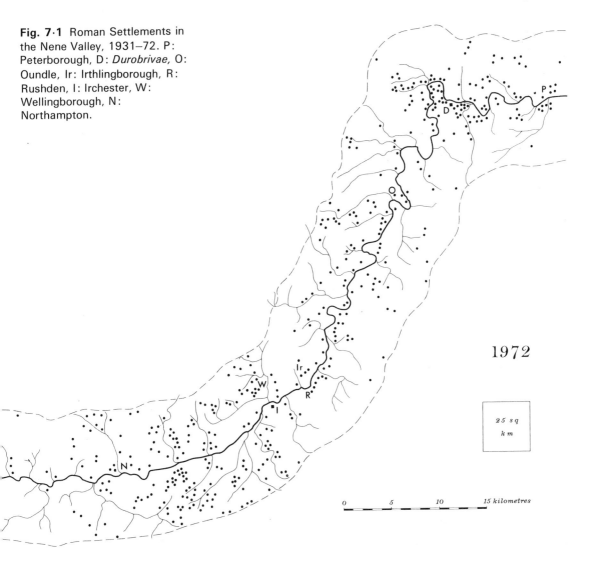

Fig. 7·1 Roman Settlements in
the Nene Valley, 1931–72. P:
Peterborough, D: *Durobrivae,* O:
Oundle, Ir: Irthlingborough, R:
Rushden, I: Irchester, W:
Wellingborough, N:
Northampton.

1972

25 sq
k m

0   5   10   15 kilometres

has produced over a dozen settlements including a major temple complex. The
effect that the lack of fieldwork can have on a distribution map is nowhere
better seen than north of Irthlingborough. There, though the bulk of the land
is covered with Boulder Clay, few settlements are known even on the lighter
sand and limestone soils around the perimeter of the clay areas. The reason
for this is an almost total lack of any fieldwork here whatsoever. In fact, it
is fairly safe to conclude that all the apparent sparsely occupied areas on the
distribution map are largely the result of inadequate or non-existent fieldwork
and that our present pattern of known settlements is reflecting only the distribution of archaeologists.

The amount of work still to be done and the vast number of sites still to be found may be appreciated by looking at areas where fieldwork has been fairly intensive. This is particularly well marked in the region south west of Irchester and south east of Northampton. Here both the topography and geology are very varied with extensive gravel terraces along the river, gentle slopes of sand and clay soils, limestone spurs and large areas of undulating highland covered by Boulder Clay. Yet over all this, and remarkably evenly distributed, many Roman settlements have been discovered in the last few years. In some places the density of settlement is as high as four per square kilometre. And even here many more settlements remain to be discovered in places where the local fieldworkers have not yet trod. The true density of Roman settlement has by no means been established yet. North of the Nene, just east of Northampton, where fieldwork has also been intensive, the apparent distribution of one settlement per square kilometre must be viewed against a further 16 settlement sites of probable Roman date, discovered from the air and not yet ground-checked. The only parts of the region where, even after detailed fieldwork has been carried out, Roman settlements appear to be few and of relatively small size are on the extremely heavy clayland of the Upper Lias and Oxford Clay deposits. Even then such areas cannot be written off as completely unoccupied. At Aldwinckle, south west of Oundle on Oxford Clay, five sites, all apparently small farmsteads, are known. Indeed, one of the largest villas in the region, at Cotterstock, north of Oundle, lies on Upper Lias Clay.

With these examples of specific areas in mind, the overall density of settlement in the region of one per 2·5 sq kms, remarkable though it may seem, is clearly a hopeless underestimate of the true situation here in the Roman period. It is very likely that the actual density of settlement was at least twice this, and that in the future archaeologists must be prepared for an overall density of perhaps one settlement every square kilometre rising to five per square kilometre in certain favourable areas. The interpretation of such densities in terms of population and economy will mean much rethinking by contemporary and future workers in this field. At the present moment such rethinking can hardly be said to have started, and all of us are still at the stage of being either largely ignorant of or amazed at the results of our own fieldwork and air photography.

Yet sooner or later the implications of this new information will have to be faced. What, for example, do such densities of occupation mean in terms of population? Certainly it would seem that all our previous estimates of the population of Roman Britain will have to be radically revised to take account of the new results. It may be that we shall have to think of a vastly greater Romano-British population in many parts of the country. If so what are the economic and social implications? How did these almost countless settlements of every conceivable size function? What were the relationships between villas, villages, hamlets, farmsteads and towns? The overall pattern is very different from that which we have previously understood to have existed. And there still remains the problem of the agricultural background to these settlements. In spite of all the fieldwork and air photography, nothing is known from the Nene

Valley which can at the present time be interpreted as fields or field systems except for what are clearly little more than paddocks around settlements. In certain places ditched trackways, up to a kilometre and more in length, can be traced on air photographs leading to, from and through settlements. But apart from these and indeterminate linear ditches which are not only undated but form no coherent pattern, nothing is known of the agricultural areas surrounding the settlements.

The work carried out on Roman settlements in the Nene Valley is also of interest when analysed in terms of the most favoured soils. Statistically the large spreads of gravel along the River Nene are not the most densely occupied. Only about 20% of all known settlements lie on river gravel, though many are of considerable size. The most frequently used soils are those derived from limestone, usually the Cornbrash and Oolitic or Lincolnshire Limestone deposits; some 30% of all known sites lie on these. Here sites covering large areas, probably villages, are common, though much smaller ones, presumably single farmsteads, also occur in large numbers. Just over 23% of sites lie on glacially derived deposits, mainly loams and clays, and here the majority, but by no means all of them, are of the small farmstead type. A further 18% of settlements, again mainly small ones, are found on light sandy soils. Only 5% are found on the heavy clay land, which is to be expected, and a further 3% are on the upper and lower Estuarine Beds whose lithology varies considerably within short distances from sands and limestones to clays. These figures are not really comparable for the actual areas of the soil types are very different. The limestone-derived soils and those on Boulder Clay are the most extensive, while the sandy, clay and gravel regions are much smaller. In addition, the uneven amount of fieldwork and the limitations of air photography mean that there are probably more sites to be found on the Boulder Clay soils than on any others. Nevertheless, there is every indication of a preference for lighter soils where possible and the suggestion that on the whole the larger settlements developed on such soils. Even so, heavier soils could be and indeed were occupied, often intensively, if only by smaller settlements.

Ideally the extent to which various soils were occupied ought to be correlated with the date of individual sites. It would be interesting to know if the heavier soils were settled later than the lighter soils. Unfortunately, as noted earlier, this is not possible to achieve except in a very subjective way, for the vast bulk of the known settlements are not dated accurately and less than 20 have been excavated to reasonably modern standards. Using the very small amount of dating evidence available in relation to the total number of sites known, no clear pattern emerges. Settlements which seem to have been occupied during the greater part of the Roman period appear to be as common on the heavier soils as on the light ones. Likewise all soils have sites which have evidence suggesting they were mainly occupied in the later Roman period.

Though this paper is concerned with Roman settlements, it is worth noting that the impact of the recent archaeological work along the Nene Valley has produced much evidence of earlier occupation as well, and this in part has a bearing on the amount of Roman material found. As yet little of the Neolithic period has been discovered, though what there is is of considerable importance. On the other hand, the number of ring-ditches, most probably the sites of Bronze Age barrows, and other evidence of burials has increased the known remains of this period by a factor of about 20 since 1945. More interesting is the vast increase in the numbers of Iron Age occupation sites, especially in areas where fieldwork has been carried out on a large scale. In the area east and south east of Northampton a host of Iron Age settlements has come to light in the last few years, many associated with the later Roman ones. In some places the density of Iron Age settlement approaches that of the Roman period and covers the same variety of limestone, sand, clay and glacially derived soils. In these areas the heavy Roman occupation seems to be merely an intensification of an earlier and almost equally heavy Iron Age settlement. This is especially important when account is taken of the survival factor of much of the friable Iron Age pottery on arable land: it is considerably less than that of the harder, better-made, Roman pottery.

One other point regarding the dense Roman settlement pattern in the region, perhaps of more significance to the historian rather than the archaeologist, is its possible influence on the succeeding Saxon period. It seems clear that the incoming Saxon settlers of the fifth and sixth centuries, to judge from the relatively few pagan-Saxon finds in the area, were in a considerable minority. The Saxons came to a very densely populated area, intensively occupied and cultivated for many centuries. Whatever political and tenurial control they achieved, most of the population is likely to have remained basically Celtic rather than Saxon for many generations. In addition, it may be of some significance that those pagan-Saxon cemeteries that do exist, while often being remote from the settlement sites of the later medieval period, are often very close to or even on top of newly discovered Roman occupation sites. The Saxon burials found in 1965 at Islip some distance from the village, for example, are now known to lie on one side of a Roman settlement discovered from the air in 1971. This suggests that the changeover from the allegedly Romano-British settlement pattern to the medieval and modern one perhaps took place well on into the Saxon period and not in early Saxon times.

These then are some of the results and problems thrown up in one small area of lowland Britain by recent archaeological work. Whether the same results are applicable over the whole country remains to be seen. Only similar detailed work will provide the answers. Results from the M5 motorway in Gloucestershire, from research projects in Somerset and from detailed area surveys in the Fens, Warwickshire, Wiltshire, Buckinghamshire and elsewhere can be seen to indicate that the apparently dense pattern of Roman occupation found in the Nene Valley is being repeated in these places. On the other hand, it may be that there are marked differences between one area and another which will come to light and need explanation. One example of this possibility must suffice here. In south Cambridgeshire, though fieldwork has not been carried out on anything like the scale in the Nene Valley, work by Dr St Joseph, the R.C.H.M., local archaeologists over many years, and more recently by investigators on the proposed motorway alignments, have consistently failed to find Roman sites in any great numbers except within the major river valleys and along the fen edges. This is in an area largely composed of rolling chalk downland where such sites might be expected and are certainly potentially easy to discover. The problems of defining and interpreting such blank areas are almost as great as those where occupation sites are numerous. Yet the necessity to define these areas of negative settlement is vital. The need for detailed work of the kind described here is imperative if even some of the questions posed are to be answered.

The problems connected with the collection and publication of these results have been immense and will continue to grow as the flood of new information inevitably increases. In the Nene Valley the remarkable co-operation between local and state archaeologists and between archaeologists and the general public has been especially noteworthy, and the methods evolved to make the new material available to a wider archaeological world are splendid. The same kind of information and publication format is appearing all over the country and there can be no doubt that ultimately there will be a complete coverage of the whole of Britain. Much remains to be done, much will be irretrievably lost, but the prospects for the future are immense. It only remains for the more academic archaeologists to emerge from their ivory towers and commence work on the interpretation of all the new material which is the great achievement of the *real* 'New Archaeology'.

Bibliography 7

Fieldwork in the Nene Valley
E. T. Artis, *The Durobrivae of Antoninus*, 1828.

Bulletin of the Northamptonshire Federation of Archaeological Societies, 1966, in progress.

B. R. Hartley, 'Notes on the Roman Pottery Industry in the Nene Valley', *Peterborough Mus. Soc. Occas. Paper* **2**, 1960.

R.C.H.M. (Eng.) *Peterborough New Town, A Survey of the Antiquities in the Area of Development*, 1969.

Ordnance Survey, *Map of Roman Britain* (2nd ed., 1931; 3rd ed., 1956).

Ordnance Survey, Archaeological Record Cards.

Fieldwork elsewhere
Bull. Wolverton and District Arch. Soc. (now *Wolverton Hist. J.*) (1956), in progress.

C.B.A., Scottish Regional Group, *Discovery and Excavation in Scotland*, 1955, in progress.

P. J. Fowler *et al.*, 'Fieldwork and Excavation in the Butcombe Area, North Somerset', *Proc. Univ. Bristol Spelaeol. Soc.* **12**, 1970, 169–94.

(ed.) 'M5, M4 and Archaeology', *Archaeol. Rev.* **4**, 1969, 13–20; **5**, 1970, 5–10; **6**, 1971, 5–10; **7**, 1972, 5–10.

'Field Archaeology in Future', in P. J. Fowler (ed.), *Archaeology and the Landscape*, 1972, 96–126.

C. W. Philips, (ed), *The Fenland in Roman Times*, 1970.

C. Thomas, 'The Present Significance of Fieldwork', in P. J. Fowler, (ed.), *above*, 1972, 75–95.

8 Continuity in the Landscape?

P. J. Fowler

A summary of some local archaeology in Wiltshire, Somerset and Gloucestershire

It is a truism that acceptable interpretations of the past change. A good example is the way in which theories have altered about what happened to people, farms and fields at supposedly crucial times like the Roman and Saxon conquests. In both these instances, views have swung back and forward between the 'blood and thunder brigade', arguing for violent change with Britons always fleeing to the West, and the 'cultural absorption' school, arguing that whatever was decided by battle or diplomacy (if indeed either occurred), the peasant continued to plod his weary way unchanged. Facetiousness apart, these are of course important historical issues: it matters a lot to our understanding of the 1st millennium AD to try and understand where people were living in the countryside and when a basic rural pattern of land units was established. Did the Saxons sweep all before them or should we look to the Roman period for the origins of some features in the medieval countryside? What can archaeology contribute to such basic problems of English history?

It is with questions such as these in mind that work summarised here was undertaken. It has produced few answers yet, and indeed this essay is intended only to outline an approach to the past in the countryside and to mention some of the lines of thought resulting from research in three small areas, respectively in Wiltshire, Somerset and Gloucestershire. Each locality provides a valid local history study in its own right but here we are concerned only to isolate some of the evidence in each relating to 'continuity', particularly with reference to settlements, fields and land-use.

Fyfield and West Overton parishes, Wiltshire

Fyfield and West Overton parishes span the Kennet Valley at the south-west corner of the Marlborough Downs. They contain, in their northern halves, a downland area with a better-preserved variety of earthworks than any other in Wessex. Over a number of years and through a combination of fieldwork, excavation and documentary research, a land-use sequence for the downs from prehistoric times to the present has been established and an attempt made to correlate it with developments in the valley.

On the downs, quite long periods are unrepresented by any evidence on the ground, suggesting breaks in the local land-use. Any continuity, from Neolithic

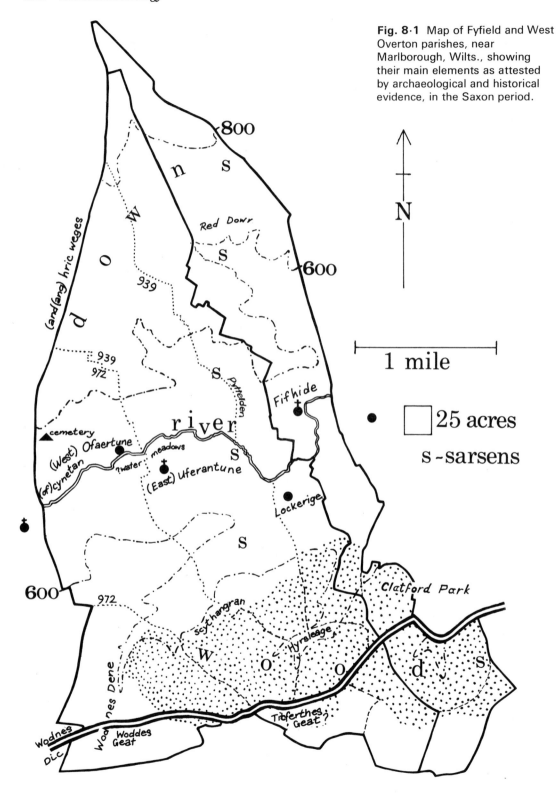

Fig. 8·1 Map of Fyfield and West Overton parishes, near Marlborough, Wilts., showing their main elements as attested by archaeological and historical evidence, in the Saxon period.

N

1 mile

25 acres

s - sarsens

800

Red Dowr

s

600

939

939
972

s
Pyttelden

Fifhide

river
s

cemetery
(West) Ofaertune

?water meadows

(of)cynetan
(East) Uferantune

Lockerige

s

600

972

s

Clatford Park

Scythangran

W   o   Hyrsleage   o   d   s

Wodnes Dene

Titferthes Geat?

Wodnes
Dic
Wodnes
Woddes Geat

on, is only general; continuity of community, or agrarian regime, through any one site's unbroken occupation, must be doubtful. On the downs, the Bronze Age shows a start of land divisions, of arable field systems and perhaps a settle-**pl. 8a** ment pattern containing elements that last to Roman times or even later; but within this continuum, there seems to have been a break—a major one—early in the pre-Roman Iron Age, when the downland landscape as a whole was re-organised for widespread exploitation in a phase that continued till about the turn of the centuries BC to AD. The next phase brought renewed exploitation **pl. 8b** in the early and middle Roman period, but again a change is detectable in the fourth century AD, when much of the arable had fallen out of cultivation. Whether it was abandoned or was now being used as pasture, the change may indicate the existence of a late-Roman villa estate as one of several land units which are perhaps subsequently reflected in the settlement pattern conventionally called Saxon. **fig. 8·1**

Even if possible Roman elements are discounted, the origins of the Saxon settlement pattern are nevertheless obscure. It is arguable that it could have been formed from an amalgamation of Saxon communities and customs with British in the sixth to seventh centuries; or that it dates only from the tenth century when good documentary evidence appears. Though one excavated settle-ment on Overton Down flourished in the late fourth century and continued into the fifth, the ancient downland settlement tradition may well have weakened in favour of river-valley locations before the end of the Roman period. And the Saxon settlements, when evidence points them out, are along the Kennet valley, fairly regularly spaced and apparently already within blocks of land simi-lar to the later system of parishes. It could well be then that, while a (Roman?) **pl. 8c** land-unit system may not only have existed but have also stayed basically unchanged, the prehistoric mode of life on the downs disappeared. No evidence yet known contradicts this view of the downs anyway: there is some evidence for Saxon downland arable but when evidence appears again for downland habi-tation, after 700 years or so, the meaning of the settlement is clear. They show a valley-based economy expanding now towards the margins of its land units, beginning in the twelfth century, and documented firmly from the middle thir-teenth century onwards. Thereafter continuity of occupation in the valleys is **pl. 8d** attested, despite many local changes, and such expansion up-hill to the downs and on to the forested land to the south was itself not continuous so much as periodic. Similarly, in the pre-documented and pre-Saxon periods, even where archaeological evidence seems abundant, there must surely have been an ebb and flow, a discontinuous land-use, characterising a rural tradition stretching from prehistory to the present.

The Vale of Wrington, Somerset

The Vale of Wrington, deliberately chosen for study partly because of its earth-work remains of ancient fields and settlements, is in the north of the county (though in south Avon from April, 1974). It embraces alluvium and river pastures as well as the thinly covered scarps of Carboniferous Limestone on the south, rising to Mendip, and on the north, rising to Broadfield Down. The **fig. 8·2** main points bearing on the 'continuity' theme to emerge here from documentary and fieldwork research are the possible relationships between pre-Roman and Roman settlement, and the survival of elements from the Roman landscape into Saxon, medieval and later times. **pl. 8e**

The prehistoric period in this area is represented most obviously by long and round barrows and hill-forts. Worked and waste flint of Neolithic and Bronze Age types is fairly common. Insufficient, however, is known to think constructively about the changing environment or settlement patterns. The discovery, however, of at least two phases of Iron Age settlement beneath a 'native' farm of the Roman period in Westmead, Row of Ashes Farm, Butcombe, offers more than the possibility of studying developments on this particular site in **pl. 8f** the 1st centuries BC/AD. It also suggests that other 'missing' pre-Roman settlements, providing the rural background to the hill-forts, may well exist beneath other Roman sites too. Furthermore, with hints of pre-Iron Age activity on the Row of Ashes settlement as well, the possibility is suggested that a few particularly favoured sites were re-used many times, and that the almost total absence of non-defended settlements from the pre-Roman distribution maps of this area is to be filled as much from the investigation of visible later sites (including extant settlements) as from the discovery of unencumbered prehistoric remains. The point was implied some years ago by the finding of Iron Age occupation material beneath a windmill mound, also in Butcombe. The discovery in 1970 of an Iron Age settlement and cemetery, of which no surface indication existed, during motorway construction at Christon, eight miles away, also points an obvious moral. Furthermore, it emphasises how difficult is the compilation of a realistic prehistoric settlement pattern map in this area, where previous widespread cultivation has presumably already destroyed much. Nevertheless, the Butcombe and Christon results suggest the existence of small farmsteads with a mixed economy outside the hill-forts, as on the Wessex chalk. They open, in particular the question of the date of the 'Celtic' fields which were once widespread, certainly high on the north side of the Vale and probably on the lower slopes too.

Previously these fields have been regarded here, largely in default of good evidence, as Roman, and their relationship to the Row of Ashes and other neighbouring settlements would appear to bear this out. But even if the visible remains are Romano-British, there surely were earlier fields, not only in the area generally but almost certainly on the same land. Earlier arable probably also occurred lower down the slopes, on land cultivated in medieval times and consequently now devoid of pre-medieval earthworks. The hill-tops themselves have, however, never been ploughed, though some parts have recently become arable.

That there was valley occupation in the Roman period is not in doubt; the questions are rather about its nature and whether or not it was a perpetuation

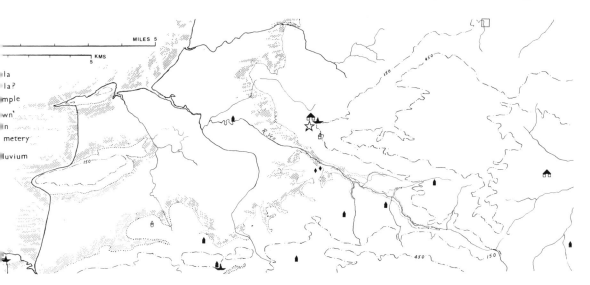

Fig. 8·2 Map of the Vale of Wrington, north Somerset, showing the main archaeological sites as known for the Roman period.

The distribution of the villas along the valley bottom is regarded as of some significance in view of the fact that each one is in a

separate Saxon estate. The star symbol, *centre,* indicates Cadbury Congresbury, a prehistoric hill-fort re-used in the fifth century AD.

of an already established pattern. Archaeologically, with one exception, it is represented not by earthworks, but by known buried villas and chance finds. Only one complex—now beneath Chew Valley Lake—has been properly excavated, but the distribution pattern of the evidence along the valley seems to be more than the result of chance. The villas particularly, certain and probable, appear to be deliberately spaced out as if representing a planned land division. This may connect with the theory that the villas themselves are the result of capital investment and settlement by Gallic refugees in the late third century, a possible occasion for the formalisation of land units as villa estates. Whether new or not, there is good reason to believe in the possibility here of an organised landscape *c* AD 300, organised to make efficient use of the natural resources by sharing them out equitably. As a suggestion of the sort of disposition that might have occurred in any one such estate, a tentative reconstruction of one such possible villa estate is offered based upon the archaeological evidence, the topography and the soils. It is, however, but an outline and makes numerous assumptions.

fig. 8·2

The Lye Hole villa and the surrounding area is nevertheless chosen as the hypothetical 'estate' for good reason. In general, its archaeological and documentary record is sound and both have recently been examined; in particular, the situation is one in which not only is there an apparent relationship between the villa in the valley and the 'native farm' on the hill above, but each of these settlements is associated with its own distinct field system, both roughly on the same axis. The Scars Farm settlement, like that half a mile east in

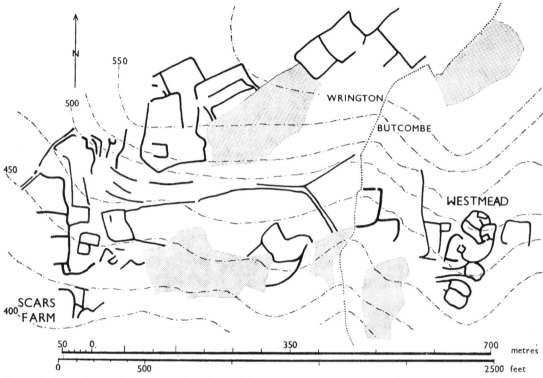

Fig. 8·3 Plan of a settlement complex at Scars Farm, Wrington, one of several settlements of the Roman period occurring along the south-facing slopes on the north side of the Vale of Wrington. It and the others can be interpreted, though without any certainty, as outlying 'native' farms on estates related to the villas in the valley. In this case, the nature of the remains, which are most probably collapsed stone walls, suggests that stock-keeping was an important part of the activity.

Westmead, Row of Ashes Farm, seems only to contain two or three buildings, and is surrounded by grass-covered stone banks. To the west, and further up the hill to the north east, these form a pattern of 'Celtic' fields, lynchetted on the slopes and presumably therefore once cultivated; but immediately north and east of the presumed buildings, the 'earthworks' are not necessarily those of cultivated fields and indeed seem to make better sense as cattle or sheep enclosures and droveways (there are similarities with some of the settlements illustrated in Chapter 6 above). The pastoral element in the local economy is well-evidenced by cattle and sheep bones at the excavated Row of Ashes settlement.

fig. 8·

fig. 6·2

A very different pattern is presented by the 'earthworks' immediately west of the villa. Again they are stone banks, very low on the plateau, lynchetted where the ground drops west and south about and below the 250 ft contour. They provide a very rare instance indeed of association between arable fields and a villa (*below* p. 133). Unfortunately, some uncertainty exists about the field layout and renewed cultivation has now further obscured the detail; but basic-

fig. 8·

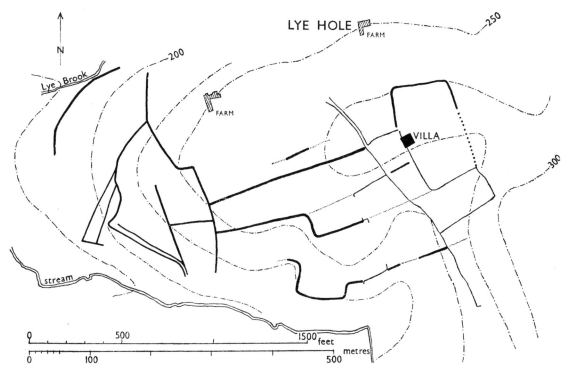

Fig. 8·4 Plan of the fields immediately west of the villa at Lye Hole, Wrington. The fields were defined by low banks and lynchets on the top and sides of a small plateau between two streams. Most were in pasture, now unfortunately reseeded after rotovating, but short lengths were and indeed still are incorporated into the sides of existing hedged fields. Though the earthworks at the west end are puzzling and not necessarily part of the complex, there can be little doubt that the series of strip-like enclosures represent arable fields attached to the villa. The thesis, however, remains to be proven.

ally there seems to have been at least eight 'strips' laid out west from the villa to the north–south boundary bank, each *c* 30 m wide and *c* 304 m long. Subdivided longitudinally, as they may well have been, there would have been sixteen fields, each of slightly less than one fifth hectare. The significance of the apparently associated lynchets on the west is not clear; but the way in which existing short lengths of existing hedge perpetuate fragments of the Roman field system is really remarkable.

In the Vale of Wrington, then, there is suggestive evidence to construct an outline sketch of what may have been the situation in later Roman times. What happened to this apparently organised, reasonably prosperous and heavily settled landscape from the late fourth century AD onwards? Nor is the question invalid here, an area beyond the zones of primary, and indeed secondary, Saxon settlement, an area where even the pro-Saxon documentary evidence does not suggest a political changeover before the late sixth century at earliest. There is as yet no archaeological evidence to contradict such a view and there is no reason to doubt the apparent lacuna of some two centuries between Roman and Saxon: plenty of time not only for things Roman to continue, but also for post-Roman non-Saxon developments to occur as the local communities, economically and doubtless socially, adjusted to the changing circumstances of the fifth century. Accepting for the sake of argument the premise that continuity is historically more likely than complete disruption in this particular area, is there any evidence, archaeological and in the landscape, to bear on it?

The nature of the late-Roman milieu from which the fifth/sixth-century communities of north Somerset developed is reasonably well-attested. There were no large towns and even Bath, at the north east corner of the area, was small by fourth-century standards. The local economy, which certainly included industries like metal-working and pottery-making as well as mixed farming, revolved around a minimum of about 30 villas and 50 'other settlements' (this latter figure should be at least doubled for a realistic picture) in an area of some 775 sq kms. The area was served by larger settlements at Charterhouse, Gatcombe and Camerton, and three temples at Brean Down, Henley Wood in Yatton and Pagan's Hill, Chew Stoke. The impression of prosperous self-sufficiency in this small area is strengthened by the fact that it is bounded by, rather than integrated with, the main Roman road system, from which in all probability branched a system of minor roads for internal communication, linked by tracks to villas, settlements and industries.

fig. 8.2

Two major local factors can be isolated in considering late-Roman developments. In the first place, the sophisticated occupation at several villas in north Somerset seems to have suffered a severe setback in the 360's. Occupation does not necessarily cease, but where it continues or re-appears it is of a different kind, to all appearances a 'squatter' occupation in a real sense. We see this at the Star villa, for example, and now, further down the social scale, at Row of Ashes Butcombe. The second factor is a possible and now disputed marine transgression, originally postulated on the basis of scattered evidence along the Somerset coast. There are many admitted problems of dating, extent, local variation and duration connected with this, but it can probably be envisaged that by the middle of the 1st millennium AD a large area of coastal Somerset was wet marshland if not actually flooded. Something like one sixth of north Somerset could have been lost to settlement and agriculture, with possibly further losses inland due to impeded drainage.

Our concern here is with the possible effects of these two factors, not their causes; and both prompt the question, where did people go? If the villas were abandoned by their owners (though not necessarily by the estate workers) then surely the instinct would be to find or create a safer place. One way would be to shelter behind defences, and the extraordinarily thick walls of Gatcombe, probably built in the mid-third century and certainly maintained later, may well have come to seem of immense importance in the eyes of the local magnates, even if the accommodation inside was not up to their accustomed standards. Another way would be to move to higher ground, and Cadbury Congresbury,

Pl. 8a This apparently shallow ditch runs across the northern end of Overton Down, Wilts., from the level ground near Avebury. Much of it has been flattened by modern ploughing but here it is well preserved as an earthwork, admittedly of slight relief, by the accident of being in a National Nature Reserve and, farther east, in a Site of Special Scientific Interest. Ironically, but of great interest, in the SSSI it has been overploughed by 'Celtic' fields and is also overlain by a possible later prehistoric settlement. This itself gives a clue to its date of origin, further supported by excavation in the area illustrated where it cut through a scatter of Beaker pottery. It was probably first dug, then, in the 2nd millennium BC, and its original function was fairly certainly as a land boundary. In fact, on the downland in the background of the photograph it specifically divides small, formerly arable fields from a 'blank' area to the north. The latter was presumably grazing land. This unassuming earthwork therefore provides us with a glimpse of land-use and land-organisation, as discussed in Chapter 3 above, some three to four thousand years ago. Then it would of course have been a much more obvious feature of the landscape: excavation showed it to have been originally as much as 2 m deep and, in parts, revetted with sarsen stones. Ditches like these have of course also been claimed as ancient trackways in Wessex: again ironically in a way, this particular one was in fact used as a track, but some 2000 years after being first dug. During the Roman period, when it had silted up almost to the existing ground level, it was used by traffic, probably including wheeled vehicles, going between the several settlements and the fields that have been surveyed in this area.

Pl. 8b These large banks, up to 3 m high, are in fact the edges of prehistoric fields, remarkably well-preserved on Fyfield Down, near Marlborough, Wilts. They were not of course built like this: these banks of lynchets represent the gradual accumulation of ploughsoil at the downhill edges of contiguous fields laid out on a slight slope. The lower photograph shows in close-up one of the lynchets on the distant slope in the upper photograph. In this case, excavation showed that the fields, round about the middle of the 1st millennium BC, were marked out with small stone walls, and it is these walls which have acted as the 'checks' against which the soil has slowly piled up. 'Slowly' is the word here, for the finds, particularly pottery, in the lynchet indicated that cultivation, discontinuous maybe, had nevertheless occurred in these fields over some six or seven hundred years up to c 100 AD. Study of the snail shells obtained from soil samples demonstrated how the local vegetation had changed over this period from a scrub-covered, perhaps even tree-covered, landscape to the open downland which persists today.

Pl. 8d Until fairly recently, it was a widespread belief that the downs had lain deserted except for the shepherd and his huge flocks from late Roman times until the present. Without in any way denying the tremendous importance of the downs for sheep-grazing in medieval and later times, the generality must not obscure the fact that a lot of the downland was brought back under cultivation, particularly in the twelfth and thirteenth centuries, and that resettlement occurred in some places. Fyfield Down near Marlborough is one such place: the photograph shows part of the twelfth to thirteenth century farm there being excavated. The stone 'walls' are in fact little more than lines of the local sarsen stone which served as the footings for what must have been essentially timber buildings. The farm, which at its greatest extent in the thirteenth century consisted of a 60 ft long dwelling house and byre, two other buildings (illustrated) and an earth closet, lay within a banked enclosure which was itself within what appeared to be a large paddock. Beyond were the arable fields, still represented on the ground by blocks of ridge-and-furrow. The site can be identified with certainty with a *Raddun* appearing in documents of the Priory of St Swithun, Winchester, between the mid-thirteenth and early fourteenth centuries, and the two sources of evidence, archaeological and documentary, combine to provide a detailed picture of life on an isolated medieval downland settlement. The name, slightly altered, has in fact persisted to the present, for settlement is called Wroughton Copse.

Pl. 8c This magnificent sarsen stone, locally known as 'Long Tom', stands in wide-open downland on the present parish boundary between Fyfield and Clatford. It is actually on a low bank with a ditch on either side, a common form of boundary earthwork which here is cutting across slight traces of 'Celtic' fields but is respected by adjacent blocks of medieval ridge-and-furrow. Such a boundary structure is very necessary on the smooth, undulating downs, conspicuously lacking in natural features which could have been used as boundary markers; the stone, which must have required quite an effort to erect and is visible from miles around, not only makes the boundary even more conspicuous but speaks volumes about its intended permanence. One of the major problems represented by such evidence, here and elsewhere, is of course that of date: when was the stone erected? when was the boundary earthwork built? are they contemporary? does either or, both represent an earlier line marked out in some other way?

And whatever the original boundary structure and its date, what was it bounding? In this area on the Marlborough Downs precise answers cannot yet be given, but firm documentary evidence, checkable on the ground, shows that the framework of the land-units which have come down to us as the ecclesiastical parishes was already in being certainly by late-Saxon times and probably a bit earlier, while archaeological evidence hints at a pagan Saxon existence and even encourages thoughts of an origin in late Roman times.

Pl. 8e Analysis of the landscape by the application of simple first principles is not a prerogative of the Wessex Chalk country. This photograph shows a typical stretch of countryside in north Somerset containing evidence, some of it fragmentary, which merely by being recognised and related to other evidence on the ground provides an outline of the history of the local land-use. Admittedly, nothing prehistoric is visible, though it has been found by excavation (*see* pl. 8f); but settlements and fields of the Roman period, an Anglo-Saxon estate boundary which is still the parish boundary, medieval strip and enclosed fields, ancient and planted woodland, medieval farms and related lanes, all these elements are there for the looking. In fact, the documentary evidence for the area has also been thoroughly investigated, and the land-use history is extremely complicated.

Pl. 8f This near-vertical air photograph shows one of the small Roman farms in Butcombe being excavated. Its position can be seen near the centre of pl. 8e, in a field called Westmead at Row of Ashes Farm. The rectangular stone building, probably the main farmhouse at the time, dates from *c* 270 AD and was surrounded by stone-walled yards probably for sheep and cattle. This arrangement lasted for about a century but, although the site apparently became ruinous in the late fourth century, occupation continued: the question is, for how long? At the other end of the Roman period the earliest occupation, which can be dated from the mid-first century, itself succeeded, though not

necessarily directly, several phases of prehistoric activity going back at least to Neolithic times. There was certainly a major phase of settlement on the same site sometime during the last few centuries BC best represented on the photograph by the dark arc to the left of the stone building. That is part of the rock-cut trench which took the upright timbers forming the wall of a circular house some 10 m in diameter with a central hearth and a porch to the south east (bottom right). Sequences like this are not uncommonly demonstrated by excavation but rarely is the evidence good enough to indicate whether we are looking at coincidence or continuity in any meaningful sense.

Pl. 8g An air view of Brean Down, Somerset, from over the Severn estuary looking inland towards Weston-super-Mare which is in the background. Remains of 'Celtic' field systems, here argued to be of late/sub-Roman date, survive on the highest parts of the Down, which is virtually an island separated from the Mendip hills by the estuary of the R. Axe. The mid-nineteenth-century fort in the foreground is matched by a hill-fort at the farther end; on the knoll in the middle distance was a Romano-Celtic temple.

Pl. 8h Excavations in progress inside the hill-fort of Cadbury Congresbury. In addition to the wide range of prehistoric evidence from these excavations, it has been shown that the hill-top was enclosed anew in the later fifth century and used perhaps until the middle of the sixth century. It is uncertain who re-occupied it and what it was used for, after 5 season's work and the accumulation of a considerable quantity of data and material. Amongst the latter, the relatively large amounts of imported Mediterranean pottery, other imported pottery and glass from western Europe, the evidence for metal-working, the various buildings and the command of labour implied by the construction of new enclosure all suggest a person, persons or community of some substance; but it is still not at all clear whether, for example, the basis of the occupation was secular or religious or both, let alone what its relationship was to the existing population. The photograph actually shows the outline, in the form of a rock-cut trench, of a circular timber building 11 m in diameter with its entrance top right opening on to a gateway through the late fifth century AD 'defences'. Part of these can be seen bottom left, with a pre-Roman Iron Age pit beside them.

Pl. 8i Air photograph from the north of Barnsley Park, Glos, showing the villa excavations in the parkland around the great house. The villa is surrounded by a Roman field system of which the evidence is so slight that its earthworks are difficult to see even from the air.

Pl. 8j The plan on fig 8·6 may look reasonably convincing but most of it is based on the field survey of earthworks of the slightest relief. This photograph shows, if that is the word, the boundary between two adjacent fields: merely a low rise of some 20 cms spread over about 8 m. In itself it is of course insignificant visually but it was only by plotting the hundreds of metres of similar evidence that fig. 8·6 was produced. Excavation rather satisfactorily produced, almost literally, nothing: a few pieces of late-Roman pottery and no structural evidence. The significant implication of this, since there cannot be any real doubt that the 'bank' *is* part of a field system, is that the fields were originally divided by an unploughed baulk.

Pl. 9a West Dereham, Norfolk. A view of the isolated church, which stands on a hill a little distance from its village. This is one of a large number of such churches in the county. Field walking around the church has produced a spread of Ipswich ware, which demonstrates the existence of a middle Saxon settlement site beside the church.

a derelict hill-fort near a Roman temple, might have been a fairly attractive place in the circumstances.

pl. 8h

Yet another factor may have simply been that all the good land was already occupied in the locality. People forced from their own lands by raids or floods would therefore simply have had to take what was available and, in this well-settled area, such would be highly marginal land. This is precisely what Cadbury Hill is; and it may well have been not only marginal in an agricultural sense, but also peripheral to any system of land division relating to villa estates (*above* p. 124). The present parish (and Saxon estate) boundary between Congresbury and Yatton crosses the Hill, in fact now separating the temple and later (fifth–sixth century?) cemetery from the hill-fort. But rather than dividing related sites, might the existing boundary not be a later formalisation of the common boundary between two contemporary (fourth century?) land units, on either side of which secondary development took place at a time of land-pressure.

Whatever the reasons for the re-use of Cadbury Congresbury hill-fort, the site now provides abundant evidence for fifth/sixth century occupation. From the point of view of our local 'continuity study' its main importance is that we now have at least one definite site in the area where people lived and worked in the fifth century, perhaps from *c* 450 onwards. Who they were, we do not yet know: former villa-owners, tenant farmers, Christians, or upstart 'British' leader and followers?—all is guesswork on that score. But this one site, even if it was fully populated, cannot account for the whole of the population of the area, so presumably other contemporary, non-defended settlements exist elsewhere. While occupation continued at some sites—the Star villa, and Row of Ashes, Butcombe—it can be argued that, henceforth, a regrouping of the settlement pattern around centres, which emerge into history as our documented late Saxon/Domesday settlements, began to take place. The only other local Roman site with evidence suggesting that activity of some sort continued later than mid-fifth century is the Pagan's Hill temple, and there indeed further excavation might show real continuity into Saxon history.

Let us return from single sites to the landscape. What happens to the Roman field systems and the partly arable economy they imply? If we accept a land-hunger as a fact of life in north Somerset in the fourth and fifth centuries, remains of contemporary fields might survive on highly marginal land. Three such examples can be considered. The Wrington/Butcombe systems already discussed could come into this category: their northern limits climb to *c* 165 m above O.D. and actually extend on to the flat plateau of Broadfield Down where the soil is very thin. This is higher than medieval cultivation came, and is encroaching on to the traditional sheep-grazing land of the area. Across the Vale on the north-facing slopes of Mendip, north east of Dolebury hill-fort, a group of at least six fields lies along the contours *c* 150 m above O.D. Almost certainly these are the outermost and highest fringes of a system now destroyed on the slopes below, yet they do not appear to be medieval. The fields are straight and parallel-sided, *c* 9 m broad and over 60 m long. Their ends are closed. They are therefore superficially similar to Romano-British fields elsewhere, though they have no associations and no direct dating evidence.

Even more marginal is Brean Down, the narrow whale-backed peninsula jutting for 1·6 km into the Bristol Channel from the mouth of the R. Axe. The Down is covered with a soil so thin that the Carboniferous Limestone frequently projects through it; and it is extremely exposed to the prevailing south westerly winds. On the Down is a late fourth-century Romano-Celtic temple and a later east/west orientated rectangular building. Nearby is a probable early Christian inhumation cemetery of the type now familiar in Somerset. There are also the remains of two separate field systems.

pl. 8g

The easterly fields close to the temple barely survive; they have been ascribed to a documented phase of cultivation in the early nineteenth century but they make better sense as survivals of a 'Celtic' field system which, if of fourth/sixth century date, would not conflict with the Romano-British pottery found in them. The plan of the westerly field group strongly suggests that that system lies in the 'Celtic' field tradition. Farmers must, nevertheless, have been hard-pressed to cultivate such an area, and a time of crisis comparable to the Napoleonic period must be sought for the fields' use. Land shortage could have been the occasion, though it is difficult to imagine the crop returns being very high. There is no direct dating evidence, but the fields do not look prehistoric, medieval or modern.

fig. 8·.

One other strand of evidence hints at what may have been happening to the fields and the economy generally. Detailed animal bone reports are available only from Row of Ashes, Butcombe, and Cadbury Congresbury. At Row of Ashes, cattle and sheep/goat are dominant in approximately equal proportions; pig is barely represented, and these two facts correlate with the earthwork evidence in suggesting an open landscape supporting widespread crop-growing and animal grazing. At Cadbury, separated only by 7 kms and possibly less than 50 years from Row of Ashes, cattle and pig are best represented, sheep have receded and deer have appeared. The suggestion is clear: a change to a mainly meat-consuming economy, with the implication that former arable and pasture were reverting to scrub and woodland. This interpretation is supported by one further piece of excavated evidence from Westmead, Row of Ashes: beneath a twelfth/thirteenth century fieldwall was a 20 cm thick layer of dark humus on top of the turf-line which had formed over the 'Celtic' field surface after abandonment. The existing soil depth of only 10 cm at abandonment emphasises the obvious fact that the overlying humus must have come from somewhere between the fifth and twelfth centuries, and an origin in a woodland environment suggests itself independently of the animal bone evidence already outlined. On the other hand, of course, extreme caution is necessary in treating such slender evidence, particularly as the Domesday evidence for Butcombe, for example, points to a clear distinction between wooded valley floor, and sheep-grazed slopes and plateau above.

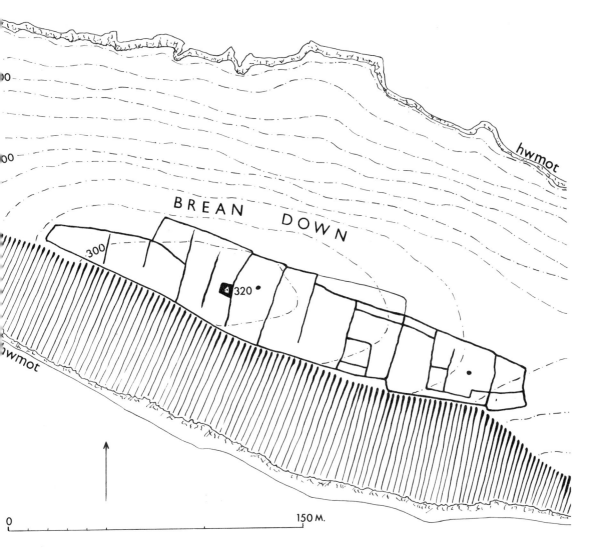

Fig. 8·5 Brean Down, owned by the National Trust, is really a continuation into the Bristol Channel of the Mendip Hills. Its Carboniferous Limestone outcrops through the thin turf even on its top within the area of the plan. This field system is towards the western end of the Down and can easily be located by the trigonometrical station near its centre and at the highest point of the Down. That there should be a field system in such an exposed and remote place is remarkable; the system itself is all the more remarkable now because it must be one of the very few remaining in southern England which is actually complete. Though the interpretative value of its completeness is somewhat lessened by the physical limits imposed by its situation, the system could have continued further down the slopes to east and north. As an 'ancient field system', it has several puzzling features, yet it is clearly in the 'Celtic' field tradition. For the purposes of this essay, it is argued to be of late-Roman or later date, though it must be stressed that there is no specific evidence of its date at all.

The documentary evidence for the Saxon period is relatively full. From the landscape point of view, the main deduction to emerge is that by the tenth century at latest the Vale was divided up into a series of estates of which the existing parishes are, by and large, a fairly accurate reflection. The Saxon charter evidence portrays a landscape of well-delineated estates aligned north–south across the Vale; and it is the correlation, doubtless deceptively simple, between these estates and Roman villas which has in part led, on the one hand, to the corollary that the Saxon estates existed here and, on the other, to the corollary that the Saxon estate themselves reflect a much older land-division. If the basic elements of a rural economy remain constant, whatever the political or tenurial arrangements, there should be no inherent improbability in the idea of a system which had been found to work at one time reappearing with different trappings at another. The existence of pre-Saxon estates and of continuity of land-division from Roman to Saxon times in this area cannot be proved, but it is one possible interpretation of the evidence.

Barnsley, Gloucestershire

Withington in Gloucestershire has for long represented the classic argument for landscape continuity from Roman to Saxon times, not just in that county but further afield. A little more can now be said about Gloucestershire, notably in the light of fieldwork and excavation at Barnsley Park, 6·5 km north east of Cirencester and 11 kms south south east of Withington.

Three points can first be emphasised about Gloucestershire itself in terms of early settlement patterns. First, although there is the fine series of hill-forts along the Cotswold scarp and the scatter of less obvious, but presumably Early Iron Age, enclosures on lower ground in the south of the county, we know next to nothing about—or even whether there were—smaller and unenclosed contemporary settlements, at least before the first century AD. Is it possible to query whether there were in fact lots of non-hill-fort Wessex-type settlements in Gloucestershire? Do the hill-forts represent the major part of the Iron Age settlement pattern (as has been argued elsewhere and is discounted *above* p. 94)? And is there any likely connection—social, political tenurial?—between the extraordinary density of hill-forts and villas? It is rather a coincidence that the greatest density of the one should be in the same area as one of the greatest densities of the other.

The second general point is that, whereas small Iron Age settlements are rare in Gloucestershire, their equivalent in the Roman period is certainly present. They are currently coming to light in a 'quantitative explosion', resulting from systematic fieldwork, air photography, widespread ploughing and motor-way-building. The large number of villas has been appreciated for a long time; now we are beginning to be able to appreciate the rural settlement pattern of which they were presumably the focal points. The landscape is filling up with the less dramatic, less tangible types of settlement in which most people lived. Now we can begin to see, in realistic terms, the populous background from which consideration of the continuity question from the fourth century AD onwards can proceed.

The Barnsley Park 'villa' fits into the background briefly outlined above. A Romanised agricultural settlement—proof of it being a villa has yet to come,—its long-term excavation indicates a structural sequence from the second to late fourth century, with the deliberate razing of at least part of the establishment at the end of that period when it was converted into a stock-yard or something similar continuing in use into the fifth century. The surrounding Park grassland contains a complex palimpsest of earthworks representing former land-uses and land-divisions from the present back to Roman times. The earliest pattern, barely discernible but over 80 hectares in extent, consists of a fairly regular system of rectangular plots defined by long, low continuous banks related to the axes of the excavated buildings and their immediately adjacent enclosures. There seems no reason to doubt that here is another villa arable field system. **fig. 8·6**

It is difficult to perceive a regularity of layout appreciably different from contemporary 'Celtic fields' associated with non-villa settlements. Here, however, with the exception at the north east edge of the system where the fields follow the contours, the fields are rectangular. The smallest unit is a field c 27 m by c 52 m (1:2), but more common are dimensions of c 27 m by c 82 m (1:3) A width of between 24 and 30 m is repeated sufficiently often (at least 14 times) to support that c 27 m was one, if not the only, of the field widths intended in the original layout. In this respect, there is a similarity to Romano-British fields elsewhere, and to the probable original width of the villa-associated fields at Lye Hole, Somerset (*above* p. 127). **fig. 8·4**

Small-scale excavation in 1969–72 began an investigation into the structure and date of the Barnsley Park field system and the enclosures around the exca- **pl. 8i** vated buildings. Suggestive evidence on both aspects has already come to light bearing directly on fifth-century continuity. A distinct structural difference between field and enclosure boundaries is apparent: the latter are stone walls but the former contain no stone structure at all. A section through a lynchetted boundary on the north east of the system showed an accumulation of ploughsoil on an original surface; a section through one of the low banks north west of the excavated buildings suggested it was an unploughed baulk between adjacent arable fields. The absence of permanent, structured field boundaries means that **pl. 8j** arable plots could have been altered in shape, size and orientation fairly easily and that the plan of the field system based on the existing earthworks might simply represent, in the same way as fossilised ridge-and-furrow, the last arrangement before abandonment.

The pottery found in the field system is predominantly late-Roman in character but includes fabrics untypical of late assemblages from the main excavation. Furthermore, two of the field boundary cuttings produced grass-tempered ware, locally considered of fifth to sixth century date. The implication is that the fields continued in cultivation after late-Roman times. If so, they would be being farmed from a settlement other than the excavated buildings, which, after

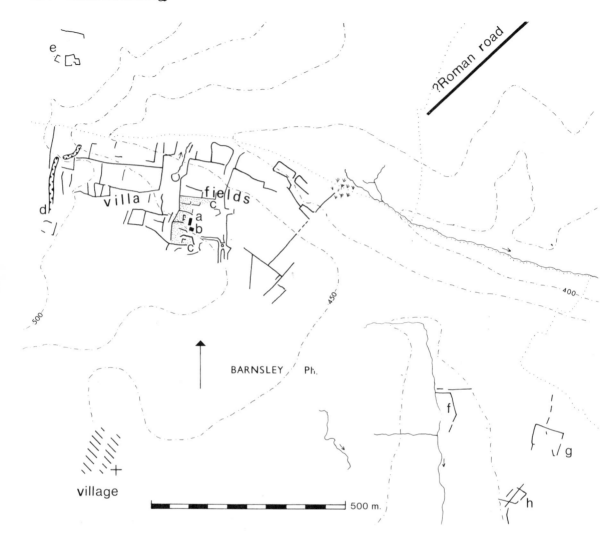

Fig. 8·6 This plan, it is argued, represents as far as is possible from surface evidence the arrangement of (stock?) yards and arable fields around an as yet undefined villa in Barnsley Park, Glos. It is based on the sort of evidence illustrated in pl. 8 which was surveyed at intervals, in differing vegetational circumstances, over five years. During the same period, selective excavation tried to establish the nature of the 'earthworks' and date them. Overall, the pattern shown here is undoubtedly Roman, though it has not been possible to date every individual element, with the additional point provided by the discovery of grass-tempered pottery in the field boundaries that cultivation continued during part at least of the fifth century. Excavation has also demonstrated that, while the structural evidence beneath the grass is more complex than that visible on the surface, the enclosures (stippled) immediately around the villa buildings are stone-walled while those further out are not. Here we seem to have a distinction between stock-yards and the like around the farm buildings and the arable fields beyond. The whole area is, incidentally, a marvellous example of fortuitous archaeological preservation as a result of emparkment. a: bath-house; b: barn; c: closes; d: boundary ditch; e, f, g, h: air photographic traces of other sites.

c 380, had been demolished. Here surely is a hint of that sort of agrarian continuity which has been suggested before: a desertion of the villa buildings about the end of the fourth century but a continuation of the food-producing activities on the estate land and, in particular, the unbroken cultivation of the arable until, and even beyond, the time when a new landlord established predominance.

The evidence allowing tentative interpretations of Roman-Saxon continuity is accumulating generally in Gloucestershire. Near Withington itself, excavation of the superficially medieval deserted settlement at Upton in Blockley has produced hints of continuity as a habitation site and even of land-division; and at Frocester Court villa, 29 km west of Barnsley, there is also evidence of post-villa cultivation associated with grass-tempered pottery. Perhaps what happened at Barnsley itself is closely related to the history of Cirencester, but a tentative hypothesis can be suggested. The 'villa' is almost at the centre of what subsequently became the parish—is this fortuitous?—with, around it, a few sites known from air photographs and only possibly Roman; while the existing village of Barnsley, **fig. 8·6** just south of the southern edge of the late/sub-Roman field system is towards the south west corner of the parish. Is it possible that the site of the village perpetuates either a new Saxon settlement in the seventh(?) century or that of estate workers on the edge of the Roman permanent arable which continued in cultivation after the abandonment and conversion of the estate headquarters? While there is no relevant evidence from the village itself for pre-Saxon settlement, such speculation need not be entirely idle. In the case of Wrington, Somerset, near Lye Hole villa (*above* p. 125), Roman material has come from the present village, prompting the thought that, when the change did come, it was the 'native' settlement which was perpetuated and the villa, bereft of its capital, which was deserted, *i.e.* the estate continues though its headquarters move, in both cases to the river bank. Since the West Overton evidence can be interpreted in exactly the same way, we may be glimpsing here one of the many clues to a fuller appreciation of that most subtle and fragile of all historical 'documents', the English landscape.

Bibliography 8

None of the projects summarised here are yet fully published, largely because they are still in progress, but the source material as far as it goes can be found, for Fyfield, in the *Wiltshire Archaeol. Natur. Hist. Mag.* throughout the 1960's, in C. Thomas (ed.), *Rural Settlement in Roman Britain* (CBA, 1966), 54–67, and in *Antiquity* **41**, 1967, 289–301; for the Vale of Wrington, one reference here will suffice to lead to most of the relevant material, viz. P. J. Fowler (ed.), *Archaeology and the Landscape*, 1972, 187–221; for Barnsley Park, there is an interim report on the villa excavations in *Trans. Bristol Gloucestershire Archaeol. Soc.* **86**, 1967, 74–83, but the fields etc. have not previously been published. See now too, in general, K. Branigan, 'The End of the Roman West', *Trans. Bristol Gloucestershire Archaeol. Soc.* **91**, 1972, 117–28.

Much of relevance is published annually as short interim notes in *Archaeological Review* **1–7**, 1966–72, *continuing*. It hardly needs saying that the stimulation in general of this work is to be found in the writings of O. G. S. Crawford, H. P. R. Finberg, W. G. Hoskins and H. C. Bowen.

Acknowledgement

Without the assistance of many hundreds of students of the Department of Extra-Mural Studies, University of Bristol, over the last dozen years, Fyfield, Butcombe and Barnsley Park would still be no more than names on a map.

9 The Origins of Rural Settlement in East Anglia

Peter Wade-Martins

'The variety of plan among the villages of England, besides affording one of the most delightful characteristics of the countryside, is profoundly interesting—and tantalising—to the historian of the landscape. It is interesting because he realises that this variety of forms almost certainly reflects very early cultural or historical differences, and it is tantalising for two reasons. First, because we cannot be sure that the present plan of a village is not the result of successive changes that had been completed before the earliest maps are available: we cannot be sure we know what the original *shape was in many instances. And secondly, even if we are sure of the original shape of a village, we are not yet in a position to say—for the subject has been so little studied in this country—what the various shapes and plans mean in terms of social history.'*

W. G. Hoskins, *The Making of the English Landscape*, 1955, 49

Introduction

These words eloquently summarise the present state of our knowledge of the birth of the English village. Much has been written about the economic and social history of the English countryside, but of the origins of the villages themselves we still know very little. How far the villages, the roads, the open fields and the parish boundaries in the different parts of the countryside are really the same as those in use during the Anglo-Saxon period is certainly one of the most fascinating and crucial questions any archaeologist interested in the medieval landscape can ask. It is still a theme where speculation based on chance archaeological finds can often be a substitute for fact.

One of the studies of the English village system which has had most influence on thought during the last 40 years is the survey by Professor Harry Thorpe of the villages of County Durham. Thorpe examined the modern plans of the villages within the county, and found that nearly half had houses grouped around greens, while the rest were without greens. Taking this classification of village patterns a stage further, he subdivided the green villages into types according to their modern shapes: 'broad greens', 'street greens', and 'greens of indefinite shape'. As all except 11 of the 101 green villages were recorded before 1200, and as 85% have names which are Anglo-Saxon in origin, he argued that the green villages of today are basically the same as those introduced into the north of England by Anglo-Saxon settlers in the pre-Christian period.

These conclusions were, of course, based on present village patterns, and they made little allowance either for the loss of village greens in more recent centuries or for more fundamental changes in settlement form since the Norman conquest. It is always helpful to question whether the situation has remained static in a region during the past thousand years, and any village classification based solely on modern information can certainly give rise to misleading conclusions. The idea that village patterns have *evolved*, in some cases into quite different forms from those in which they began, has been a rather neglected aspect of settlement studies.

The discovery of two thousand deserted medieval villages has made us see the landscape in a new light. It is now viewed very much as a changing scene in which the rise and fall of rural communities has become an integral part of landscape history.

We have also seen a fundamental re-thinking of the long held views about the date of our earliest Anglo-Saxon place-names: those ending in *-ingas*. It has been shown that the distribution of these names does not coincide with the pattern of fifth and sixth century Anglo-Saxon cemeteries. Rather, the two actually complement one another. These names are therefore unlikely to be primary in the settlement period. Place-names especially allow little room for the survival of the Romano-British population. We ought to question how much it is good to rely on them to provide accurate data about the cultural background of many early village populations; we should try to look beyond this Anglo-Saxon population which formed the dominant, but not always numerically superior, element in early English society.

Can villages ever be traced back to reveal continuity with the Roman period? Do recent village plans necessarily bear any relation to their pre-conquest forms? In any given area, what was the order in which the pre-conquest villages were formed? Archaeology can do much in the different parts of the country to contribute to these and many other questions which concern everyone interested in the origins and development of the English countryside.

In East Anglia there are, of course, many features which are peculiar to that area. There are vast numbers of isolated churches often far removed from their villages. Does this separation within a parish demonstrate a movement of the population at some time, or has the church in many instances always been an isolated landmark? An examination of the nineteenth-century enclosure **pl. 9a** maps of the region shows that many villages were green settlements until that time. Was this also true in the Middle Ages, and more especially, at what time did these green villages come into existence? What were the reasons behind the creation of such a distinctive form of rural settlement?

No reliable answers can be given to these questions unless a tremendous amount of time-consuming fieldwork is carried out and detailed records made.

The rest of this chapter describes an attempt made by the writer to unravel a small part of the East Anglian landscape. Similar studies have rarely been attempted elsewhere, partly because the landscape in some of the other regions is not so favourable for this type of work. The study by Professor Barry Cunliffe of the parish of Chalton, Hampshire, is an important example of how such a survey can be carried out for all periods of human settlement.

We certainly know far too little to postulate any general theories of English village development; *much* more fieldwork will have to be done in many more areas before we can reach this stage. In every major region we may find that village development has followed quite different lines.

Methods of Survey

In 1967 when this work began it became clear that much intensive fieldwork would have to be done before any reliable understanding of post-Roman settlement could be achieved in any part of the East Anglian region. For much of central Norfolk there was almost a complete absence of recorded archaeological finds which could be of use in this work. If the fieldwork was to be sufficiently detailed it would have to be limited in area. Therefore one medieval 'hundred', consisting today of 29 parishes, was chosen. This was the 'Launditch Hundred' in west central Norfolk. The writer had already excavated part of the deserted village of Grenstein which lay within this hundred, and large-scale excavations of the Anglo-Saxon cathedral settlement at North Elmham had just begun. Therefore within this single area both fieldwork, excavation and a study of the relevant documents could be combined. It is an area of medium soils, not especially heavy or infertile, and the settlement pattern could well be compared with many other parts of the region.

East Anglia offers an almost unrivalled opportunity for archaeologists interested in settlement history; it is one of the most extensively cultivated regions in the country, and permanent pasture is a rare sight. Although this brings great problems for the preservation of archaeological sites, especially deserted medieval villages which often cover large areas, it nevertheless provides almost unlimited opportunities for anyone to search fields for pottery scatters and to work out the history of settlement from the Roman period right through to the present day. Of course, the further one goes back in time, the less the settlements are related to the existing framework, and therefore the more difficult they are to locate. In this region one finds that settlement patterns have certainly never remained static, and even a hundred years can usually see significant changes. However, the advantages of this constant shift of village plans is that only the most recent habitation sites are unavailable for study. By collecting surface pottery, by examining earthworks, by excavating selected sites of different periods, and by using documents, a relatively clear-cut picture of the evolution of villages within an area can be obtained as far back as the seventh century, and possibly earlier. The region offers great opportunities for this work, yet fieldwork along these lines has hardly begun.

The other advantage which East Anglia offers is the fact that there has been a relatively plentiful and uninterrupted production of pottery from the Roman period to the present day. So far only pagan Saxon cemeteries have really influenced thought about the general distribution of pre-conquest settlements, yet archaeology can do much more than this. Our knowledge of the seventh- to eleventh-century pottery is now quite sufficient to provide not only general distribution maps of settlements, but also much more detailed information about the form and size of many village sites from their earliest days. The location, the sizes and the shapes of many pre-conquest villages came to light during this survey, when previously none had been recorded in the area. The important excavation of the pagan Saxon village at West Stow in Suffolk has done much to provide some detailed information about pagan Saxon villages, and the work at North Elmham and also Wican Bonhunt in Essex is helping to fill the gap for the later period.

For East Anglia the study of wheel-made Anglo-Saxon pottery was put on a firm footing in the late 1950's. First there was *Ipswich ware* which was used throughout the middle Saxon period between *c.* 650–850 AD. It was the first mass-produced wheel-made pottery to be made in East Anglia, and the knowledge for this new technique must have come from the Rhineland. The arrival of the Danes saw the introduction of three more Saxon pottery types into Eastern England, all dated between *c.* 850–1100; in central Norfolk it was *Thetford ware* which was used almost exclusively.

In fieldwork the distribution of pottery is the only type of evidence which can be used for the Anglo-Saxon period. But careful collection and detailed recording of pottery scatters on 25-inch Ordnance Survey maps can reveal much about village sites; smaller scale six-inch maps are really not suitable for this purpose. For the medieval period earthworks of villages and moated manor houses survive. The pottery collected from the medieval sites has revealed the final stage of growth of settlements at the height of the Middle Ages, when enormous village communities thickly covered the Norfolk countryside.

No survey of this nature is complete without the use of documents. These villages seldom have the wealth of documentation which is available for towns, although North Elmham has a very useful and very detailed parish survey which describes the village and all the fields as they were in 1454–5. Of great importance are the manuscript maps; nine of the parishes in the Launditch Hundred contained farms owned by the Holkham Estate, mostly acquired by Chief Justice Coke in the sixteenth century. For most of these parishes there are maps of several dates from the sixteeenth century onwards. The earliest map for the Launditch Hundred is a parish map of West Lexham dated 1575. These sixteenth-century maps are very detailed, if somewhat stylised, and they are quite adequate enough to provide an accurate picture of the villages as they were at the end of the Middle Ages.

Three Sample Villages

Longham. The three villages illustrated in this section have been chosen because they represent three ways in which village development has taken place in the region. Longham has really proved to be a classic example, because it reveals so well the migratory habits of the East Anglian village.

In Longham today hardly any trace of the medieval landscape survives. Most of the parish belonged to the Holkham Estate in the nineteenth century, and at the enclosures in 1815–16 all its three farms were completely re-organised as a part of the land improvement schemes initiated by Thomas William Coke. In fig. 9·1 the nineteenth-century pattern of rectangular fields can be seen. After   **fig. 9·1** these improvements hardly any trace of the medieval field patterns survived. None of the areas of medieval common remain, because they were all enclosed at this time, and even their outlines were largely obliterated in the new field system. The church, which was partly re-built in Victorian times, and the two eroded moated manor sites are all that remain of the medieval landscape. Certainly none of the houses standing in the late sixteenth century are left today.

Fig. 9·2 has been drawn from an undated late sixteenth-century map of the   **fig. 9·2** parish. This early map is absolutely vital for the understanding of the medieval settlement pattern, because it shows in detail the layout of the late medieval village, and it also provides a starting point from which one can work backwards in time through the Middle Ages to the Saxon period.

Our first positive evidence for occupation in Longham comes from the middle Saxon period. Although it is not easy to be precise about how much a pottery scatter can be used to represent the pattern and the extent of an Anglo-Saxon village, it is still possible to pinpoint the main concentration of middle Saxon houses, and to distinguish this from the later Saxon settlement areas. This has been shown in fig. 9·2. The late Saxon village occupied a similar position, but one can see that during this time the settlement expanded to occupy a much larger area. All the Anglo-Saxon pottery comes from near the church, and the earliest sherds collected from around Southall Green show that people did not move to this new site until the twelfth century. We can see from the pattern of the occupation that by this time the pre-enclosure pattern of roads and commons had become stabilised.

In the thirteenth and fourteenth centuries the main village area was around Southall Green. Almost all around Southall Green large quantities of medieval pottery can be collected from the fields which lie over the perimeter of the old common. In fig. 9·2 the shaded areas representing medieval occupation were compiled solely from the information collected in the course of this fieldwork.

There is really very little trace of medieval occupation around Kirtling Common and by closely comparing the parish maps of the sixteenth, eighteenth and nineteenth centuries a secondary shift during the last five hundred years from Southall Green to Kirtling Common becomes apparent. All the material collected from the house sites around Kirtling Common confirm the suspicion   **figs 9·1** that this area did not develop until the fifteenth century. We therefore have   **and 9·2**

Fig. 9·1 Longham in 1816, showing the layout of the village after the enclosures. The old greens and commons are stippled.

two deserted areas of settlement in the parish, one largely pre-conquest and the other medieval.

Today the church stands on one of the highest points in the parish, surrounded only by nineteenth-century houses and farm buildings. Before the erection of these houses (after the 1815–16 enclosures), there had been no settlement there since about the thirteenth-century when the dwindling medieval occupation on this spot came to an end.

How much earlier than the seventh century this early village at Longham might be is a very exciting question which can only be adequately answered by large-scale excavation. One Roman coin of AD 270–274, two Roman sherds and two handmade sherds of uncertain date are the only clues.

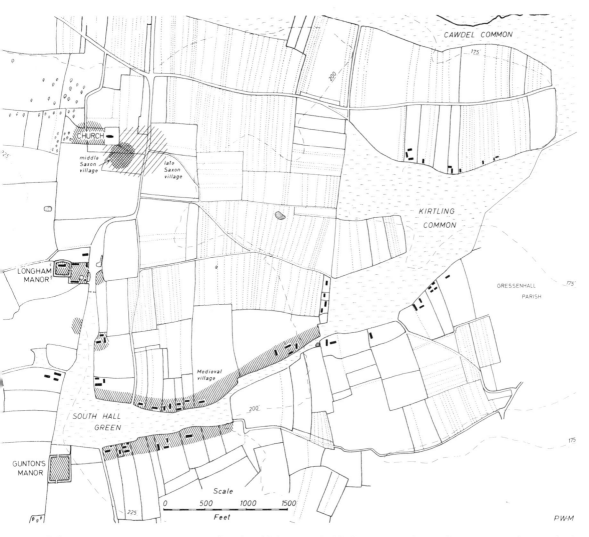

Fig. 9·2 Longham village from the middle Saxon period to the late sixteenth century. The map is based on an undated late sixteenth-century map. There was a middle Saxon village near the church which expanded in late Saxon times. Then in the twelfth century settlement started around Southhall Green, and the shift to this green was almost complete by the fourteenth century. By the sixteenth century settlement had started to shift again, this time from Southhall Green to Kirtling Common. This second wave was almost complete by 1816.

The late Dr O. K. Schram's interpretation of the place-name 'Longham' was that it was derived from *Lawingaham*, a clear *-ingaham* place-name. Yet, we have seen that there is no evidence whatever for *Anglo-Saxon* occupation on this original village site. This place-name must therefore either be later than one would normally suppose or, alternatively, this village was founded by a sub-Roman community who at some time adopted a place-name which ended with an unmistakable Anglo-Saxon element.

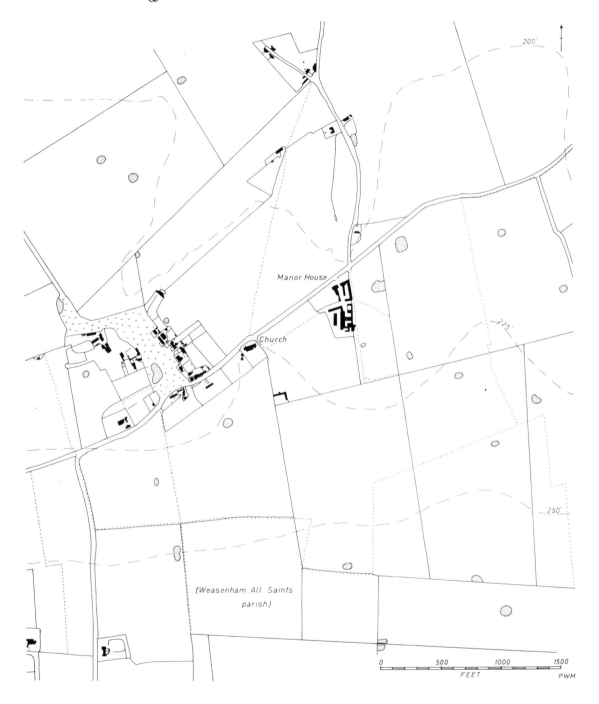

Fig. 9·3 Weasenham St Peter 1905. The village consists of a cluster of eighteenth- and nineteenth-century cottages around Thorpe Green, and the church stands on a small hill to the east.

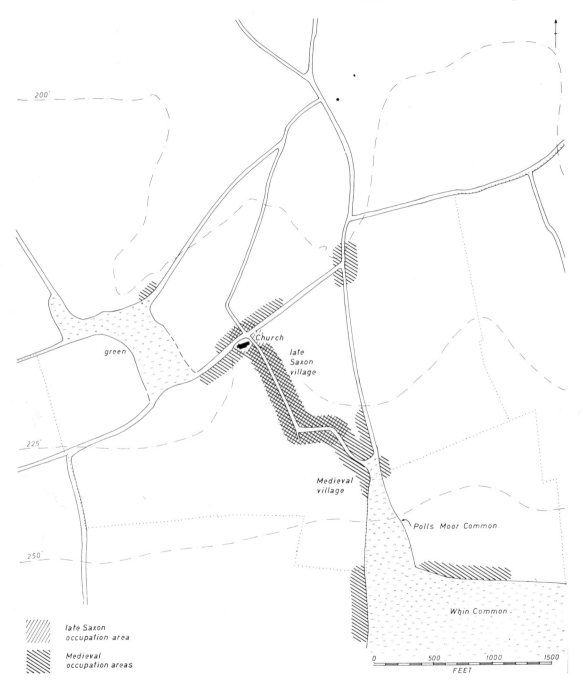

200'

225'

250'

green

Church

late
Saxon
village

Medieval
village

Polls Moor Common

Whin Common

late Saxon
occupation area

Medieval
occupation areas

0   500   1000   1500
FEET

Fig. 9·4 Weasenham St Peter during the late Saxon and medieval periods. During this time Thorpe Green was not an important element in the settlement pattern. The late Saxon village started where the church now stands; it then expanded up the hill away from Thorpe Green, and during the Middle Ages it reached as far as the large open heathland of Whin Common. Today no trace remains of this site, except for the church.

Running down the western side of the parish is a Dark Age linear earthwork, called the Launditch, which gave its name to the Launditch Hundred. The names of the dyke and the village certainly suggest that the two were in some way associated. Along the north end of the parish there runs the main east–west Roman road which crossed Norfolk from the Fens near Denver Sluice probably to the Roman port at Caister-on-Sea on the east coast. The Launditch intersects the Roman road in the north-west corner of this parish. The dyke must have been constructed to control traffic moving along the road from the west; the dyke itself faces *westwards* and it was built as a defensive earthwork for exactly the same distance (600 m) to either side of the Roman road. It is possible that this dyke and a very similar one farther south, called the Panworth Ditch, are both either late Roman or sub-Roman in origin and were intended to prevent the passage of unwanted Anglo-Saxon settlers moving inland from the areas of dense settlement bordering the Fens. By contrast the two great west Norfolk dykes, the Bichamditch and the Fossditch, face *eastwards*, possibly as a defence for the Anglo-Saxon Fenland communities.

The very fact that the Launditch was constructed could indicate that a well-organised sub-Roman community was living somewhere nearby to make effective this gateway across the Roman road. Although this is the point where interpretation may be reaching into the realms of fantasy, it is right that we should at least consider the origin of the Launditch and Longham village in these terms. Perhaps one day an excavation of the early village will find the answer to these questions.

Weasenham St Peter. The continuing process of settlement change can be seen many times all over East Anglia, even by glancing at the one-inch Ordnance Survey maps. Isolated churches, scattered hamlets and enclosed village greens are all the end products of this fluctuation. There was apparently neither the geographical or social factors to prevent the movement of villages. The flat gently undulating scenery provides so many places which are suitable for settlement, and the high proportion of free peasantry in the region gave people the opportunity to change their mode of life and the way they farmed to adapt to the changing economic and climatic conditions.

Another example of the changing village is Weasenham St Peter, which lies 9·5 kms to the north-west of Longham where the soils become lighter towards the Goodsands region of north west Norfolk and the chalk upland of west Norfolk. Today there is a cluster of eighteenth- and nineteenth-century cottages around a small green beside the Fakenham to Swaffham road, and the church stands up high on a small hill nearby. As the church and the village lie so close together, we might expect that here one would find a relatively stable history of village growth. In fact the picture is quite different. **figs 9·3 and 9·4**

This village began probably in the ninth century as an offshoot of its neighbouring village of Weasenham All Saints, where the site of a very substantial middle Saxon village has been found. In the ninth century occupation began at Weasenham St Peter on a spur of land where the church now stands. Then, during the succeeding centuries, the village spread *up* the hill towards Whin Common, along a road which was closed in the nineteenth century. A comparison between figs 9·3 and 9·4 will show how much the medieval road pattern was obliterated by the enclosures.

It was in the twelfth century that occupation first began around the small green near the church (known as Thorpe Green on the sixteenth-century map). Most of the village expansion, however, continued to take place in the upland village which overflowed on to Whin Common by the thirteenth century. Then, in the later part of the Middle Ages, this village suffered a severe decline; there is a little pottery on the upland site which can be dated after the fifteenth century. On the sixteenth-century manuscript map there are no houses shown in this area; a small hamlet is shown around Thorpe Green, and a new scattered roadside hamlet had become established 0·5 km to the north-east of the church. Since the sixteenth century this secondary hamlet has also considerably declined, leaving a few scattered houses and the small community around Thorpe Green. Longham and Weasenham St Peter both show very well how the concept of stable village patterns and terms like 'deserted villages' may often be difficult to apply to East Anglia.

Mileham. The development of this village was very different from that seen in the two previous examples. Mileham lies near the centre of the Launditch Hundred, and a motte and bailey castle stood at one end of the village which grew up on the road which was the main medieval east–west route between Norwich and Kings Lynn. Its importance during the early Middle Ages must have been due largely to this location. No maps earlier than the nineteenth century for Mileham survive, but it has certainly been a typical street village since the late Saxon period. There were small greens at either end of the village, but the houses apparently did not extend this far in either direction.

figs 9·5 and 9·6

The one feature which does not fit into the medieval pattern is the church which stands well back from the main street. Here a middle Saxon village covering nearly seven acres has been found. Once again we can see that the church pin-points the original nucleus of the village, and no middle Saxon pottery is to be seen anywhere else in the medieval village. This early site was comparatively short-lived, and even by the tenth century the people had moved northwards onto the main road, leaving a church on the site of this pre-Danish village.

fig. 9·6

The new site on the main road rapidly developed from a tenth-century core opposite the church, spreading out both ways down the main street. Domesday Book records a total working male population of 111, a large number which compares well with the archaeological evidence. The church is actually not recorded in the survey, but neither is the fine late Saxon church at Great Dunham a few miles away. The Domesday records are not in fact a reliable guide to the distribution of eleventh-century churches in the region.

Soon after the Norman conquest the castle, consisting of a motte and bailey standing within an outer circular ringwork, was built at the west end of the village. It was no doubt placed at this point to control the movement of traffic

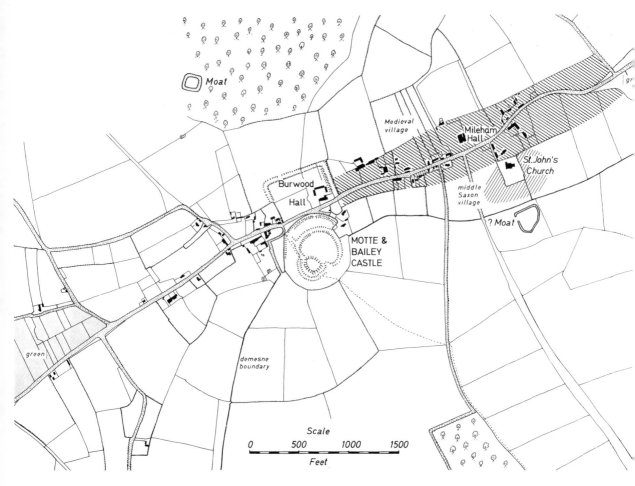

Fig. 9·5 Mileham village from the middle Saxon period to the nineteenth century, based on the enclosure map of 1814. The middle Saxon village site is near the church. By the tenth century the settlement had moved north to the main road. It then expanded east and west. To the west it reached as far as Mileham Castle. Since the Middle Ages gaps have developed along the street and settlement has expanded a little to the west. In the south east part of the map is part of the demesne land bounded by a hedge line which still survives (shown as a thick line).

Fig. 9·6 Mileham: the area of middle Saxon settlement near the church (to the same scale).

along this important routeway, and a rectangular enclosure abutting onto the north side of the castle was built across the main street. The old hedgerows outlining the area of the demesne land on the south side of the castle can also still be seen. No documents for the castle have come to light, and the only record shows that Henry I granted this manor to the Fitz Alan family.

fig. 9.5

Set back from the streets on either side are two meandering hedgelines which were the rear boundaries of the medieval village 'tofts'. Within this belt of occupation the area is thickly strewn with finds. The many gaps in the street frontage, where properties stand empty, show how this village centre has decayed since the Middle Ages.

Like so many of the early village sites in the area, the original occupation is difficult to date with any accuracy. The early success of this village must have been due especially to its location first close to and then on the important Anglo-Saxon routeway which replaced stretches of the east–west Roman road. A thin scatter of Roman finds have come from the vicinity of the village, especially at the eastern end near the church. This might point to the beginning of occupation sometime during the fifth, sixth or early seventh centuries, but again no trace of pagan Saxon pottery has been found. The earliest datable Anglo-Saxon find is a sherd of Ipswich ware with a boss pressed out from the inside: a pagan Saxon method of decoration which must have lasted into the beginning of the middle Saxon period.

These three sample villages, out of the much larger number which have been examined, show the great wealth of information which is available to the persistent fieldworker. All one needs to do this work is a good pair of wellington boots, a supply of polythene bags to collect the finds and a set of 25-inch Ordnance Survey maps to record the results. It is also important to see the limitations of the fieldwork evidence; sooner or later there comes a point where knowledge can be advanced little further without excavation. One type of evidence is little use without the other, and it is important that a balance should, if possible, be achieved.

Discussion

With the end of Imperial rule in Britain in the fifth century, a true Dark Age descended upon East Anglia. Contemporary commentators and the Anglo-Saxon Chronicle are almost totally silent about events which took place within the region before the ninth century. Despite considerable fieldwork, no settlement in the Launditch area dateable either to the fifth, sixth or early seventh centuries has yet been positively identified. None of the nine Roman sites examined has produced any *recognisable* post-Roman (i.e. Anglo-Saxon) pottery, and none of the later village sites has yielded anything except very enigmatic evidence for pre-seventh century activity. Somehow this gap of two hundred and fifty years must be bridged.

The linear earthworks in west Norfolk are of the greatest importance for the post-Roman period. It seems certain that they form two pairs of opposing defensive systems designed to interrupt east–west communications, particularly along Roman roads. They were constructed at some date between the collapse of Roman rule and the foundation of the East Anglian kingdom in the second half of the sixth century when all East Anglia was united. The distribution of Anglo-Saxon cemeteries shows that, during the initial settlement period, the main weight of the migrations was around the Wash and into Breckland. It is, therefore, best to see the Fossditch and the Bichamditch as a defensive line established by these settlers to consolidate their hold over the eastern side of the Fenland basin at the end of the fifth century if not earlier. The eastern pair, on the other hand, consists of two shorter dykes which lie across Roman roads; they may have been an attempt by the predominantly sub-Roman population of central Norfolk to stem the tide of Anglo-Saxon advance into the interior. The very existence of these four dykes suggests that there was a prolonged period of stalemate in the political turmoil of the fifth century, with the western region firmly under Anglo-Saxon control, while the *civitas* of the Iceni lingered on for a while in the heartland of East Anglia no doubt supported by federate troops. The line of Saxon shore forts around the east coast may have inhibited similar incursions from the other direction.

The lengthy west Norfolk dykes would be quite ineffective against sustained infantry attacks, but as a method of forestalling the cavalry of a sub-Roman army over the open Breckland, these earthworks could have been successful. These linear earthworks are the best pieces of evidence we have for a controlled Anglo-Saxon movement into the area in the fifth and sixth centuries. With such a slow Anglo-Saxon expansion there is little reason why some Roman sites could not have continued for long into the fifth century.

J. Dodgson has cast doubt on the long held theory that *-ingas* place-names indicate the settlements of original Anglo-Saxon migrants in the fifth and early sixth centuries. He demonstrated in 1966 that the pagan Saxon cemeteries and the *-ingas* names are in fact complementary in their distribution. In East Anglia the place-names occur most often in the central and eastern districts, while the distribution of cemeteries has a western orientation over the lighter soils of west Norfolk, Breckland and Cambridgeshire. Dodgson suggested that the majority of *-ingas* place-names actually belong to a time *after* the migration phase and the abandonment of pagan Saxon cemeteries. The *-ingas* place-names were in vogue when the settlement was being expanded from the original migration areas; these names were given to Anglo-Saxon colonies during the secondary expansion phase in the sixth and presumably seventh centuries. He set a final limit for the frequent adoption of place-names of this nature at the widespread conversion to Christianity; by then, they had already become an archaic word-form in the German homeland.

We must consider, however, whether these settlements were *necessarily* Anglo-Saxon in origin, for the distribution of *-ingas* names and that of the pagan Saxon cemeteries is so totally different. The fertile soils of Norfolk, which gave rise to the largest population per square kilometre of any county in England in the eleventh century, must have supported a great number of people by the fifth century. It would, therefore, seem unwise to talk in terms of these early names denoting a purely, or even predominantly, Anglo-Saxon population after several centuries of prosperity under Roman rule.

It could be argued that the explanation for the absence of pagan Saxon objects on village sites, even on those with -*ingas* place-names, was because people were frequently shifting their settlement under the unstable conditions. Such an argument, however, cannot explain the *complete* absence of Anglo-Saxon material in all the early sites which have been examined. Where the place-name is linked to a topographical feature, as in the case of Wellingham (which probably relates to the adjacent stream), there clearly could not have been much movement of the settlement since the name was first introduced.

In Breckland and west Norfolk the population was undoubtedly Anglo-Saxon by the fifth century. But over much of central Norfolk and High Suffolk there is still a very prominent gap in our understanding for the first two and a half centuries after the end of Roman rule. There was possibly still a largely Celtic population, although later no doubt it became dominated by an Anglo-Saxon minority. How long the Romano-British settlement sites continued is at present unknown; we can only guess. Except possibly for the latest types of Romano-Saxon pottery, we cannot at present recognise any finds of Roman character made after the early fifth century. The matter cannot at present be taken much further through fieldwork; the question of the survival of Romano-British settlements must remain unanswered until the upper levels of settlements sites have been excavated as they have been at Wroxeter. Only in the seventh century, with the introduction of Ipswich ware, does this apparently a-ceramic population make its appearance again in the archaeological record.

During the survey of the Launditch Hundred, twelve villages have been located which were in existence during the time that Ipswich ware was in use in the seventh, eighth and ninth centuries. These were not the only middle Saxon villages in the area, for there are several likely sites which are inaccessible. Four of these twelve sites also produced a thin scatter of Roman pottery. As Roman pottery is very seldom found sealed in middle Saxon deposits at the excavation at North Elmham, these Roman finds belong to an earlier phase of settlement.

In the Launditch area are eight place-names containing -*ingas* elements (Bittering, Wendling, etc.). Except for two, these villages are in one of the tightest clusters of -*ingas* place-names in East Anglia, and this is deep in central Norfolk, well away from the general distribution of pagan Saxon cemeteries. There is no archaeological evidence that any of the early centres of these villages were founded by *Anglo-Saxon* people. It is therefore at least possible that many of these villages were originally made up of sub-Roman Celtic people who gradually mingled with the Anglo-Saxon settlers in the sixth century. The Romano-British population no doubt continued for a while to maintain their old traditions, and only gradually moved to new sites. It is quite clear that by the end of the sixth century all vestiges of the old economic and social orders had disappeared. The evolution of the new way of life was no doubt created alongside a gradual secondary colonisation of Anglo-Saxon peoples.

These ideas are, however, extremely difficult to reconcile with the almost complete absence of Celtic village names in the region. Nevertheless, it is possible that the names as recorded in Domesday Book were adaptations of earlier word forms dating from the time that Old English became the dominant language. In much the same way during both World Wars the local place-names overseas were frequently adapted to suit the English tongue.

The place-names which followed on closely behind the *-ingas* names were those ending in *-ham* (Litcham, Elmham etc.). In Launditch there were about eight of these, of which half have produced Ipswich ware sites, and most of the other possible sites are inaccessible. The archaeological evidence therefore confirms the widespread belief that *-ham* villages were relatively early; they were founded no later than the ninth century. It is usually these villages which occupy choice locations, and they frequently became market centres during the Middle Ages.

The next names in the accepted sequence are those with *-ton* endings. In Launditch there are six (Beeston, Kipton etc.). Archaeology shows that with this class of settlement the date of the earliest occupation varies enormously between the eighth and eleventh centuries; nevertheless, as a group they are later. Unlike the two previous types, two thirds of these villages are now deserted; they mostly, therefore, belong to the period of settlement expansion into more marginal land after the ninth or early tenth centuries. When the rural population declined in the fourteenth and fifteenth centuries, these were the first ones to decay.

Roughly contemporary with this group are names ending in *-leah* (Brisley, Gateley), *-halh* (Gressenhall) and *-feld* (Stanfield). Almost without exception, archaeology has demonstrated that they began in the tenth- and eleventh-century phase.

During the tenth and eleventh centuries the population of East Anglia, both in the urban and rural areas, rose rapidly. Many small farms in marginal lands grew into villages, and entirely new settlements came into being. It is the impressive size of many of the eleventh-century villages, such as North Elmham, Mileham and Weasenham, which is surprising, even though we know they lay in the most heavily settled part of England at this time.

One of the most interesting results to come out of this survey is the recorded absence of pre-conquest occupation around all the village greens which have been examined. Thorpe argued from continental examples that the green villages of Lowland England had been introduced by the Anglo-Saxons as the typical types of settlement pattern during the migration period. This research, however, has shown that green villages, as we normally understand them in East Anglia, did not come into existence until the twelfth century. Before that villages were usually clustered around crossroads or along streets. The medieval settlements in East Anglia are mostly secondary developments and therefore should in no way be equated with migration period village patterns in north west Europe.

Green villages were the most common form of rural settlement. The greens were frequently in the wetter parts of the parish, either in the damp valleys or on the poorly drained boulder clay plateau soils. Because these places were difficult to cultivate they may already have been set aside for common grazing before the Norman conquest, but they did not usually become focal points for settlement until later.

The origin of green villages is a fascinating subject. As the rural economy and the population expanded in the twelfth century, and as the conversion of waste land into arable intensified, so people became more dependent upon these pieces of common grazing for their farm animals. Excavations at Thuxton and Grenstein, two deserted villages in the area, have shown that medieval villages were full of relatively prosperous small farmsteads, each with a living-house and separate outbuildings, and not landless labourers living at subsistence level. Every household had at least one animal that needed room to graze.

An analysis of the 1334 Lay Subsidy returns for East Anglia and Lincolnshire reveals that Norfolk was one of the richest as well as the most prosperous counties in medieval England, and these figures actually represented a county already on the decline. The depopulation of the Norfolk countryside is perhaps best seen in the numbers of ruined churches. There are 659 surviving churches built before 1700 and an additional 245 are in ruins. Most of these date from the medieval period, when more churches were built per square kilometre than anywhere else in England. In Norfolk, including the large areas of open Breckland, there was an average of one church for every two thousand acres. Over a quarter of these have since been abandoned, while many now serve very diminished communities. These figures alone both exemplify the size and the prosperity of the medieval population and the extent of the subsequent decline.

In the Cambridge area the number of people dropped by nearly half between 1279 and 1524. In one Norfolk manor in 1565 only 57 dwellings held in bond tenure were standing, while vacant plots numbered no less than 87; during the period 1376–1565 the population of this one manor was less than half what it had been at the beginning of the fourteenth century. Such a reduction in the rural population in the fourteenth and the second half of the fifteenth centuries was apparently being repeated all over Western Europe. In Norfolk this depopulation was a gradual process. Some villages were deserted by the early fourteenth century, while others remained until the seventeenth century. This abandonment was a slow retreat over a period of several centuries. While villages in more marginal situations, such as Grenstein, disappeared entirely, others were left with gaps between the surviving dwellings.

We can, therefore, see a fairly rapid rise in the number of village people up to the middle of the thirteenth century; then followed a long overall decline, accentuated at times by plague. Only from the mid-eighteenth to the mid-nineteenth centuries was there any marked reversal in this trend. In the twentieth century depopulation has continued. In Launditch, an area without especially difficult soils, fieldwork has demonstrated that 45% of all medieval village sites have been abandoned. If this figure is used to estimate a county total, the figure would be in the region of 400, as against an earlier calculation of 130. If we include in this total pre-conquest villages as well, then the numbers would be phenomenal; the archaeological potential for further fieldwork and excavation in East Anglia is enormous.

In the next few years we shall see an enormous wealth of detailed information about Anglo-Saxon villages come to light as more government funds for rescue archaeology become available and the excavation of large areas becomes normal practice. Let us hope that alongside this there will be a similar upsurge of detailed fieldwork. The need for government finance for this work is just as great and just as urgent as it is for excavation. Excavated settlements not placed in their regional contexts and field surveys not supported by selected excavations are of limited value. Only when both techniques are employed can we hope to achieve a good understanding of the origins and the evolution of the land-scape.

Archaeological fieldwork can make a major contribution to the history of settlement patterns; it certainly helps us to realise that the history of village development is a far more complex and intricate subject than the classification of present-day village patterns would suggest. Let the story of the English calf be a lesson to those who would find logic and order in the development of the countryside!

The Calf Path

One day through the primeval wood
a calf walked home as good calves should;
But made a trail all bent askew,
A crooked trail as all calves do.
Since then, three hundred years have fled,
And, I infer the calf is dead.
But still he left behind his trail
And thereby hangs my moral tale.
The trail was taken up next day
By a lone dog that passed that way;
And then a wise bell-wether sheep
Pursued the trail o'er vale and steep,
And drew the flock behind him too,
As good bell-wethers always do.

And from that day, o'er hill and glade,
Through those old woods a path was made,
And many men wound in and out
And dodged and turned and bent about,
And uttered words of righteous wrath
Because 'twas such a crooked path.
But still they followed—do not laugh—
The first migrations of that calf,
And through this winding roadway stalked
Because he wobbled when he walked.

This forest path became a lane
That bent and turned and turned again;
This crooked lane became a road
Where many a poor horse with his load
Toiled beneath the burning sun,
And travelled some three miles in one;
And thus a century and a half
They trod in the footsteps of that calf.
The years passed on in swiftness fleet.
The road became a village street;
And this, before men were aware,
A city's crowded thoroughfare.
And soon the central street was this
Of a renowned metropolis;
And men two centuries and a half
Trod in the footsteps of that calf.

Each day a hundred thousand rout
Followed this zig-zag calf about;
And o'er his crooked journey went
The traffic of a continent.
A hundred thousand men were led
By one calf near three centuries dead.

They followed still his crooked way,
And lost one hundred years a day;
For thus such a reverence is lent
To well established precedent.

Samuel Foss, 1895

Bibliography 9

J. K. Allison, 'The Lost Villages of Norfolk', *Norfolk Archaeol.* **31**, 1955, 116–62.

R. Rainbird Clarke, 'Norfolk in the Dark Ages', *Norfolk Archaeol.* **28**, 1940, 233

'The Fossditch—A Linear Earthwork in South-West Norfolk', *Norfolk Archaeol.* **31**, 1955, 178–96.

East Anglia, 1960.

F. G. Davenport, *The Economic Development of a Norfolk Manor 1086–1565*, 1906, 98–105.

Deserted Medieval Village Research Group, Annual Reports.

J. M. Dodgson, 'The Significance of the Distribution of the English Place-Name in -*ingas*, -*inga* in South-east England', *Medieval Archaeol.* **10**, 1966, 1–20.

D. Dymond, 'The Suffolk Landscape', in L. Munby (ed.) *East Anglian Studies*, 1968, 17–47.

H. P. R. Finberg, 'Continuity or Cataclysm?', *Lucerna*, 1964, 1–20.

'Roman and Saxon Withington', *Lucerna*, 1964, 21–65.

P. J. Fowler (ed.), *Archaeology and the Landscape*, 1972.

R. E. Glasscock, 'The Distribution of Wealth in East Anglia in the early fourteenth century', *Trans. Inst. Brit. Geogr.* **32**, 1963, 113–23.

J. G. Hurst, 'Saxo-Norman Pottery in East Anglia', Pts 1, 2 and 3, *Proc. Cambridge Antiq. Soc.* **49**, 1956, 43–70; **50**, 1957, 29–60; **51**, 1958, 37–65.

G. Jones, 'Settlement Patterns in Anglo-Saxon England', *Antiquity* **35**, 1961, 221–32.

J. M. Lewis, 'The Launditch: A Norfolk Linear Earthwork', *Norfolk Archaeol.* **31**, 1957, 419–26.

N. Riches, *The Agricultural Revolution in Norfolk*, 1967.

J. Saltmarsh, 'Plague and Economic Decline in England in the later Middle Ages', *Cambridge Hist. J.* **7**, 1941, 23–41.

O. K. Schram, 'Place-Names', in *Norwich and its Region*, 1961, 142.

C. T. Smith, 'The Cambridge Region: Settlement and Population', in J. A. Steers (ed.) *The Cambridge Region*, 1965, 142–50.

C. Taylor, *Dorset*, 1970.

H. Thorpe, *The Geography of Rural Settlement in the Durham Region* (University of Durham dissertation, 1936).

'The Green Villages of County Durham', *Trans. Inst. Brit. Geogr.* **15**, 1949, 155–80.

'The Green Village as a Distinctive Form of Settlement on the North European Plain', *Bull. Soc. Belge d'Etudes* **30**, 1961, 5–133.

P. Wade-Martins, 'Excavations at North Elmham, 1967–8 and 1969; (each) An Interim Report', *Norfolk Archaeol.* **34**, 1969, 352–97; **35**, 1970, 25–78.

The Development of the Landscape and Human Settlement in West Norfolk from 350–1650 AD, *with particular reference to the Launditch Hundred* (Ph.D. thesis, Leicester University, 1971). Copies are deposited at the University of Leicester and the Local History Section of Norwich Library.

'The Linear Earthworks of West Norfolk', *Norfolk Archaeol.* forthcoming.

Index

Places are indexed alphabetically by their first element, e.g. Mount Pleasant is under 'M', Dun Ardtreck is under 'D'. No attempt has been made to accommodate the county references to the new (1974) local government boundaries. Author's names and bibliographical references are not indexed.

Abbot's Way, Som 14, 15, 20, 21
Agriculture 21, 27, 28, 31, 32–3, 34, 36, 63, 64, 68, 95, 116–17
  arable 16, 17, 23, 27, 32, 39, 40, 50, 51, 63, 104, 123, 130, 133
  cattle/stock *see* cattle
  continuity in 132, 135
  cultivation by plough 63
  — by spade 34, 39
  forest clearance 17, 21–3, 24, 29, 31, 32–3, 36, 38, 40, 45, 63, 104
  increase in information on 21
  'landnam' 22–3
  mixed farming 128
  pasturing/grazing 16, 17, 27, 45, 63, 67, 130
  reversion to woodland 32, 130
  ridge and furrow 48, 111–12
  rigg and furrow 100
  stone clearance 34–6, 38–9
  strip cultivation 100
  terrace systems 100
  use of marginal land 128, 130, 152
Air photography 44, 45, 48–9, 94, 95, 107, 109, 110, 111, 112, 113, 114, 116, 132
Antler picks 61, 70
Apple 63
Archaeology 12, 107–19
  amateur 107–8, 110–11
  chronology *see* radio-carbon dates
  destruction of evidence 57, 111
  excavation 17, 18, 44, 57, 109, 121, 139, 154
  field work 44, 58, 107, 108, 109, 110–11, 112, 114–16, 118–19, 121, 124, 132, 138–9, 149, 154
  'new' 119
  recording 16, 17–18, 25, 107, 109
  rescue 57
  topographical 44–55, 154
Ard-marks *see* plough
Arrowheads 17, 34, 36
Askrigg, Westmor 100
Astronomical observations 55, 66–7
Avebury, Wilts 59, 61, 66, 68
Avenue, Stonehenge, Wilts 45, 47
Axes 17, 33, 34, 36, 58, 64
  bronze 37
  iron 84
  stone 17, 33, 34, 58, 64

Axe factories
  Cornwall 33, 36–7, 64
  Lake District 36, 64
  Netherlands 36

Banks 44, 45, 47, 57, 64, 67
Barnsley Park, Glos 132–5
Barrows 45
  chambered cairns 72
  earthen long 45, 47, 51, 55, 57, 58, 60, 63, 68, 124
  round 45, 57, 58, 59, 118, 124
  stone long 58, 68
Bath, Som 128
Beads
  glass 84, 88
  shale 39
Beakers *see* pottery
Bell complex, Som 15, 20
Boar 31
Bodmin Moor, Cornwall 31, 32, 38
Bokerley Dyke, Dorset 51, 54
Bone
  analyses 28, 101–4
  animal 28, 29, 67, 79, 101–4, 126, 130
  combs 89
  dice 89
  tools 30, 58, 67
Boundaries *see* ranch boundaries
Boundary banks 27
Bracken 21, 23, 32
Brean Down, Som 128, 130–31
Bristle cone pine 29
Brochs 72–90
  architecture of 73–5, 81–5, 88
  construction of 73, 75–7
  defence of 75, 77, 81
  distribution of 72–3
  engineers 73, 88
  entrances of 75, 77, 82–3
  excavations of 79
  fortifications 75
  galleries 75, 81–2
  guard-cells 76, 77, 88
  height of 73–5, 77–8, 79
  measurements of 73, 81, 85–89
  origins of 81–5
  pottery 85
  roofing of 76–7
  secondary use of 79, 81
  semi-brochs 83–4
  undefended 81
Bronze 58
  axes 39
  palstave 39
  pins 37
  spiral finger rings 88

Buildings 130
  circular timber 61–3, 64, 67, 68, 69
  construction of 61–2
  transmutation into stone 68
Building materials 61–2
Burial *see also* cemeteries
  collective 59
  crouched 68
  —ground 45, 107
  inhumed 58, 130
  — practices 57, 58–9, 63, 64
  Saxon 107, 118, 138, 140
  single 59
Burtle, Som 12, 16, 24
Burwens, Westmor 98, 100, 101
Butcombe, Som 124–6
  Row of Ashes Farm 124, 126, 128, 129, 130
  windmill mound 124

Cadbury Congresbury, Som 128–30
Caithness 72, 82, 83, 85
Calluna 19, 20, 23, 32
Cambridgeshire 119
Camerton, Som 128
Carn Brea, Cornwall 33, 34–6
Carrowburgh, Northumb 100
Cathedrals 72, 139
Cattle 16, 17, 27, 32, 33, 37, 40, 52, 63, 102–5, 126, 130
  improved breeding
  supply of as food 102, 104
  winter feeding of 22, 101, 105
  winter stalling of 105
Castles 72
  motte and bailey 147–9
'Causewayed camps' 34, 57, 60–61, 63, 64
Cemeteries *see also* burial
  Early Christian 130
  Iron Age 124
  pagan Saxon 118, 138, 140, 150, 151
Cereals 32, 34, 37, 63, 105
  barley 33, 63, 104
  bread wheat 33, 63, 105
  einkorn 33, 63
  emmer 33, 63, 104
  oats 104
  spelt 63, 104, 105
Ceremonial 64, 67, 70
Cess-pit 79
Channel Ports, Iron Age use of 52
Charcoal 28, 29, 63, 84
Charterhouse, Som 128
Chert 32
Chew Valley Lake, Som 125
Chilton Moor, Som 23–4

Cholwich town, Plymouth, Devon 37–8
Christon, Som 124
Church Hill, Findon, Sussex 33
Churches 138, 141, 142, 146, 147
  ruined 153
Circles
  earthen 49
  stone 64, 66, 68, 87, 89
  wood 64, 67
Cirencester, Glos 135
Cladium 18, 20, 23
Clickhimin, Shetland 79
Climate 40
  climatic zones 29–30
Comb 89
Communities *see* population, settlement
Copper 58
Corn storage *see* pits
Cornovii 95
Cornwall 31, 93
Cranborne Chase, Dorset 57, 60
Croft Moraig, Perth 68
Crosby Garrett, Westmor 95, 97, 98–9
Crosby Ravensworth, Westmor 98–9
Crosskirk 79
Crucibles 89
Cult 64
Cumberland 95, 101
Cursus 45

Dartmoor 28, 30, 32, 36, 37, 39
Dating *see* radio-carbon dates
Deer 31, 33, 104, 130
Devon 93
Dice 89
Din Lligwy, Anglesey 101
Ditches 37, 44, 47, 48, 57, 60, 61, 64, 67
Documents 121, 124, 139, 140
  Domesday Book 129, 130, 147, 152
  historical 16, 17
  Saxon charters 129
Dog 33
Dolebury, Som 129
Dorset 104
Dorset cursus 45, 46, 51
Dorset Downs 57, 60
Dozmary Pool, Bodmin Moor, Cornwall 31
Drains 39
Dun Ardtreck, Skye 75, 83–4
Dun Carloway, Lewis 73
Dun Dornadilla, Sutherland 73
Dun Mor Vaul, Tiree, Argyll 79–80, 88

Dun Telve, Inverness 73, 76, 78, 82, 83
Dun Troddan, Inverness 73, 78, 82, 83
Durham County 137
Durobrivae *see* Water Newton
Durrington Walls, Wilts 61–4, 67, 68
Dykes 98–9
  boundary 98
  defensive 146
  Norfolk Dark Age *see* linear earthworks

Earthworks 45–55, 58, 61, 63, 67, 121, 123, 139
  linear 146, 149–50
East Anglia 137–54
Easton Down, Wilts 64
Economy 27, 57, 93
Eden Valley, Cumb 95
Eller Beck, Cumb 101
Enclosures 47, 61, 63, 64, 98, 100, 132
  'banjo' 47–8, 52
  defended 94
  dyked 100
  non-defensive 94, 98
  oval 93–4
  polygonal 93–4
  rectilinear 95, 100, 101
  stock 27, 28, 48, 100, 126, 133, 135
  stone-walled 94
Environment 12, 15–16, 18–19, 27–8, 29, 30, 57, 58
Eriophorum 19
Ewe Close, Westmor 95, 98
Exmoor, Som 16

Farming *see* agriculture
Farmsteads 95, 99, 101, 112, 116, 124, 126, 133, 153
Fens 48, 118, 146
Fields *see* field-systems
Field-systems 28, 37, 38–9, 121, 123
  Bronze Age 51
  'Celtic' 45, 47, 48, 51–2, 53, 124, 126, 130, 133
  medieval 141
  Romano-British 48–9, 100, 101, 129–30, 133–4
  strip 48–9, 100, 127, 129–30, 133
  tofts 149
  villa 126–7
Fish 16, 17
Fishing 16
Flax 63
Flint mines 33, 57, 64
  tools 31, 34, 39, 58, 60, 124
Flooding 15–16
Forest 32, 34, 36, 37, 130
  submerged 31
Forts *see* hill-forts, Roman forts
Foss, Samuel 155
Fotheringhay, Northants 113
Fowl 16, 17
Frisia 102
Frocester Court villa, Glos 135

Fruits 18, 19, 31
Fuel 17
Funerary monuments *see* monuments
Fussell's Lodge, Wilts 58
Fyfield Down, Wilts 121–3

Garden-plots 38–9, 149
Gatcombe, Som 128
Geology
  boulder clay 108–9, 111, 114–15, 153
  bluestones 64, 68
  chalk 63, 119
  granite 31–2, 36, 39, 40
  gravel 108, 111, 116, 117
  igneous rock 64
  ironstone 109, 111
  lias 12, 16, 108
  limestone 16, 64, 108–9, 111, 116, 117, 124, 130
  sand ridges 12, 16, 24, 37, 40, 116
  sarsen 64, 67
  shale 39
  volcanic rocks 33
Glastonbury, Som 16
Gloucestershire 118, 121–35
Goats 33, 63, 104, 130
Gold 58
Grasses 32
'Greenstones' 33, 36, 37, 38
Grenstein, Norfolk 139, 153
Grimes' Graves, Norfolk 36
Gussage All Saints, Dorset 48, 67
Gwithian, Cornwall, 31, 36, 37, 38, 39, 40

Hadrian's Wall 95, 98, 100
Haldon Hill, Devon 33
Haltonchesters, Northumb 100
Hambledon Hill, Dorset 60
Harlyn Bay, Cornwall 31
Hazard Hill, Devon 33
Heathland 38
Hebrides 82, 83, 85
Hedge patterns 127, 149
Hedgehog 31
Hembury Fort, Devon, 33, 34, 60, 63
Henge monuments 57, 64, 67
Henley Wood, Yatton, Som 128
Hides 52
Highland Zone 93
High Peak, Devon 33, 34
Hill-forts 47, 50, 68, 70, 72, 84, 90, 94, 98, 124, 132
  re-occupation of 129
Holkham Estate 140, 141
Horridge Common, Cornwall 39
Houses 33, 37
  Iron Age wooden round 77–8
Housesteads, Northumb 100
'Hunter gatherers' 30–2, 36, 39
Hunting 33, 36, 40
Huts *see* buildings, houses
  circular 38, 101
Hut-circles 100

Industrial activity 64
Irchester, Northants 109, 113, 116
Ireland 19, 93
Iron 109
  ring 75, 84
  working 75, 112
Iron Age 73, 75, 81, 118
  pre-Roman 90, 123

Jarlshof, Shetland 77, 78, 79

Kirkby Stephen, Westmor 99, 100

Land allotment/division 52, 55, 60, 68, 121, 123, 125, 129, 133, 135
  survey 45, 133
Landscape 44–55
  continuity in 121–35, 138
  organisation of 44–55, 68
Launditch Hundred, Norfolk 139–54
Levels, Somerset 12–26, 28, 32, 39
  creation of 18–19
  'hangings' 16, 17
  'Limpet-scoops' 30
Little Woodbury, Wilts 48, 50, 52
Lizard Peninsula, Cornwall 64
Llandegai, Caernarvon 64
Longham, Norfolk 141–3, 146
Lowland Zone 93
Lye Hole villa, Wrington, Som 125–7, 133
Lynchets 27, 37, 45, 47, 55, 100

Maiden Castle, Dorset 60, 68–70
Man
  Neolithic 17, 21, 88
  medieval 17
  modern 17
  prehistoric 18, 25, 27, 44
Manors 141
Manuring 37
Marden, Pewsey, Wilts 61, 67, 68
Margidunum, Notts 103–5
Marine transgression 128
Marlborough Downs, Wilts 57, 60, 121
Martin Down, Hants 51
Maryport, Cumb 98
Meare Heath, Som 12, 39
Medieval villages *see* villages
Mendip, Som 16, 19, 124
Metalworking 128
Microliths 30, 31, 32, 34
Midden 30–31
Mileham, Norfolk 147–9, 152
Monuments 58
  funerary 46
  ritual 45, 107
Motorways 132
  M5 118
Mounds 44, 68
Mount Pleasant, Dorchester, Dorset 61, 67, 68–70

Mousa, Shetland 73, 75, 77, 78, 81, 82
Mumrills, Stirling 102

Nene Valley 107–19
  geology of 108–9, 117, 118
Newstead, Roxburgh 102
Norfolk 139
Norman Conquest 138
Normangate Field, Peterborough, Northants 112–13
Northampton 116, 118
North Elmham, Norfolk 139, 140, 151, 152
North-Western England 93–103
Nuts 28, 31, 63

Occupation 34
Orkney Isles 72, 82, 84
osmunda regalis 20

Pagan's Hill, Chew Stoke, Som 128, 129
Palaeobotany 12, 18, 25
Palisaded settlements 94
Palstave 39
Peacock's Farm, Shippea Hill, Cambs 30
Peat 12, 16, 17, 18, 28, 32, 39
  blanket 39
  building material 17
  commercial exploitation of 12, 13, 25
  fen-woodland 18, 19, 20–21
  fuel 17
  raised bog 15, 19, 20, 21, 29
  reed swamp 18, 19, 20
Pebble tools 30
Peterborough, Northants 109
Pig 31, 33, 37, 63, 64, 102, 104, 105, 130
Pins 37
Pits 44, 57, 64
  alignments 50
  storage of corn in 50
Place-names 138
  -ham 152
  -ingas 138, 150–2
  -ingaham 143
  Saxon 138
  -ton 152
Plant fossils 12, 18, 19, 28
plantago lanceolata 21, 23, 31
Plough 28, 34–5, 37, 40
  marks 27, 34–5, 37, 63
Poldens, Som 12, 16, 17, 24
Pollen analysis 16, 19–25, 28, 29–30, 32, 36, 39
  diagrams 20–25
  grains 18, 28, 29, 31, 32, 39
Population 27, 28, 31, 39, 55, 58–9, 60
  Celtic 50, 95, 132, 151
  decline in 153–4
  increase in 50, 52, 58, 61, 64, 68, 116, 132, 152
  pressure of 51
  Romano-British 116, 138, 145, 151–2
  Saxon 138, 150–51
  and storage pits 50

Pottery 17, 28, 34, 36, 39, 58, 60, 63, 67, 79, 85, 139, 140
  collecting 139, 140, 141
  manufacture 109, 112, 113, 128
  types—beaker 37, 67, 68
  Clettraval 88
  early medieval 140, 147
  Glastonbury 88
  grass-tempered 133, 135
  'grooved ware' 61, 64
  Hembury 36
  Ipswich ware 140, 149, 151, 152
  Iron Age 118
  late Romano British 133
  Lizard type 34, 64
  Romano-British 84, 109, 113, 118, 130, 142, 151
  Romano-Saxon 151
  Saxon 140, 141, 147, 149
  Thetford ware 140

Quantocks, Som 16
Quarley, Hants 51
Querns 37, 84, 89

Radio-carbon dates 14, 30, 31, 33, 34, 58–9, 60, 63, 64, 67, 68, 83, 84
  and dating 19, 25, 29, 94
Ranch boundaries 47–8, 50, 51
Rath 93, 94
Religion 57–70
'Religious observance' 47
Ridge and furrow *see* agriculture
Ridgeway, Dorset 59–60
Rigg and furrow *see* agriculture
Rijkholt, Maastricht, Neths 36
Risehow, Cumb 98
Ritual 45, 66, 67
Roman forts 72, 94, 100, 107
  roads 98, 128, 146, 149, 150
  towns 112, 128
Round 93
Rudchester, Cumb 100

Salisbury Plain, Wilts 57, 60
Sanctuary, Overton, Wilts 61, 68
'Sauveterrian' 30, 31
Saxon 127
  estates 132
  shore forts 150

Scars Farm, Wrington, Som 125–6
Scotland 72–90, 102
Seeds 18, 19, 28
Settlement patterns 15, 16, 44–55, 93, 121, 152–4
  history of 44, 121–3, 137–54
  Iron Age 48, 67, 124, 132
  late Roman 123, 128
  Neolithic 34–5
  prehistoric 27, 47, 57–70, 123–4
  Romano-British 48, 93–105, 107–19, 123
  rural 93–105, 108, 128, 132–3, 137–54
  Saxon 118, 123, 127, 135, 139
Severn Basin 95
Shale 39
Sheep 17, 33, 37, 63, 64, 102, 104, 105, 126, 130
Shell fish 31, 63
Shells 28, 32
Shetland Isles 72, 82
Shovel 37
Sidbury, Wilts 51
Silviculture 22, 24
  coppicing 24
  pollarding 22
Snail Down, Wilts 45
Snails 28, 29, 32, 63
Social development 57, 58, 64
Soils 28, 34, 38, 63
Solway Firth 19
Somerset 104, 118, 121–35
Somerset Levels *see* Levels
South Street long barrow, Wilts 34, 63
South West England 27–40
Spade 17, 34–6, 39
  marks 27
Sphagnum 19, 20, 23
Stannon Down, St Breward, Cornwall 38–9
Stanwick, Yorks 105
Star villa, Shipham, Som 128, 129
Stone
  axes *see* axes
  circles *see* circles
  hoes 37, 38
  mauls 67

piles 37
row 37–8
settings 64, 67, 68
share 28
tools 67
Stonehenge, Wilts 45, 47, 55, 59, 64, 66, 68, 72
Studland Heath, Dorset 49
Sussex 33, 104
Sutherland 72, 82, 83, 85

Temples 128, 129, 130
Terrace systems *see* agriculture
Thatcham, Berks 31
Thelypteris palustris 20
Tools 27, 58, 67
Torwoodlee, Selkirk 79
Tracks 47
Trade 34, 52, 64
Trees
  alder 14, 15, 17, 19, 20
  ash 15, 17, 23
  birch 14, 15, 17, 19, 20, 23
  elm 21–2, 23, 24, 25, 31, 32, 33
  hazel 15, 23–4, 31
  holly 17
  lime 23
  oak 17, 31, 32, 34, 37, 61–3, 69–70
  willow 17
  yew 15
Tree rings 29

Units of measurement 66, 85–9
Upton, Blockley, Glos 135

Vaul *see* Dun Mor Vaul
Villa 101, 112, 113, 116, 123, 125, 126, 127, 128, 132, 133
  desertion 135
  economy 93
  field-systems *see* field-systems
Village 38–9, 135, 137–9, 141–54
  deserted 107, 114, 135, 138, 139, 152, 154
  development 135, 138, 148
  with greens 137–8, 152–3
  medieval 107, 114, 135
  patterns 138

Roman 112, 116, 138
Saxon 138
street 147

Waitby, Westmor 95, 99, 100
Wales 93, 101
Walesland, Pemb 94
Warwickshire 118
Water-meadows 48
Water Newton, Hunts 109, 113–14
Weasenham St Peter, Norfolk 144–5, 146–7, 152
Wedmore, Som 12, 16, 17, 24
'Weed' pollen 21, 22–3, 24, 32, 33
Welsh Marches 94–5
Wessex 35, 44–55, 57–70
West Kennet, Wilts 58
West Kennet Avenue, Wilts 68
West Overton, Wilts 121–3, 135
West Stow, Suffolk 140
Westhay, Som 12, 20, 24, 39
Westmorland 95, 98, 101
Western Isles 72, 88–9
Westward Ho! Bideford, Devon 31
Wheelhouses 72, 77, 78
Whitchurch, Shrop 102–3
Whitsbury, Hants 51, 53
Wican Bonhunt, Essex 140
Wiltshire 118, 121–35
Windmill Hill, Wilts, 60, 63
Withington, Glos 132, 135
Wolsty Hall, Cumb 95, 98
Wood 18–19 *see also* trees
  bow 17
  as building materials 17, 29, 36
  door 75
  fragments 12, 28
  as fuel 17, 29
  mallets 15
  plough 28
  spade 17, 37
  tablet 102
Wooden trackways 12, 13–15, 17, 20, 24, 39
  corduroy road 14–15
  methods of construction 14, 15
Woodhenge, Wilts 61
Wrington, Vale of 123–32, 135